D1582079

CONSTITUTIONAL POLICY IN UNIFIED GERMANY

CONSTITUTIONAL POLICY
IN UNIFIED GERMANY

Edited by
Klaus H. Goetz and Peter J. Cullen

FRANK CASS • LONDON

First published in 1995 in Great Britain by
FRANK CASS AND COMPANY LIMITED
Newbury House, 890-900 Eastern Avenue,
London IG2 7HH, England

and in the United States of America by
FRANK CASS
c/o ISBS, Inc.
5602 N.E. Hassalo Street, Portland, Oregon 927213-3540

British Library Cataloguing in Publication Data
Constitutional Policy in Unified Germany
I. Goetz, Klaus H. II. Cullen, Peter J.
344.302

ISBN 0-7146-4631-8 (hardback)
ISBN 0-7146-4204-5 (paperback)

Library of Congress Cataloguing-in-Publication Data
Constitutional policy in unified Germany/edited by Klaus H. Goetz, and
Peter J. Cullen.
p. cm.
ISBN 0-7146-4631-8
1. Germany—Constitutional law. 2. Germany (East)—Constitutional law. 3.
Germany—History—Unification, 1990. I. Goetz, Klaus H., 1961–.II.
Cullen, Peter J., 1663–.
KK4450.C67 1995
342.43—dc20
(344.302)

This group of studies first appeared in a Special Issue of *German Politics,*
Vol.3, No.3 (December 1994), [*Constitutional Policy in Unified Germany*].

Printed in Great Britain by Antony Rowe Ltd, Chippenham, Wiltshire

Contents

PREFACE

The high hopes of many in 1990 that the achievement of unification would be crowned by a new Constitution for the unified Germany have been dashed, and there is little prospect of a popular referendum to affirm the Basic Law. Instead, continuity seems to prevail. The changes to the Basic Law contained in the Unification Treaty were restricted to those immediately necessitated by unification, and subsequent constitutional amendments, whilst important, have left the essential features of the Basic Law intact. There is little prospect that this will change in the foreseeable future. The proposals put forward by the Joint Bundestag–Bundesrat Commission on the Constitution in its report of October 1993 (see Appendix) were, on the whole, so cautious that some questioned whether the energy invested in the Commission had not been wasted. A dispute between the Federal Government and the Bundesrat concerning the Commission's recommendations on the strengthening of the role of the Länder in Federal legislation threatened, in August 1994, to block the adoption of the whole package of constitutional reform legislation. Although most of the recommendations were eventually passed into law in October 1994, the resultant changes to the Basic Law are not very far-reaching. They do not incorporate some of the more radical proposals to alter the constitutional order made by the Social Democratic Party and others during the debate, for example the introduction of plebiscitary decision-making.

However, the degree of continuity, or even stagnation, can easily be overestimated. The constitutional amendments adopted at the time of unification, the amendments passed in December 1992 in connection with the ratification of the Maastricht Treaty, the new Article 16a on asylum of June 1993, and the amendments to pave the way for the privatisation of the public railways and the Bundespost have all had substantial constitutional implications. Perhaps more importantly, change to the text of the Basic Law is only one element of constitutional policy. Just as significant are judgments by the Federal Constitutional Court, the most recent example being the decision of 12 July 1994 on the deployment of German armed forces outside the NATO area. It should also be remembered that Federal constitutional law forms only one, albeit the most important, part of German constitutional law, as it is complemented by 16 Länder constitutions. Finally, the Europeanisation and internationalisation of the legal system imply constitutional change which is not necessarily reflected in textual amendments to the Basic Law.

The present collection seeks to identify some of the central tasks of constitutional policy and analyses how, and with what degree of success, they are being fulfilled. The first contribution by Goetz and Cullen looks at internal and external challenges to the Basic Law which, they argue, threaten to undermine its centrality and directive capacity in the longer term. They include, in particular, the increasing importance of international legal frameworks and changes in state–society relations, which have the potential of marginalising national constitutional regulation. The most decisive external influence on the Basic Law is discussed by Georg Ress. He provides a critical assessment of the new Article 23 of the Basic Law (Article on European Union) as a means of responding to European integration and examines the judgment of the Federal Constitutional Court of 12 October 1993 on the Maastricht Treaty.

The implications of German membership in the European Union also play an important role in the contribution by Uwe Leonardy, who assesses the recommendations of the Joint Constitutional Commission, and the Bundesrat Commission on Constitutional Reform which preceded it. Leonardy highlights aspects of the federal system where further constitutional reform is required and points to the difficulties of achieving reform legislation.

Some of the reasons why such reforms prove so difficult to achieve are discussed in Arthur Benz's analysis of the Joint Constitutional Commission. He argues that the lack of innovative and forward-looking proposals in the Commission's report can in part be explained by reference to the Commission's institutional features and, in particular, the predominance of bargaining behaviour as opposed to rational arguing in its negotiations. Instead of providing for the open deliberation of constitutional issues, the Commission largely reproduced the established political framework and, thus, encouraged bargaining processes amongst the political élite. That more innovative constitutional ideas can find their way into constitutional law is underlined in Christian Starck's article on the constitutions of the new Länder. Although Starck is sceptical about the usefulness of some of the new regulations, his analysis nonetheless points to the vitality and political relevance of this second layer of constitutional regulation in Germany.

The following two contributions point to elements of continuity and discontinuity in constitutional policy. In his article on the Federal Constitutional Court, Nevil Johnson discusses the new problems and challenges which the Court has faced since unification, but concludes that continuity in approach has clearly prevailed. The Court, he maintains, has been exceptionally successful in acquitting itself of the contentious and often delicate exercise in which it is engaged. Whereas, for the Court, the emphasis has been on 'business as usual', albeit more of it than before unification, Neil Walker, placing the German debate in the context of a wider discussion about constitutional purposes, points to developments which may change the significance of constitutional law in unified Germany. He argues that, on the one hand, the emergence of a politics of cultural identity suggests an increasingly pivotal role for constitutional law, which has always been closely concerned with identity questions. On the other hand, insofar as it makes constitutional actors the focus of political controversy and encourages a distorted view of law's regulatory potential, this same development might in the longer term undermine the legitimacy and effectiveness of constitutional law. The latter argument is also taken up in the concluding theses of Cullen and Goetz, which seek to identify some of the key themes emerging from the preceding papers. They argue that the constitutional debate in Germany overlooked a number of important theoretical questions concerning the proper scope of constitutional regulation and the form it should take.

With two exceptions, first versions of the papers collected in this volume were presented at a conference hosted by the Europa Institute, University of Edinburgh, in March 1994. The conference brought together an interesting mix of experts on German and British constitutional law and government drawn from the fields of law and political science in both countries. It took place in the splendid surroundings of Edinburgh University's Old College, whose Raeburn Room proved an ideal venue for the conference discussions. Our thanks go to the staff of Old College and to Mr Ronnie Galloway of UnivEd Technologies for their assistance with the conference arrangements. This event was jointly sponsored by the Europa Institute and the European Institute of the London School of Economics. The major financial contribution came from the Europa Institute, but we are also very grateful for the generous support of Dr Klaus Funken, Director of the London Office of the Friedrich Ebert Foundation; Mrs Susanne Abegg, Director of the Goethe-Institute in Glasgow; Dr Britta Baron, former Director of the DAAD in London; and the Government Department at LSE. Without their help, this volume could not have been published. The conference benefited greatly from the comments of the discussants of the papers, and we would like to thank Professor A. W. Bradley, Professor James Cornford, Christopher Himsworth, Charlie Jeffery, Nevil Johnson, Isobel Lindsay, Professor Peter Malanczuk, Geoffrey Marshall and Andrew Morton for their perceptive comments. Special thanks are also due to Lord Rodger of Earlsferry, Her Majesty's Advocate, for opening the conference with his interesting address on the contacts between members of the Scottish Bar and German universities in the nineteenth century. We thank Professor Colin Munro, Dean of the Faculty of Law at the University of Edinburgh, for his talk on 'Britain's Changing Constitution'; the subject matter of this paper did not lend itself to inclusion in this volume, but his discussion of British constitutional developments gave the proceedings an important comparative perspective. Finally, the conference would not have been possible without the encouragement and enthusiastic support of the Director of the Europa Institute, and now founding Director of the Institute for German Studies at the University of Birmingham, Professor William E. Paterson. He made sure that the conference was both an academic and a social occasion, and the wonderful dinner which he arranged for the participants at Dalmeny House, ancestral home of the Earls of Rosebery, topped by one of his inimitable after-dinner speeches will, no doubt, linger in the memories of all present for some time to come.

Klaus H. Goetz and Peter J. Cullen, September 1994

The Basic Law after Unification: Continued Centrality or Declining Force?

KLAUS H. GOETZ and PETER J. CULLEN

Throughout the history of the Federal Republic, the Basic Law and its interpretation by the Federal Constitutional Court have played a central role in shaping the German polity. It is, therefore, not surprising that the process of unification has also been decisively influenced by constitutional considerations. However, the Basic Law is confronted by internal and external challenges which threaten to undermine its centrality in the longer term. They include, in particular, the increasing importance of international legal frameworks and changes in state-society relations, which have the potential of marginalising national constitutional regulation. Constitutional policy since unification, whilst seeking to respond to some of these challenges, has found it very difficult to address them effectively.

I. *Weltstunde* of the Constitutional State and the Basic Law: Centrality Reaffirmed?

The late 1980s and early 1990s have been described as the 'Weltstunde des Verfassungsstaates'.[1] Although the affirmation of constitutionalism was less universal than this notion might suggest, it certainly encapsulates recent European developments. With the collapse of the Communist regimes of central and eastern Europe, opportunities for meaningful constitutional debate opened in a region where, at least since the late 1940s, democratic constitutional government had been suppressed.[2] The round-table talks between the Communist rulers and opposition movements in countries such as Poland, Hungary and Czechoslovakia in the late 1980s marked the beginning a period of extremely intensive constitutional discussion across central and eastern Europe.[3] In fact, at least during the initial stages of the political transition process, debate about political reform was, to a large extent, synonymous with constitutional argument; and the de-Communisation of the inherited written constitutions, which involved, for example, the removal of all references to the leading role of the Communist Party in state and society and the explicit acknowledgment of the right to private property, signalled the completion of a first, highly symbolic, period of democratisation.

In some central and eastern European states, reconstitutionalisation has, so far, not been as wholesale as many would have wished. Poland and Hungary, for example, have not yet adopted completely new constitutional documents, and the constitutional reform debate in these countries is gradually moving down the political agenda. None the less, post-Communist reconstruction has undoubtedly provided powerful evidence for the pivotal role of constitutional reform in the processes of democratisation, pluralisation and economic liberalisation. Perhaps most critically, the central and eastern European experience has highlighted the close link between constitutional reform and the legitimation of the emergent post-Communist political order.

Viewed in the context of European regime change, the intensity of constitutional argument associated with the collapse of Communist power in the GDR can, therefore, occasion no surprise.[4] What distinguishes the German case is that the debate about reconstitutionalisation in the GDR became quickly entangled with and, eventually, superseded by the controversy over the road to unification and the form and substance of the constitutional framework for the united Germany. In this respect, the spectrum of political and academic opinion ranged from what might be called maximalist positions, advocating unification under Article 146 of the Basic Law (GG) and a popular referendum on a new constitutional document for the whole of Germany, to minimalists, who argued in favour of unification under Article 23 GG, wanted constitutional amendments restricted to those directly necessitated by unification, and rejected the view that the Basic Law required confirmation through popular referendum.[5]

The vigorous constitutional debate engendered by the collapse of Communism and the prospect of unification manifested a perhaps surprisingly strong belief in the power of constitutional regulation. However much proponents and opponents of far-reaching reform differed in their views on the necessary extent and content of constitutional change, few doubted the centrality of national constitutional law for the political, economic, social and cultural life of the country and its capacity to influence and guide, if not, in fact, determine the course of the polity. Similarly, the Joint Bundestag–Bundesrat Commission on the Constitution (Joint Constitutional Commission), set up in late 1991, was principally concerned with what German constitutional law ought to achieve, but paid little attention to the question of what it is (still) capable of accomplishing and under what conditions.

This more or less unquestioned belief in the directive capacity of the Basic Law is, of course, a key theme in the legal-political history of the Federal Republic, and it is closely related to a number of other well-known traits of the German polity, such as the tendency to couch political argument in constitutional terms and to seek authoritative answers to political questions through constitutional review.[6] The trust placed in the power of constitutional law to guide and shape political, economic and social reality might, however, appear misplaced in the light of external and internal challenges to national constitutional regulation which have become increasingly evident over the last two decades or so. Externally, the growing importance of international legal frameworks has the potential of undermining the primacy of national constitutional law. In this respect, the law of the European Union is of special significance. At the same time, some of the central preconditions and assumptions on which constitutionalism and constitutional government have historically been based are increasingly being undermined by internal changes affecting state, society and their interrelationship. Briefly, the ever closer integration between state and society threatens the functional and empirical identity of the state; as the latter is the Basic Law's prime addressee, constitutional law is confronted with increasing difficulties in trying to determine the allocation and uses of state power and in delimiting the boundaries of legitimate state interference with civil society and the individual. A leading commentator on the German Constitution has raised the prospect that, as a result, the Basic Law might be 'relegated to the margins of social life'[7] and degenerate into a 'partial order'.[8] Seen from this perspective, the intensive constitutional debate since the late 1980s, which the present volume documents, might obscure the gradual decline of the Basic Law's centrality to the polity.

    It is, then, possible to formulate two sharply differing perspectives on the German Constitution. The first emphasises its crucial importance for the life of the polity by providing a central point of reference for political, economic and social actors. The constitutional debate provoked by unification; the influence of the Basic Law on the process and substance of unification; the sometimes decisive role played by the Federal Constitutional Court in the unification process; the deliberations of the Joint Constitutional Commission and its suggestions for constitutional change; and, finally, the constitutional amendments of October 1994 – all provide evidence for the resilience of the Basic Law. The Constitution might, in parts, be in need of reform; but it has lost none of its vitality, centrality and directive capacity. By contrast, a much more pessimistic view highlights the implications of external and internal challenges to which the Constitution can adapt only within closely defined limits. Far from attesting to the health of the Basic Law, the many proposals for extending constitutional regulation to an ever wider range of matters are indicative of the diffuse sense of unease about the Basic Law's declining ability to perform its traditional functions. The loss of functionality in relation to the historic core tasks and objectives of constitutional regulation may not be explictly acknowledged, or even recognised, by the reformers; but it forms the backdrop of their efforts to regulate ever more and increasingly remote matters through constitutional law. This use of the Constitution for purposes for which it is ill-suited not only leads to excessive regulation; more critically, it might promote, in the longer term, the delegitimation of the Basic Law.

Evidently, both positions represent stark simplifications of what are often complex and nuanced arguments, and they merely mark the extreme poles in the discussion. None the less, they point to genuine and profound differences of opinion on the long-term future of the Basic Law. Put briefly, is the role of the Constitution declining, a process which constitutional reform might, perhaps, temporarily halt, but cannot ultimately arrest? Or will the Basic Law remain, for the foreseeable future, the central source of authority not just for Constituting, distributing and controlling state power and for granting and protecting basic rights, but also for guiding the political, economic and social life of the German polity?

The following does not claim to provide a detailed and exhaustive answer to these questions, but it examines at least some of the arguments advanced in the debate on the future of the Constitution. The starting point of this analysis is a re-examination of the role which the Basic Law, and, importantly, constitutional interpretation through the Federal Constitutional Court have played in the process of unification (II.). Much of the evidence presented in this connection bears out the decisive role of the Constitution in the political process. But it could be argued that the special constitutional implications of regime transition might overshadow a process of long-term weakening. The following part of the analysis is, therefore, concerned with the external (III.) and internal challenges faced by the German Constitution (IV.). The former relate, in particular, to the changing international legal environment of the Basic Law, whilst the latter are principally connected to changes in the state and its relations with society. Next, the discussion turns to the question of how the constitutional legislator seeks to respond to perceived adaptive pressures. In this context, the report of the Joint Constitutional Commission deserves particular attention (V.). Finally, the paper considers the likely future direction of constitutional policy in Germany and highlights the limits of constitutional adaptation (VI.).

II. Unification and the German Constitution

1. Process

The application of the Basic Law to the territory of the former German Democratic Republic (GDR) proceeded from the option of the *Volkskammer* to seek accession to the Federal Republic under Article 23 of the Basic Law. The political decision to pursue unification by this means had been taken by those parties which had campaigned on a 'unification ticket' in the March 1990 elections to the *Volkskammer*. Their decision curtailed discussion about the possibility of separate constitutional arrangements for a new eastern German state, but constitutional developments in the GDR in the months following the fall of the Berlin Wall played an important role in paving the way for the adoption of the Basic Law. The GDR's Constitution, which survived the political upheaval of November 1989, was amended in a number of respects to reflect the revolutionary changes which had taken place. The reference in Article 1 to the leading role of the Socialist Unity Party (SED) as the Marxist-Leninist party of government was the first clause to be removed; other laws that followed included provisions which introduced the possibility of private ownership of the means of production, defined trade union rights and provided for free and democratic elections to the *Volkskammer*.[9] An amending law of 17 June 1990 expunged all traces of a 'socialist concept' of law and justice from the Constitution and committed the GDR to uphold the principles of 'a free democratic, federal and ecologically oriented state based on the rule of law'. This law, in particular, was fundamental in creating the legal conditions necessary for the adoption of the Basic Law and the coming into force of the Treaty on Monetary, Economic and Social Union of 18 May 1990 and the Unification Treaty of 31 August 1990.[10]

These alterations were a direct and swift response to the Communist monopoly of power in the GDR, just as the Basic Law was in many respects a response to the dictatorial government of the Nazi period. But the East German constitutional debate, in fact, went a significant step further than these important, yet piecemeal, amendments would suggest. In April 1990, the constitutional working group of the Round Table (which represented reform-oriented citizens' groups and parties in the GDR) proposed a fully fledged draft of a 'New Constitution for the German Democratic Republic' to the *Volkskammer*.[11] This took the Basic Law as its point of departure, but built upon it in a number of ways. For example, it contained provisions for a wider range of fundamental rights divided into several categories, beginning with classical liberal freedoms, but extending to a series of rights related to economic activity, including a right to work, a right of co-determination in the workplace, protection of property rights and special provisions regarding environmental protection. Another category would have conferred special constitutional protection upon citizens' groups and associations such as those which took part in the GDR's political revolution. The role of political parties, on the other hand, was to be less strongly emphasised than under the Basic Law. Notable among the other provisions of this draft document were the regulations regarding direct democratic participation in government under Article 98 which foresaw the possibility of legislation being proposed, and even adopted directly by the people (though only in the case of proposals supported by at least 750,000 voters). That so much importance should have been attached to constitutional reform was in itself revealing. For the system of government in the GDR, the Constitution never played more than a symbolic or declaratory role. It obviously lacked the normative quality which the Basic Law possesses,[12] and the GDR's reformers were determined to place government on a new and firm legal basis.[13]

For the Federal Government negotiating the Unification Treaty, there was a strong interest in avoiding recourse to Article 146 – as the alternative to Article 23 – which would inevitably have resulted in protracted constitutional debate and delayed the unification process at a time when rapid unification seemed the only answer to the critically unstable political and economic situation in the GDR.[14] Foreign policy considerations also played a role, particularly the growing concern about the stability of the Gorbachev administration. Moreover, to follow the Article 146 route might have prejudiced the legal position regarding East German entry to the European Communities; by using Article 23, it was easier to maintain the legal fiction that no new state was being created and, therefore, no formal accession to the Community would be required.

It would be misleading, however, to account for the decision to apply the Basic Law to the former GDR on grounds of political expediency alone. The constitutional steps taken in the GDR after unification reflected a desire to opt for much of what the Basic Law had to offer: human rights, protected by an independent judiciary headed by a Constitutional Court, a multi-party system, political freedoms to assemble, form associations, demonstrate and express opinions freely and access to education, jobs or professions regardless of political affiliation.

2. The Unification Treaty

Wolfgang Schäuble was Minister of the Interior in Chancellor Kohl's government from April 1989 until November 1991 and as such he was responsible for leading the negotiations on the Unification Treaty on behalf of the Federal Government. From the account he has provided on the negotiations with the GDR,[15] it is clear that the Basic Law was a major constraining factor in the negotiations, as the extension of the West German constitutional order eastwards posed a number of difficult challenges for both sides. The most awkward questions raised for discussion included the voting system to be used in the first all-German elections; the distribution of seats in the Bundesrat; the reorganisation of the financial arrangements underlying the federal system; abortion law; property rights; and proposals for the inclusion of new state objectives in the Basic Law (environmental protection was thought to be a prime candidate for inclusion). Schäuble was concerned that debate on these wide-ranging and potentially divisive issues would seriously delay conclusion of the negotiations. The situation in the GDR was clearly volatile; speed seemed of the essence as East Germans continued to flood west.[16]

In the light of these pressures, it was decided to restrict constitutional debate and especially the adoption of constitutional amendments to the minimum necessary. This is the explanation behind Article 5 of the Unification Treaty, which postponed debate on the wider implications of unification for the federal system, on the restructuring of the Berlin–Brandenburg area, on state objectives, on the possible application of Article 146 and on all other general questions posed by unification until after conclusion of the Unification Treaty. This solution also had an advantage from a democratic standpoint, in that it gave the legislative bodies of the united Germany the chance to consider possible constitutional amendments on these matters individually. By contrast, the Unification Treaty, including the constitutional amendments which it contained, could only be accepted or rejected in its entirety, as the Federal Constitutional Court was to confirm in response to a challenge by a number of Bundestag deputies.[17]

The constitutional changes made by the Unification Treaty were, therefore, confined to matters directly associated with the process of unification and dictated by pressing domestic and international political and legal considerations. These included changes dictated by the Two-plus-Four Treaty (see below) and a restructuring of votes in the Bundesrat which secured a continued blocking majority for the four largest Länder of Baden-Württemberg, Bavaria, Lower-Saxony and North-Rhine Westphalia. The postponement of final decisions on some constitutional questions required the adoption of certain holding or transitional provisions. Two issues in particular, the highly contentious abortion question and the constitutional regulation of property rights, stood out in this respect.

The abortion question threatened to derail the negotiations.[18] The GDR's representatives demanded the preservation of its liberal abortion clause allowing termination of pregnancies without restriction during the first three months of pregnancy. This clause could not be reconciled with the law applying in the Federal Republic which was, at least on paper, much more restrictive and had the backing of the Federal Constitutional Court. A compromise was eventually reached in the Unification Treaty which effectively bypassed the Basic Law. Each law would be kept for two years on the respective territories of East and West Germany and women from the west would be able to take advantage of the eastern rule. Within two years after unification, a new law would have to be passed to resolve the issue (Article 41, Unification Treaty). The new Article 143 of the Basic Law introduced by the Unification Treaty expressly to allow a deviation from the Basic Law to cater for the interim solution was of dubious constitutional validity.[19] After unification, the parties in the Bundestag, following lengthy and heated debate, did produce a new abortion law for the whole of Germany. It went some considerable way towards the former East German law, although it added an obligation regarding special counselling. This law, however, was overturned by a judgment of the Federal Constitutional Court of 28 May 1993.[20] Some might have expected the Court to exercise restraint in its judgment, perhaps taking account of the strength of public opinion, particularly in the east, for whom the liberal law on abortion was part of the socialist inheritance deemed worthy of preservation.[21] In issuing its critical opinion, the Court eschewed calls for such restraint and, in holding that the right to life as enshrined in Article 2 GG required abortion to remain in principle illegal throughout pregnancy, reasserted itself as the supreme interpreter and guardian of constitutional values.[22] The Court's decision caused considerable public discontent, but parliament bowed to the Court's opinion fairly quickly, perhaps with undue deference.[23] New legislation, redrafted to accord with the Court's judgment, was adopted by the Bundestag on 26 May 1994, but, by the end of June 1994, had still to pass through the Bundesrat.

Whereas abortion law was not part of the general political consensus represented by the unification settlement, the rules regarding return of property expropriated under Soviet or GDR authority after the Second World War did fall under this heading. Here, there is evidence to suggest that the Court was very much alive to the dangers of interfering with carefully constructed political compromises. In its decision of 23 April 1991,[24] the Court upheld Article 41 of the Unification Treaty which enshrines the terms of the Joint Declaration of 15 June 1990 on the Settlement of Open Property Questions issued by the governments of the Federal Republic and the GDR. The property declaration provides that expropriations of property carried out without compensation under Soviet authority between 1945 and 1949 are irreversible. This was the subject of a constitutional challenge in Karlsruhe on the basis that it conflicted with Article 14 GG. The Court dismissed the complaints by holding that the Federal Republic could not be held responsible for the expropriations carried out under the auspices of the Soviet Union, because, before unification, the jurisdiction of the Basic Law had been practically limited to the territory of the 11 Western Länder and, moreover, the Basic Law had not been in existence when they took place.[25] But the Court clearly also attached considerable importance to the evidence of Klaus Kinkel, the then Minister of Justice who had negotiated for the Federal Republic on the property question, and to that of Lothar de Maizière, the first and last freely elected Prime Minister of the GDR, who each testified that the Soviet Union and the GDR had made their consent to unification conditional upon legal recognition of the post-war expropriations. It is now being seriously questioned whether these foreign policy considerations were quite as compelling as these witnesses made them appear, and the Court may yet take a second bite at the cherry.

3. The Post-Unification Agenda

Post-unification discussions of the Basic Law have divided on lines remarkably similar to those reflected by the debate on the best way to unify. The elements of conservative opinion, represented in parliament by the CDU, CSU and the FDP, who have favoured leaving the Basic Law essentially untouched, are the same who supported the Article 23 route to unification; the more audacious reformers, who seek substantial revisions of the Constitution to adapt to new challenges, are the SPD and further left-of-centre groupings who wanted Article 146 to be used on unification. The political battle-lines were, in fact, drawn already before the substantive discussions began, namely on the question of the most appropriate forum to debate constitutional reform. The Unification Treaty spoke only of 'the legislative bodies of the united Germany' in Article 5. There was little controversy surrounding the convening of a separate Bundesrat Commission on Constitutional Reform, whose 32 members, consisting of the 16 Länder Minister-Presidents and another member from each Land government, debated possible reforms in the federal system necessitated by unification and the process of European integration.[26]

The conception of the Joint Bundestag–Bundesrat Commission on the Constitution was less easy. The SPD called for a Constitutional Convention or Council (*Verfassungsrat*) to lead the discussion on constitutional reform.[27] This reflected a desire for a wide-ranging constitutional debate going beyond the issues immediately raised by unification, and it also showed that the party wished to stimulate a broad public debate. The members of the Convention would have included persons with a role in public life, not only political party representatives. The parties of the governing coalition, on the other hand, were anxious to limit membership to Bundestag deputies and delegates of the Bundesrat. They won the argument, even if the Commission was double the size they would have liked (64 rather than 32 members). This victory proved crucial as it strongly influenced both the public perception of the Commission's work and the scope and character of its deliberations. In particular, the exercise of party discipline in respect of positions taken by Commission members was a feature of the proceedings.[28]

With regard to the substantive agenda, the more ambitious reformers could at least claim success in broadening the scope of discussions beyond matters which may be said to relate closely to unification. In consequence, the Commission found itself looking at more than half of the provisions of the Basic Law to see if they required amendment or expansion.[29] However, as will be discussed below, the range and substance of the recommendations finally adopted by the Commission were very much more modest in character.

In sum, the role of the Basic Law during the unification process was pivotal. Unification confirmed the centrality of the Basic Law for the German polity. A number of the most difficult political questions raised by unification were, at the same time, constitutional questions which could only be solved with the help of the Basic Law and, rather frequently, the Federal Constitutional Court. Fundamentally, unification resulted in the transplantation of the Federal Republic's constitutional order in an ailing GDR which had actively sought the political freedoms and successful economic system with which the Basic Law had, over 40 years, become closely identified. But unification, especially its aftermath, also raised expectations of the Basic Law and of constitutional regulation in general which might seem rather inflated. The Joint Commission, for example, remarks with some pride upon the large number of petitions presented by ordinary citizens (some 800,000), and interprets this as evidence of the 'exceptionally great importance which the public attaches to constitutional law for the life of the community and the individual'.[30] The capacity of the Basic Law to satisfy such high expectations seems, for the most part, to have gone unquestioned in the debate, and more and more seems to be expected of it in meeting future challenges. At the same time, it is possible to identify both international and domestic developments which could severely limit the Constitution's capacity to respond effectively to these challenges. Unification may, as a result, turn out to have been the Basic Law's finest hour.

III. Challenges to the German Constitution I: The Changing International Legal Environment

1. International Law and Unification

The interdependence amongst nations which today characterises international relations has had a profound impact on the relationship between national and international (including European) legal orders. Such interdependence has vastly increased the scope for regulation by international legal norms of matters which were formerly the exclusive preserve of national legal systems.[31] In relation to Germany, the regulation of external aspects of the unification process provides a particularly clear illustration of this close interrelationship between national and international legal regimes. The end of the division of Germany was bound to raise a series of questions which required to be resolved, in the first instance, at an international rather than national level. This did not, however, necessarily mean that national constitutional rules would be subordinated to international norms. Indeed, in relation to the fundamental question of Germany's legal status, the German constitutional position determined the approach adopted under the wider frameworks of international public law and European Community law. Germany's Community partners and the broader international community accepted the German theory of the legal identity of the Federal Republic in its pre-unification guise with the united state, though this was not a foregone conclusion, as the application of the principle of moving treaty frontiers to the process of German unity was a novel one and not free from doubt.[32] Germany's fellow member states might have thought fit to call into question the possibility of the former German Democratic Republic becoming part of the European Community without following the process of formal accession envisaged under Article 237 of the former EEC Treaty. As it was, the German constitutional perspective was adopted by the EC, with the Dublin European Council meeting leading the way.[33]

German constitutional law may be said then in one sense to have 'triumphed' in its interaction with international legal regulation on unification. In another respect, it was subordinated to that wider context: under the terms of the Treaty on the Final Settlement with respect to Germany ('Two-plus-Four Treaty'), the Basic Law had to be adapted to take account of the fixing of Germany's borders. Article 1 of this treaty declares that 'The United Germany shall comprise the territory of the Federal Republic of Germany, the German Democratic Republic and the whole of Berlin. Its external borders shall be the borders of the Federal Republic of Germany and the German Democratic Republic ...'. This was designed to make it quite clear that Germany's external eastern border was to be the border between the former GDR and Poland. A specific obligation was imposed on Germany under Article 1 (4) of the Two-plus-Four Treaty to ensure that 'the Constitution of the united Germany' would conform with the recognition of the current borders as 'definitive'. This obligation required the deletion of the former Article 23, in order to exclude the constitutional possibility of expansion of German territory by further 'accessions' after unification. The preamble and the former Article 146 were also reworded to indicate that Germany was, after East German accession, territorially complete.

The European Community's decision that German unification simply resulted in territorial rather than legal redefinition of the Federal Republic of Germany fitted with the Federal Government's preferred option of the former Article 23, as opposed to Article 146 GG, as the route to unification. One of the European Commission's officials closely involved in the negotiations concerning East German entry to the Communities has remarked on the 'parallel' between the internal German constitutional mechanisms used to secure unification and the legal means of integrating the GDR into the European Communities.[34] The Community showed considerable flexibility in its reaction to German unification, both in institutional–procedural terms and the transitional arrangements made and in relation to the derogations it allowed, and continues to allow, from substantive Community rules.[35] Fundamentally, German membership of the Communities greatly eased the achievement of unification, whereas it was formerly thought by some that the dual constitutional goals of closer European integration and German unification were mutually exclusive.[36]

Although the special circumstances of German unification produced the need for an exceptional international legal response, the process illustrates the general point that the Basic Law is embedded in a network of interconnected legal dimensions to which it may relate in a variety of ways – the relationship may be one of co-operation and mutual respect rather than conflict – and from which, subject to dramatic political change, it is inextricable. The mode and extent of application of German constitutional law, but also its substance, must take account of these wider dimensions. Whilst, after unification, Germany possesses – in the words of the Two-plus-Four Treaty, 'full sovereignty over its internal and external affairs', such sovereignty is clearly limited by her attachment to a range of European and international alliances and organisations. It is in the context of this limited legal sovereignty and the framework of international obligations which characterises it that new external challenges for the Basic Law are posed.

2. Asylum

Germany experienced a rapid and dramatic expansion in the number of persons seeking asylum throughout the 1980s, but the rise was especially steep over the period from 1989 to 1992, when applications rose from 121,000 in 1989 to 439,000 in 1992.[37] The pressure felt as a result of these numbers, which were far higher than those experienced by Germany's Community partners, coincided with the considerable economic and social upheaval associated with unification. Consequently, asylum became increasingly politicised and moved to the top of the German political agenda in 1992/93. The dilemma which faced German policy-makers was how to reconcile their commitment to the principles of free movement of persons and the protection of human rights (attested by their accession to international and European legal instruments enshrining such principles) with the calming of (perceived) public fears about the effects of uncontrolled immigration.[38]

In Germany, the constitutional dimension stood at the heart of this dilemma and of the political debate. Article 16 GG had been drafted in the light of the tragic experience of the Third Reich, and obliged the Federal Republic to offer asylum to all 'persons persecuted on political grounds', without restriction. During the late 1980s and early 1990s, however, Article 16 became exposed to pressures which the framers of the Basic Law could hardly have predicted. In response, the Federal Government, in common with other Western governments, adopted a defensive and restrictive stance on asylum, both at national and international levels.[39] In its efforts to secure a restrictive amendment to Article 16, Chancellor Kohl's administration was forced to fight a battle on two fronts. It found itself faced, in the early stages of the debate, by firm resistance to reform of Article 16 by the SPD opposition. In response, it initially concentrated its efforts on achieving a European solution to the problem, arguing for a harmonisation of the substantive and procedural rules relating to asylum requests across the member states of the European Community. Germany was a driving force behind the conclusion of the Schengen and Dublin Conventions, both of which introduced jurisdictional rules in order to render one state alone responsible for dealing with asylum requests. These international agreements did not in themselves affect the substance of national laws on asylum, although, for Germany, the prohibition of 'asylum shopping' raised questions of compatibility with the Basic Law.[40] The possibility of such incompatibility allowed Chancellor Kohl to argue before the Bundestag that the European solution required Germany to change her Constitution: 'We must establish the conditions in Germany [for a European solution]. We cannot allow ourselves to act in such a way that we stand in the way of European decisions'.[41]

Article 16 was finally amended in July 1993 (see Appendix), largely in accordance with the Chancellor's wishes and in such a way as to limit severely the accessibility to asylum.[42] The new clause excludes entirely from protection the would-be asylum seekers reaching Germany from 'safe countries', resulting in heavy burdens for Germany's eastern neighbours in particular. The Government denies claims, repeated in the discussions of the Joint Constitutional Commission,[43] that the new provisions breach obligations of international law imposed under the Geneva Convention of 1951.[44] Doubts, however, persist on this question and will not be easily dismissed.[45]

The asylum episode is instructive in a number of respects. It was clear that this particular external challenge bit deeply into the basic rights, that is cherished constitutional values, which have, in contrast to other parts of the Basic Law, only rarely been subject to amendment. These basic rights clauses have been viewed as under attack from developments in the context of the European Communities. There the concern has been to ensure the full application of the basic rights or their European equivalent. Here, on the other hand, one has seen an express and generally welcomed watering down of basic rights protection which has been justified at least in part by the need to conform to European requirements. Evidently, even the most highly esteemed constitutional values may have to be sacrificed to external pressures. The limited capacity of the Basic Law to provide legal solutions to policy issues with such international ramifications is also illustrated by this experience, where one has seen European and national constitutional frameworks of law mutually influencing each other's development. Policy-makers have sought to juggle with different legal systems or arrangements in order to see which might better secure their objectives. In fact, it would seem that the answer in this case is that neither the national nor the international or European legal systems, operating on their own, are adequate for the purpose.

Article 16, in its revised form, may also yet prove a model for the wider substantive harmonisation of laws which the Federal Government continues to seek, for example by virtue of the 'communitisation' of the third pillar of the Maastricht Treaty on European Union concerning co-operation in the fields of justice and internal affairs. If such additional measures are thought necessary this is itself an admission of the limits of national constitutional autonomy. In the new international legal environment it thus appears increasingly anachronistic to speak of discrete constitutional 'spaces'.

3. Germany's Military Role

As well as requiring express amendment of the Basic Law on the subject of territorial integrity, the Two-plus-Four Treaty established another important link between itself and 'the Constitution of the united Germany' in Article 2. This provision refers to the Basic Law's prohibition, contained in Article 26 GG, that 'acts tending to and undertaken with the intent to disturb the peaceful relations between nations, especially to prepare for war of aggression, shall be unconstitutional'. The incorporation by reference of this vital commitment by Germany to peace was an important element of the final settlement of military questions reached between the two Germanies and the Four Powers in the treaty. It was accompanied by a declaration that the 'united Germany will never employ any of its weapons except in accordance with its Constitution and the Charter of the United Nations'. These provisions, together with more concrete commitments to reduce her armed forces to a strength of 370,000 within three to four years of the conclusion of the treaty, and undertakings of economic assistance for withdrawing Soviet troops, helped to persuade the Soviet negotiators to agree to a united Germany within the NATO alliance.[46]

Soviet agreement to all-German NATO membership is reflected in

Article 6 of the Two-plus-Four Treaty which confirms that 'the right of the united Germany to belong to alliances, with all the rights and responsibilities arising therefrom, shall not be affected by the present Treaty'. Framed on the face of it in terms which suggest complete freedom to form and adhere to military or other alliances, this provision was adopted on the understanding that the united Germany would be a full member of the Western security framework. German membership of that system, and in particular of NATO, entails limitations of sovereignty. Article 24 of the Basic Law expressly recognises this when it says (in paragraph 2) that the Federation 'may enter a system of mutual collective security' and 'in doing so it shall consent to such limitations upon its rights of sovereignty as will bring about and secure a peaceful and lasting order in Europe and among the nations of the world'. So it is against the background of limited or, as Steiger has put it, 'relativised sovereignty',[47] that the Basic Law's provisions on Germany's military role should be considered.

The need for scrutiny of the constitutional bases for military actions by Germany arises from the increased expectations placed upon her as a contributor both to NATO and to United Nations actions in the areas of peacekeeping and peacemaking. Among Germany's partners, the United States, in particular, has entertained high hopes of an enhanced security role for the Federal Republic. These hopes were disappointed by the German response to the Gulf War,[48] when Chancellor Kohl explained the failure of Germany to contribute militarily to the Gulf War campaign on constitutional grounds.[49] Since then, the security crises in Somalia and in Bosnia have brought the constitutional dimension into even closer focus. The constitutional debate centres on the interpretation of Articles 87a and 24 of the Basic Law. Article 87a stipulates that 'the Federation shall establish armed forces for defense purposes'. This is interpreted as being in keeping with the fundamental rejection of military aggression contained in Article 26.[50] Article 87a goes on to provide that explicit permission is required under the Basic Law for use of the armed forces for purposes other than defence. 'Defence' in this context means defence of the territory of the Federal Republic against military attack.[51] Article 24 is thought by some commentators to offer an example of an explicit authorisation for Germany's armed forces to act beyond defence purposes, namely in the context of supportive military action under the 'system of mutual collective security' established by NATO or the United Nations, although Article 24, in fact, makes no express reference to use of military force.[52]

The political parties were long divided on the interpretation of these provisions, as is most vividly illustrated by the AWACS case. German military personnel had been taking part since October 1992 in surveillance operations over Bosnian airspace following the adoption of United Nations

Resolution 781 banning flights of military aircraft belonging to the combatants in the region ('no-fly-zone'). The surveillance flights were carried out on behalf of the United Nations by NATO's AWACS (Airborne Warning and Control System) personnel, of whom German soldiers comprised over 30 per cent. The political and constitutional controversy about German involvement in these operations came to a head when the United Nations decided in March 1993 to allow full enforcement of its earlier resolution by use of 'all necessary means'. This, of course, meant that German soldiers could be involved in the shooting down of aircraft and, thus, military action. Whilst Chancellor Kohl's party, the CDU, and its sister party in the governing coalition, the CSU, saw no constitutional obstacle to German participation, the FDP members of the cabinet argued that the Constitution did not authorise such action. On this they were at one with the Social Democratic Party who had for some time been blocking coalition proposals (supported by the FDP) which would have amended the Constitution to allow just such military action. The CDU/CSU had maintained that such an amendment was desirable to clarify the constitutional position, while arguing that it would merely be of declaratory force.[53]

Despite the FDP's objection, the Federal Government authorised German involvement in the AWACS operation on 2 April 1993. Immediately afterwards, the FDP requested an interim injunction (or interdict) from the Federal Constitutional Court to prevent implementation of the Government's majority decision; the SPD joined the action. In the main proceedings, which to date (June 1994) have not been concluded, the FDP and the SPD seek a declaration of the unconstitutionality of the Government's decision.

The Court rejected the FDP/SPD interim application.[54] The Court's denial of an interdict was based on its concern not to prejudice the position of Germany *vis-à-vis* her NATO partners. It pointed to the loss of trust which would result from German withdrawal from the AWACS operation. A German pull-out at this stage would have caused major practical problems, making enforcement of the no-fly-zone extremely difficult. Were the interdict to be granted and the Court in the main proceedings then to find German participation in conformity with the Constitution, Germany would have severely jeopardised the confidence of its NATO allies which it had gained by its participation in the AWACS operation to date.[55]

The substantive constitutional question is an 'open' one, as the Court admits;[56] but it argues, in effect, that where there is doubt about the constitutionality of a measure, the Government may still act, albeit provisionally, if the policy reasons are strong enough. Here, there were important foreign policy considerations at stake. Uppermost amongst these was the question of Germany's international responsibilities. The Court pointed to declarations of the North Atlantic Council and WEU of 1991 and 1992, to which the Federal Republic was party, which emphasise a common commitment to support UN peacekeeping and peacemaking operations.[57] The Court was clearly influenced, then, by considerations of international comity. And it also paid careful attention to the international public law dimensions. Germany should be wary of disturbing the implementation of measures approved by the *Völkerrechtsgemeinschaft*.[58] The interpretation of the Basic Law by the Court is thus squarely placed in the international context.

It will be interesting to see how the Court decides the main proceedings. In particular, one wonders whether the Court will place the same emphasis in its interpretation of the Constitution on the new international situation (legal as well as political) in which the united Germany finds itself. Traditionally, the Federal Constitutional Court has construed national constitutional law, where possible, to be in conformity with international law (*völkerrechtsfreundliche Auslegung*).[59] But there are limits to this approach. The Court cannot use this canon of construction to override the hierarchy of norms which places the Constitution above provisions of international public law.[60]

Uncertainty about the meaning of the Basic Law's provisions on action by Germany's armed forces has not prevented the Federal Government from committing German soldiers to international action in the context of her alliance commitments. The Government chose to act on a secure international law basis notwithstanding clear doubts as to the compatibility of such action with the Basic Law. The Government's approach has been vindicated, if only provisionally, by the Constitutional Court, whose judgment displays considerable respect for the application of international law. It remains to be seen how the Court will finally decide the questions asked of it, but it would be surprising if its interpretation of the Basic Law did not again favour international comity. The Two-plus-Four Treaty provides a normative international framework into which the Basic Law must be fitted. Its impact extends beyond the admittedly crucial effect it had on the constitutional ramifications of the unification process.[61] As with asylum, the debate about Germany's future military role shows that it is becoming ever more difficult to separate national constitutional development from the international legal dimension.

4. The European Union

The Basic Law might well have proved the downfall of the Maastricht Treaty on European Union. Chancellor Kohl, one of the architects of the Union, cannot have been well pleased to see the entry into force of the treaty delayed by an appeal to the Federal Constitutional Court. His government was, understandably, relieved when the judgment went its way, clearing the constitutional path for Germany to ratify.[62] The German Foreign Ministry responded to the judgment by saying that it 'confirms the course of European policy of the Federal Government'.[63] In fact, the Court's opinion suggests that the Basic Law might make it rather harder than the Federal Government previously thought to pursue the strongly *communautaire* or integrationist line that has been a hallmark of Kohl's chancellorship. It is possible to identify some constitutional themes from the judgment which may well dominate the future debate about the relationship between the German constitutional order and the European Union.

It should first be noted that, perhaps surprisingly, the Court did not have much to say about the effects of the European Union on the German federal system. This was in part because solutions of a kind to this problem had already been worked out by the constitutional reform commissions and had been subsequently adopted by parliament. Both commissions devoted considerable time and energy to elaborating a new constitutional provision which, it was hoped, would reconcile or at least reduce the tension between Germany's pursuit of closer European integration and the preservation of her federal system. The product of these deliberations, the new Article 23, gives the Länder considerably enhanced influence over federal policy and decision-making in the European Union. It eats into the Federal Government's traditional monopoly of representation of the Federal Republic on the international plane by allowing Länder government representatives to sit and speak for Germany in the Council of Ministers (see Article 23, section 6). The new clause threatens to weaken the coherence of German European policy, and the Federal Government is particularly concerned that a 'situation should not arise where the particularist interests of 16 Länder prevent a vote which is in the interests of Germany as a whole'.[64] More will be said below about the new Article 23 in Section V.

Described as 'a Europe of bits and pieces' by a leading commentator,[65] the European Union created by the Maastricht Treaty wins the rather more respectful epithet of *Staatenverbund*, or League of States, from the Federal Constitutional Court. Some of the commentators who joined the unusually lively debate among German constitutional scholars before the Court gave judgment thought the treaty represented a qualitative change of direction for the Community towards independent statehood.[66] The creation of new rights of citizenship at Community level was viewed as effectively removing similar rights at the national level and, therefore, threatening national (constitutional) identity.[67]

The Court's findings that a European state was not on the doorstep relied heavily on its view that the member states remain in control of Community competences as 'masters of the Treaties'. Maastricht did not change the system of distribution of Community competences under which the Community only enjoys such powers as are expressly conferred upon it by the member states. To use the words of the Court, the Community does not possess the ability to found its own competences or *Kompetenz-Kompetenz*.[68] More controversially, in an express challenge to the authority of the European Court of Justice, the Federal Constitutional Court has asserted its own authority to assess whether the Community institutions have acted within their competences. In so doing, it makes an implicit criticism of the European Court for failing to guard carefully enough against expansive interpretation of Community powers.[69]

In an even more surprising statement, the Court seems to depart from political reality when it raises the possibility of Germany withdrawing from the Community altogether in certain circumstances, for example if there is a real possibility of full currency stability not being achieved.[70] The Court, however, backs up the assertion of such a right by referring to the need for Union action to remain within the boundaries set by the member states. This reasoning is, in turn, linked to the issue of democratic legitimacy. In the Court's view, the legitimacy of Union actions stems from the authority lent it by national parliaments. Under the Basic Law, the democratic principle is one of the fundamental structural principles of German Government contained in Article 20. That principle may not be surrendered to the European Union, though the Court accepts that in such a supranational structure democratic requirements fall to be interpreted differently than in a national state, with the result that majority voting and a greater role for executive as opposed to parliamentary decision-making are permitted. The Court, nevertheless, makes it clear that the democratic rights of the citizen under Article 38, in combination with Article 20 of the Basic Law, would be breached were the competences of the Bundestag, in relation to legislative and control functions, to be substantially lost to an organ of the European Union or Community consisting of the governments of the member states.[71]

We see the Court then reasserting the autonomy and authority of national German institutions – itself and the Bundestag – over European ones – the European Court of Justice and the European Parliament. The latter will not have been pleased to see itself relegated in the Court's opinion to playing a 'supporting role' in providing democratic legitimacy in the Union.[72] The Court has placed limits on the expansion of the European Parliament at the expense of the Bundestag; this may have an effect on the level of support given by the Federal Government to the expansion of the European Parliament's powers.[73]

As to the protection of Germany's much-vaunted basic rights against encroachment from European law, the Court's judgment is rather reserved. It views with relative equanimity the exclusion of the European Court of

Justice from jurisdiction over decisions taken in the framework of the Maastricht Treaty's intergovernmental pillars on foreign and security policy and justice and home affairs and confirms its previous case law to the effect that it regards the protection offered under Community law to fundamental rights to be substantially equivalent to the protection offered to the basic rights under the Basic Law.[74] The possibility of conflicts between the respective legal orders in the field of fundamental rights cannot be ruled out, however. Indeed, as the scope of Community law continues to expand, it is possible that deficits of human rights protection within the European Union will be highlighted.[75]

Where once the constitutional debate about the relationship between the Basic Law and European integration focused on the question of compatibility of the respective constitutional goals of unification on the one hand and closer European integration on the other, now the main issue is how the Federal Republic can preserve the essentials of its constitutional identity in the face of increasing Community powers.[76] Challenges are faced in relation to all of the fundamental structural principles of German Government. The above discussion shows this in relation to federalism, democracy and basic rights. The challenges need not always be seen as threats; there is also clearly scope for German conceptions to gain a foothold in the Union – the influence of the German 'model' can be seen in a number of institutional features of the Maastricht Treaty, such as the co-decision legislative procedure or the Committee of the Regions. But the Federal Constitutional Court's judgment tends to suggest that the developing constitutional order of the European Union is being seen increasingly as a source of danger rather than an opportunity for the Basic Law.

5. The European Convention on Human Rights

Under German law, the European Convention for the Protection of Human Rights and Fundamental Freedoms enjoys the status of an ordinary Federal statute under the legal hierarchy of norms.[77] It is not covered by Article 25 GG as part of the 'general rules of public international law' which take precedence over statutes.[78] In theory, therefore, the Federal legislator could enact domestic legislation in contravention of the Convention without there being any constitutional objection. The Federal Constitutional Court has, however, held that the legislator is presumed not to wish to depart from obligations undertaken under international law, with the result that national legislation falls to be construed in accordance with such obligations.[79] Specifically in relation to the Convention, the Federal Constitutional Court has also made clear that the interpretation of the Basic Law itself must take account of the nature and level of protection of fundamental rights guaranteed thereunder.[80] This lends the Convention a far higher significance than its categorisation as equivalent to an ordinary Federal statute would suggest. The Convention has affected German domestic law in a number of areas, principally as a result of German courts taking account of the terms of the Convention when interpreting and applying such law. The influence of the Convention has been felt particularly strongly in the field of criminal law. A detailed study of the impact of the Convention on substantive and procedural criminal law demonstrates this with reference to decisions of the German courts, as well as acts of the legislature.[81] The ordinary criminal courts in Germany have frequently relied on the terms of Article 6 of the Convention, which sets out elementary conditions for a fair trial of persons charged with criminal offences.[82] Article 6 sets out such conditions in more detail than the equivalent provisions of the Basic Law. This is typical of the Convention; its greater precision in detailing requirements on fundamental rights protection is one of the reasons why it can be helpful in national courts.[83]

The Federal Constitutional Court has also stressed the importance of looking to the jurisdiction of the Strasbourg-based Court of Human Rights when interpreting the guarantees set out in the Basic Law. Many of the provisions of the Convention and the Basic Law overlap. There is also, of course, the possibility of conflict. In one notable case, the jurisdiction of the Strasbourg court was invoked in order to challenge the Constitutional Court's interpretation of the protection of personal privacy. Article 10 of the Basic Law had been amended to enable the security services to carry out telephone tapping without judicial scrutiny. The amendment was contested in reliance upon the Basic Law's protection of privacy and the right of recourse to the courts, but Karlsruhe held in favour of the amendment on public security grounds.[84] The complainants then sought redress under Articles 8 and 13 of the Convention. On this occasion, the Court of Human Rights interpreted the Convention in a similar fashion to the Constitutional Court's interpretation of the Basic Law.[85] The case, however, illustrates that the protection of fundamental rights in Germany takes place under a European umbrella. The German basic rights may be tested against a common European standard; their interpretation and application are not solely a German affair.

In sum, whilst unification has freed Germany 'from nearly all the dependent features which defined the role of the Federal Republic in the international arena',[86] the Basic Law remains tightly caught in a web of European and international legal relationships. The process of unification and the continuing moves towards closer European integration pursuant to the Maastricht agenda have served to emphasise the limitations upon German constitutional sovereignty. The broader legal frameworks superimposed on

Germany's domestic laws not only significantly affect the interpretation and application of German constitutional rules; these frameworks have been known to dictate the content of German norms and, in the case of conflict, may even override them entirely. There is no doubt that the expansion of Community powers poses the most serious challenge to the authority of the Basic Law. The new Article 23 attempts to ensure that the essential structural principles of the Basic Law are not undermined by future transfers of sovereign powers to the European Union. But Article 23 also shifts attention to the shaping of the constitutional order of the European Union and in so doing seems to recognise that, to some extent, the constitutional battle with the European Union has already been lost. It responds by calling upon the emerging constitutional framework of the European Union to respect the principles of democracy, federalism, the social state and the rule of law, in the image of the *Grundgesetz*.

IV. Challenges to the German Constitution II: State and Society

External challenges raise the possibility of a partial substitution of the Basic Law, as competing or superior legal frameworks assume authority which had hitherto been the preserve of the national Constitution. The central concerns in this respect are, therefore, hierarchy and replacement. By contrast, internal challenges relate principally to constitutional relevance and capacity, most notably in relation to the establishment, distribution and control of state power and the ordering of state-society relations. As Grimm points out, the Constitution is addressed to the state and its presupposes the difference between state and society.[87] However, the organisational and functional distinctness of the state, and, by implication, the public-private boundary, are increasingly called into question by, *inter alia*, shifts in institutional arrangements, tasks and forms of state-society interaction. To a large extent, the internal threat to the centrality of the Constitution is, therefore, a result of the changing empirical identity of the modern state.[88] What is more, it is by no means certain that the serious problems for constitutional regulation which they pose can effectively be dealt with through constitutional reform strategies.

(a) *Institutional arrangements*: In respect of institutional arrangements, the contemporary German state seems to deviate ever more from one of the key characteristics traditionally associated with the modern state, that is that it constitutes 'a recognizably separate institution or set of institutions, so differentiated from the rest of society as to create identifiable public and private spheres'.[89] There are at least two dimensions to this: first, demarcation problems arising from the growing reliance on para-government institutions, 'hybrid organisations', and indirect administrations which undermine the legal and organisational coherence of the administrative state; and, second, the growing 'internal privatisation' of the public sector, as it takes on organisational properties once traditionally identified more or less exclusively with the private sector.

Given the importance of public law in constituting a recognisable public as opposed to a private sphere, the growing role of private law institutions for public governance is constitutionally problematic. Public action through private law institutions has, of course, long been an established and also increasingly well-documented feature of the German administrative system,[90] and the public–private demarcation problems arising from the ubiquity of private law institutions in public governance have often been highlighted. However, they are becoming more accentuated as a consequence of the ever-growing number of such institutions and, more importantly, their extension into areas of administration which had previously been the domain of authorities under public law. The decentralisation (or regionalisation) of economic policy-making, as one of the most widely discussed trends in the German federal system during the 1980s, provides just one example.[91] Here, the strengthening of sub-central administrative capacities has not only gone hand in hand with the establishment of new para-public institutions, but has largely been synonymous with it. Consequently, both at the Länder and local levels, almost the entire management of regional economic policies is by now the responsibility of private law institutions, including publicly owned banks and regional development agencies. Such 'organisational privatisation' has further gained in momentum since unification at Federal, Länder and local levels,[92] a development that is, for example, clearly evidenced in the field of transport policy.[93]

This transfer of public tasks from public law to private law institutions is complemented by a process through which the public sector takes on organisational features originating in the private sector. Although, in Germany, in contrast to the United Kingdom, the discussion about a shift from a public administration culture to a public management paradigm is of relatively recent origin,[94] signs of a growing political interest in introducing private sector organisational techniques into public administration are unmistakable at all levels of the administrative system.[95] Given the German public sector's well-known capacity to withstand adaptive pressures, the chances for a wholesale transformation of public administration and its remoulding on private sector lines appear slim; on the other hand, there is increasing evidence for moves at all levels of the administrative system to introduce private management principles and techniques.[96] In short, the growing reliance on private law institutions, combined with internal debureaucratisation, challenges a core determinant of the distinct empirical identity of the state.

(b) *Tasks:* Organisational arrangements undermining the empirical distinctiveness of the state as well unorthodox forms of public–private interaction (see below) are, in large part, a consequence of changes in the scope of state activity. Empirically, the German state has never closely approximated the image of the liberal *Nachtwächterstaat*, content with policing the ground rules which allow society the highest possible degree of self-regulation; on the other hand, it is equally clear that the 20th century has been characterised by a steady extension of the scope of state activities, which has resulted in a profound qualitative reorientation in state–society relations. Two developments stand out in this respect: the growth of the welfare state and the rise of the anticipatory and protective state, the task of which is 'future-oriented risk anticipation to steer the process of scientific-technological change in society'.[97] Historically, the rise of the welfare state precedes the growth of the anticipatory-protective state, and, in purely quantitative terms, it has had a more profound impact upon state-society relations. Thus, the need for financing distributive and redistributive measures for the benefit of mass social welfare accounts for much of the growth of public spending (as percentage of national GDP) during the post-war period, and it has also been a crucial factor behind the expansion in the number of public personnel (welfare bureaucracy). Perhaps more critically, provision has been linked to social planning and organisation, so that 'social spheres which would be entirely removed from state influence can no longer be found.'[98]

The continuous strengthening of the organising, steering and controlling functions of the state is given further impetus by the need to contain and, where possible, minimise the risks connected with the steadily accelerating rate of scientific-technological innovation.[99] Prevention, risk assessment and risk management become central tasks of the modern state, which can only be effectively carried out on the basis of a comprehensive authority of the state to monitor, direct, and, where considered necessary, discontinue the societal process of the production and application of scientific-technological knowledge. In particular, *Vorsorge* is a central feature of environmental protection, which may cut deeply into personal liberties.[100]

(c) *State–society interactions:* The assumption by the state of comprehensive responsibility for societal development has necessitated new forms of state–society interaction and new instruments of state activity. Put briefly, the etatisation of society, or the state's permeation of society, is paralleled by the socialisation of the state. The latter refers, first, to the permeability of state institutions and decision-making processes which allows social actors to gain decisive influence on the definition of state activities; and, second, the increasing importance of 'public–private partnerships' for the implementation of state programmes. That state activity should, ultimately, be controlled by society is, of course, a basic tenet of constitutional democracy; however, a democratically elected parliament as the central institution for transmitting society's will into the state has long been increasingly complemented, and, in many ways superseded by other institutions, notably political parties and associations. The frequent, typically negative, characterisation of Germany as a *Parteienstaat* and *Verbändestaat* both highlights the extent of this phenomenon and points to its problematic constitutional consequences.[101]

Whilst extra-parliamentary channels of societal influence on the definition of state activity have long been recognised, the interaction between state and society in the implementation of public policy has only relatively recently come under more intensive and systematic scrutiny. As the state has taken on new tasks, legal regulation, backed up by the coercive power of the state, has proved of limited use, and has been partly replaced by instruments such as direct and indirect provision, motivation (through material and immaterial incentives and disincentives), negotiation, persuasion, dissuasion, or information.[102] The rise of the 'co-operative state',[103] however, appears to go even further: even the implementation of regulatory legislation would often seem dependent on co-operative public–private arrangements, including, for example, negotiations, understandings, agreements and public law treaties, a fact which further promotes 'informal administrative action'.[104] Thus, not only law-making, but also the implementation of law become enmeshed in bargaining or negotiation processes between public and private actors.[105]

The picture of the state and state-society relations which emerges from the preceding discussion is complex and not free of contradictions. Changes in institutional arrangements appear to undermine the state–society distinction, whereas the extension of state responsibility could be interpreted as the etatisation, or perhaps even marginalisation, of society. All signs, however, point to the pluralisation of the state (encompassing structures, procedures, tasks, forms and instruments) and a high degree of interpenetration between state and society, as a result of which their analytical-theoretical and empirical differentiation becomes more and more problematic.

The challenges to the Basic Law resulting from internal pluralisation and state–society interpenetration go to the heart of the Basic Law's role. Given the puzzling multiformity of modern arrangements of governance, which

seem to show less and less respect for traditional notions of public and private, it is increasingly questionable whether constitutional law is still able to
determine authoritatively the organisational structure of the state and to control state power. Thus, to the extent that the state takes on private forms, constitutional limitations on the exercise of public authority are in danger of
becoming increasingly obsolete; where the state acts through private law
entities, public law declines in importance. At the same time, the extension
of state tasks makes for a degree and intensity of state intervention into the
private sphere which is difficult to reconcile with the idea of constitutionally
limited government, in particular if intervention implies the restriction of
basic rights and liberties. Finally, the socialisation of the state makes it
increasingly impossible for constitutional law to demarcate with any precision the state sphere from society or even to provide a basic normative structure for their patterns of interaction.

V. Options of Constitutional Policy

The threat of substitution, growing ineffectualness and marginalisation, as a
result of a changing international legal environment and the long-term transformation of public–private relations, confronts constitutional policy with a
formidable task. Passive acquiescence in the gradual decline in constitutional capacity is, of course, a possible option, and it may seem more attractive than strained attempts at adapting the institution of constitutional law,
which developed in response to historically very specific tasks and circumstances, to fundamentally altered conditions and requirements. However, at
least in the German context, such an option is unlikely to be politically
acceptable. Where the Constitution has to provide 'the decisive point of
crystallising communality in the socio-political order of the Republic'[106]
and where all aspects of political, economic, social and cultural life are
deemed worthy of being discussed in the light of constitutional law, constitutional policy through inactivity is not a practicable course of action. With
benign neglect ruled out, two options remain: to try to shore up the Basic
Law's capacity to continue to fulfil its core functions, and thus maintain its
centrality to the life of the polity; and to attempt to give it new functions,
which may, at least in part, compensate for a loss of directive capacity in
other respects. Both reaffirmation and adaptation are, of course, strategies
which are fraught with difficulties, and neither is assured of success: external and internal challenges may be of a quality and magnitude which preclude more than symbolic adaptive reactions, and, like any social institution,
constitutional law is not necessarily capable of being put to use for different
purposes than those for which it came initially into existence. None the less,
to the extent that the threats of substitution and marginalisation are consid-

ered real rather than imaginary, these strategies, solely or combined, need to form the core of a reformist constitutional policy.

Although, as argued above, the debate on the Basic Law is dominated by arguments concerning constitutional substance rather than capacity, elements of both reform strategies have, in recent years, featured prominently in the German reform discourse. One of the latter's most striking features has been the sheer breadth of the reform proposals that have been under discussion. In view of the many ringing endorsements for the Basic Law as 'the best Constitution Germany has ever had' published on the occasion of its 40th birthday, the range of reform proposals discussed appears surprising,[107] as virtually no area of constitutional regulation is beyond the would-be reformers' reach.

The scope of the reform discussion on the Basic Law over the last decade or so has been very clearly reflected in the deliberations of the Joint Constitutional Commission. The main headings under which the Commission considered possible amendments included:

– Europe (that is the adaptation of the Basic Law to the European integration process and, in particular, to the Maastricht Treaty);
– Intergovernmental relations;
– Basic rights;
– State objectives (*Staatsziele*);
– Plebiscitary elements;
– Constitutional law relating to parliament;
– Electoral law;
– The military;
– The constitutional position of the churches;
– The Preamble and Article 146 of the Basic Law; and a number of
– Miscellaneous issues (including the law of nationality; the termination of international state treaties; fiscal relations; the privatisation of the public railways and the Federal Post Office; state liability law; and finally, attitudes to the former GDR).

Evidently, the Commission's extensive, and not uncontroversial[109] interpretation of its own remit under the label of *Selbstbefassungsrecht*[110] allowed for wide-ranging deliberations. By contrast, the amendments proposed by the Commission were, on the whole, modest, with the important exception of the changes adopted in connection with the ratification of the Maastricht Treaty. Thus, the Commission proposed no changes relating to plebiscitary instruments, law relating to parliament, electoral law, the military, state–church relations, the preamble to the Basic Law and Article 146, or any of the 'miscellaneous issues' listed above. As far as basic rights are concerned, the Commission adopted a single proposal, relating to the equality of men and women. Thus, Article 3 (2) of the Basic Law, which reads 'Men and women shall have equal rights' is to be extended through a provision which states that 'The state promotes the accomplishment of the equality [*Gleichberechtigung*] of women and men and seeks to eliminate existing disadvantages'. Under the heading of state objectives, two constitutional amendments were proposed. The first, which occasioned little debate in the Commission, concerned the rights of ethnic minorities of German nationality. Here, a new Article 20b should guarantee that 'The state respects the identity of ethnic, cultural and linguistic minorities'.

Much more controversially, the Commission also decided to propose an amendment which would make environmental protection a state objective.[111] For more than a decade, the protection of the environment has been at the heart of the intensive debate about the inclusion of state objectives into the Basic Law[112] and it was also one of the most hotly debated issues in the Commission.[113] The many facets to the discussion cannot be explored in this context;[114] however, the exceptionally tortuous formulation of the new Article 20a eventually adopted by the Commission betrays the difficulties involved in finding a compromise solution acceptable to both Christian and Social Democrats:

> The State protects, also in recognition of the responsibility for future generations, the natural foundations of life within the framework of the constitutional order through legislation and, according to statute and law, through the executive and the judiciary. (Proposed Article 20a)[115]

It will, however, remain to be seen what practical impact this new Article, which was approved unchanged by the constitutional legislators in the Bundestag and the Bundesrat, will have in future years.

By contrast, the constitutional changes advocated by the Commission in the remaining two closely related areas – intergovernmental relations and the constitutional implications of the creation of a European Union – were bound to have a far more immediate impact. Judged in terms of the number of amendments put forward, the field of intergovernmental relations accounts for the bulk of the Commission's proposals. Thus, amendments have been proposed affecting legislative powers and legislative procedures; administrative organisation; territorial reorganisation (including the Berlin–Brandenburg area); and the strengthening of local government. Whilst these proposals went some way, though not very far, towards meeting some of the demands of the Länder for a strengthening of their role, they provided no basis for the much-discussed 'refederalisation' of the German intergovernmental system.[116] Moreover, in the subsequent political discussion, the proposals for a tightening of the conditions under which the

Federation can use its concurrent legislative powers were watered down at the insistence of the Federal Government. As a result, none of the working principles of the German federal system is seriously called into question. This applies to the emphasis on the intergovernmental sharing of powers, responsibilities and resources; the stress on vertical and horizontal joint policy-making; the dominance of central legislation; the general presumption in favour of subcentral implementation; and the domination of the intergovernmental processes by the political and administrative executives.[117] It would, therefore, seem justified to talk of a 'non-reform' of the German federal system,[118] in particular in view of the inability to achieve any breakthrough in the field of intergovernmental fiscal relations.[119]

However, the overall effects of the Commission's recommendations on federal relations cannot be fully gauged without reference to the constitutional changes relating to the European Union, which were already incorporated into the Basic Law prior to conclusion of the Commission's work.[120] Partly, these amendments were designed to bring the Basic Law into line with the provisions of the Maastricht Treaty. Thus, an amendment to Article 28 grants citizens of the European Union the right to vote in local government elections and an amendment to Article 88 allows for the transfer of responsibilities and powers from the Bundesbank to the European Central Bank. The majority of new provisions, however, whilst closely linked to the European integration process, were not strictly necessitated by the Treaty on European Union. They include:

– *a new Article 24 (1a)* which allows the Länder to transfer sovereign powers to transfrontier institutions in neighbouring regions with the consent of the Federal Government in areas where they have the right to exercise governmental powers and discharge governmental functions;

– *an amendment to Article 50*: whereas previously this read: 'The Länder shall participate through the Bundesrat in the legislation and administration of the Federation', it now stipulates: 'The Länder shall participate through the Bundesrat in the legislation and administration of the Federation and in matters concerning the European Union'.

– *a new Article 52 (3a)*, which lays down that for matters concerning the European Union the Bundesrat forms a Chamber for European Affairs, permitted to take decisions for the Bundesrat as a whole (note that this provision merely provides a clear legal basis for existing constitutional practice);

– *a new Article 45* which stipulates that the Bundestag appoint a Committee on European Union, which can be empowered to fulfil the Bundestag's rights according to Article 23 of the Basic Law; and

– *a new Article 23*, commonly referred to as the 'Article on European Union'.

The Article on European Union, in particular, is of great significance for intergovernmental relations. It constitutionalises, specifies and extends the Bundesrat's participatory rights in Union-related policy-making; most importantly, where essentially the Länder's legislative powers, the establishment of their authorities or their administrative competences are affected, the Bundesrat's opinion needs to be given 'due consideration' in the formulation of the Federation's negotiating position in the Union. As the 'Law on the Co-operation between the Federation and the Länder in Matters Concerning the European Union' of 12 March 1993[121] makes clear, a decision taken by the Bundesrat with a two-thirds majority is, ultimately, binding on the Federation if no agreement can be reached between the Federal Government and the Bundesrat. It should, however, be noted that even proponents of the new co-operation procedures admit that the new regulations are 'fairly complicated' and can only work if the Federation and the Länder show the capacity and willingness for 'mutual co-operation and mutual compromise',[122] whilst more critical voices have questioned the practicality[123] and even the legality[124] of key elements of the new legal framework.

Predictably, the Commission report has been met with a mixed reception, both amongst academic and political commentators. In their reaction, the lines of division which emerged during 1990 clearly resurfaced. Representatives of the Social Democrats,[125] the Greens[126] and many constitutional experts who at the time of unification had called for a popular referendum on a more or less revised Constitution for the whole of Germany[127] have criticised the Commission, which could only adopt recommendations with a two-thirds majority, for its overly timid approach.[128] It is interesting to note here that the most outspoken critics have included prominent members of the Commission, such as its co-chairman, the Social Democrat Henning Voscherau, and the former leader of the Social Democratic Party, Hans-Jochen Vogel. By contrast, Christian Democrat members of the Commission[129] have praised the Commission's work, with the Free Democrats somewhere in the middle.[130] And one of the leading constitutional scholars, who had strongly argued in favour of unification under Article 23, has commented that major damage to the Basic Law has only just been avoided.[131]

Assessed in the light of the external and internal challenges to the Basic Law outlined above, it would, indeed, seem that the Commission's amendments will, at best, make a limited contribution to avoiding the dangers of substitution and marginalisation. As regards external challenges, the Europeanisation of the German Constitution deserves particular attention.

The changes adopted in December 1992 commit the Federal Republic explicitly and unequivocally to the development of the European Union and are designed to ensure the compatibility of German constitutional regulations with Union law. Moreover, they recognise the degree to which the process of European integration affects the distribution of state power within member states, both horizontally – notably between the executive and the legislature – and vertically between different levels of government. Accordingly, executive–legislative relations and intergovernmental relations have partly been constitutionally redefined in an attempt to reverse, or at least halt, the power shift towards the Federal executive with which European integration has long been associated.[132] Thus, an important step has been taken to try to ensure that the principles of state organisation originally envisaged by the Basic Law, insofar as they concern intergovernmental and legislative–executive relations – are not, in practice, undermined by the integration process. To the extent that they seek to adapt German constitutional law to the implications of European integration, the amendments adopted in connection with the ratification of the Maastricht Treaty could be described as reactive.

However, what is, perhaps even more important is the attempt, supported by the Federal Constitutional Court, to tie the process of European integration more closely to the Basic Law. The underlying objective would seem to be to compensate for the loss of national constitutional autonomy by binding supranational constitutional structures and decision-making to the Basic Law and its prime interpreters. Thus, Article 23 (1) GG commits the Federal Republic to advancing a Community committed to 'democratic, rule-of law, social and federal principles as well as the principle of subsidiarity'; the latter three principles are politically highly contentious amongst the Union member states. By constitutionally obliging the Federal Republic to their pursuit, the future course of European integration is tied in a very specific manner to the Basic Law. The German Constitution is thus used as an instrument for determining the core of the Union's Constitution.

The resolve to maintain, if not increase, the Basic Law's relative weight in the Europeanised constitutional space can also be seen very clearly in the Federal Constitutional Court's ruling of 12 October 1993 on the constitutionality of the Maastricht Treaty (see above). Here, the Court not only stipulated a connection between the powers of the European Parliament and any further extension of the powers and responsibilities of the Union; it also affirmed its right to examine 'whether the legal acts of European institutions and organs remain within the boundaries of the sovereign rights conceded to them or exceed these rights'. The challenge to the authority of the European Court this poses is evident.[133]

Can the explicit opening of the Basic Law for the development of the

European Union, combined with a Federal Constitutional Court seemingly determined to play an active role in shaping the Union's constitutional arrangements, effectively prevent the substitution through subordination which the process of internationalisation would seem to imply? In other words, can the relative loss of weight of the German constitution as a result of the Europeanisation of the constitutional space be effectively prevented through a policy of 'Germanisation'? Leaving aside reservations about the desirability of such a policy, there are political and legal factors which severely limit its chances of success. Politically, the Federation will be put in an untenable position if institutional arrangements or policies approved by other Union member states are blocked on the basis of the Federal Constitutional Court's interpretation of their compatibility with 'social and federal principles as well as the principle of subsidiarity'. This can be avoided either through non-application; or through an interpretation of these principles by the Court which leaves them so unspecific as to deprive them of their formative capacity; or through constitutional amendment, removing references to social, federal and subsidiarity principles from the Constitution. The latter might seem rather far-fetched; but given the clear signs in Germany and the Union as a whole for a move away from a federal European construction with a strong 'social' component, as exemplified by the Social Chapter, such a reversal is probably not as unlikely as it may appear. Political obstacles are reinforced by legal considerations. In this connection, one need only mention the possible implications of a conflict between the European Court and the Federal Constitutional Court regarding the compatibility of legal acts of the Union with the treaties.

Overall, it seems doubtful whether recent constitutional policy can help to prevent the further reduction in the directive capacity of the national Constitution due to European integration. The partial loss of external sovereignty which Europeanisation and supranationalisation necessarily imply affects the Basic Law's ability to determine constitutional reality; and efforts to maintain the Basic Law's centrality whilst allowing for further political integration seem ultimately doomed.

Turning to the internal challenges outlined above, the proposed changes to the Constitution do little to address them effectively. Thus, one looks in vain for innovative approaches to the growing institutional diversification of the state, which is exemplified by 'organisational privatisation'. True, in the cases of the privatisation of the Federal postal services and the public railways, constitutional law has played an important role, as their transformation into public listed companies required constitutional amendment; but both instances also illustrate the difficulties of devising a constitutional framework which allows for an adequate response to the perceived need for organisational change. If the analysis is widened to include the many instances in which policy-making and implementation responsibilities are shifted from public law to private law institutions, the assessment of constitutional capacity becomes even more sceptical. It could, of course, be argued that constitutional provisions should leave broad scope for adjustment in state practice; however, it must be realised that such discretion can only be achieved at the price of the Constitution's reduced ability to distribute and control state power authoritatively.

Whereas the constitutional reform debate has had little new to say about state organisation, state tasks have – under the labels of 'state objectives' and 'basic rights' – played a central role in the deliberations. The clear trend has been to interpret constitutionally recognised obligations ever more extensively and, at the same time, to constitutionalise new obligations on the state. The wisdom of a constitutional policy which seeks to stipulate state tasks through constitutional legislation rather than concentrating on maintaining the conditions under which these can be politically defined through democratic contest is, of course, debatable. Of more immediate concern in the context of the present discussion are the implications of the extended constitutional interpretation of state tasks for the Basic Law's directive capacity. To the extent that tasks are constitutionalised which are politically uncontroversial, constitutional regulation merely recognises existing political commitment, and practical adherence is ensured through self-binding by policy-makers. However, where an attempt is made to constitutionalise politically contentious tasks, the Constitution's directive capacity is immediately challenged. In this connection, it will be particularly interesting to see what the practical impact of the new article on the environmental protection as a state objective will be.

Amongst the three internal challenges to the Constitution outlined above, the Joint Commission has had least to say about changes in state–society interactions; and it is in this area where constitutional law and constitutional practice would seem to deviate most significantly. Thus, a much-needed reconsideration of the position of political parties is not part of the constitutional reform agenda. Neo-corporatist state–interest group arrangements have evolved without constitutional guidance or control, and although they have a fundamental influence on state organisation and state–society relations, the Basic Law remains curiously 'blind' to their existence. This non-recognition of state practice on the side of policy formulation is matched by a failure to address new forms of public–private interaction in policy implementation. True, the Basic Law would seem to provide broad scope for the 'co-operative state'; but constitutional changes to recognise, and provide a normative framework for, such arrangements are not part of the constitutional reform agenda.

In summary, in comparison to the external and internal challenges to the

Basic Law that we have identified in this paper, the Joint Constitutional Commission's recommendations seem inadequate; central problems facing the Basic Law have either not been addressed at all or the proposed responses fall short of what would appear to be required. Such an assessment should not, however, necessarily be read as a criticism of the Commission's work; rather, it raises the question whether constitutional reform is capable of halting or reversing the decline in the normative–directive capacity of the Basic Law.

VI. Constitutional Futures

With the collapse of Communist power in central and eastern Europe, constitutionalism and constitutional government appear stronger than ever before. The transition processes have underlined that legitimacy of state power on the one hand, and its establishment, distribution and control through constitutional law on the other, are by now inseparable in the vast majority of democratic states. Although Germany's specific form of regime transition, unification, was associated with political and constitutional challenges which differed significantly from those in her central and eastern European neighbours, here, too, the importance of a solid constitutional foundation to stabilise the transition process has been clearly demonstrated by events. The very broad constitutional discussion accompanying the unification process, the significant amendments to the Basic Law since 1989, the proposals of the Joint Constitutional Commission, and finally, the constitutional amendments approved in October 1994 further testify to the importance attached to the Constitution and constitutional policy in Germany.

   Against this background it might at best seem over-pessimistic, and at worst simply misdirected, to raise the spectre of the growing substitution and marginalisation of the Basic Law; to suggest, moreover, that there might be an element of inevitability about such a decline would seem to invite scornful derision. Certainly, for the foreseeable future, the Basic Law is assured of a central role in the political, economic, social and cultural life of the German polity. At the same time, however, one needs to be careful not to equate the dominance of constitutional argument in the political process with the capacity of the Basic Law effectively to shape 'the political and social life of the community' which its 'claim to a comprehensive validity'[134] would suggest. The ever-increasing number of political and social controversies ending up before the Federal Constitutional Court, the very considerable political energy invested in the constitutional reform discussion, and the undiminished disposition of political and social actors to highlight the constitutional angle of issues under debate underscore the centrality of constitutional discourse in the German polity; however, in themselves, they provide little evidence for the Basic Law's capacity to fulfil the expectations placed upon it.

That the Basic Law's directive capacity might not be sufficient to fulfil comprehensive validity claims is suggested by the growing importance of international legal orders on the one hand, and challenges to central premises of constitutional regulation on the other. The internationalisation of the constitutional space has not yet led to the 'crowding out' of the Basic Law or to its relegation to a subordinate position; but the contextualisation of the Basic Law through other positive legal frameworks acts as a power-ful force which limits claims of supreme authority and restricts national judicial interpretation. This challenge to the Basic Law is ultimately a con-sequence and reflection of the restricted external sovereignty of the contem-porary German state. Likewise, the internal challenges to the Constitution which we have identified are in large part to be explained by the partial loss of internal sovereignty of the state in relation to society. At the heart of this process is the inextricable interweaving of state and society through the mutually reinforcing processes of the etatisation of society and the sociali-sation of the state, which progressively undermine the functional-organisa-tional distinctiveness of the state. From the perspective of constitutional analysis, this implies that the key functions of organising state power and controlling its exercise, especially in relation to society, become increas-ingly difficult to fulfil.

How has constitutional policy reacted to these developments? Examining the German experience since the late 1980s, constitutional policy seems pri-marily to rely on two strategies: 'damage limitation' and, to a lesser extent, the redefiniton of constitutional teleology. In the present context, damage limitation refers to those adjustments in the text or the interpretation of the Basic Law which seek to protect key constitutional functions and objectives by adapting the normative framework to changing circumstances. Adjustment in this context is essentially about conservation. By contrast, the call for a new constitutional understanding (*ein neues Verfassungsverständ-nis*) points to the need for endowing the Constitution with new substance, new objectives and new functions if its centrality and capacity are to be maintained. Although elements of both strategies can be found in recent German constitutional policy, conservation preponderates; the very limited success of the Social Democratic and Green Party representatives in the Joint Constitutional Commission to open up the Basic Law for what they perceive as novel requirements and demands is evidence of the strong polit-ical resistance against any far-reaching redefinition of the purposes of con-stitutional regulation.

Changing political circumstances may, at some stage, result in a climate that is more favourable to comprehensive constitutional reform along the

lines suggested by the current opposition parties; moreover, the reform
debate so far has shown that even proponents of constitutional conservation
are open to suggestions of endowing the Basic Law with new purposes. It is,
therefore, not unlikely that even after the adoption of most of the Joint
Constitutional Commission's recommendations, constitutional reform will
remain high up on the political agenda. This raises the question whether the
amendments which might result from such discussions would be any more
effective in addressing the constitutional challenges that we have outlined.

As far as the international legal environment of the Basic Law is concerned, any strategy which seeks to tie processes of political Europeanisation and internationalisation very closely to substantive norms laid down
in the Basic Law is fraught with practical and legal difficulties. The Federal
Government may, of course, refer to national constitutional regulations in its
efforts to influence the course of international co-ordination and co-operation; however, attempts to 'hide behind' the Basic Law, or to impose its principles on Germany's European and international partners, will create more
problems than they might solve. In this connection, the principles of
European integration laid down in the new Article 23 GG and the very
extensive interpretation of the Federal Constitutional Court's powers emerging from the ruling on the Maastricht Treaty set precedents which may best
not be followed. It is, of course, not easy to strike a balance between maintaining the fundamentals of the national constitutional order as laid down by
the Basic Law, on the one hand, and allowing for a dynamic European and
foreign policy on the other. However, to the extent that a policy of interdependence is associated with restrictions on sovereignty, any constitutional
policy which seeks to emphasise the primacy of national constitutional law
is bound to clash, sooner or later, with political realities.

In comparison, constitutional policy would seem to enjoy a rather broader
scope for discretion in relation to internal challenges. True, the Basic Law
cannot constitute a unity of state power and organisation at variance with
empirical developments; nor would it be advisable to use constitutional regulations as a means for pursuing the de-etatisation of society or the de-
socialisation of the state. However, constitutional law has a role to play in
providing a framework for these processes which helps to ensure their compatibility with the principles of constitutionalism and constitutional democracy. If the Basic Law is to remain the fundamental framework for
constituting, distributing and controlling state power, then changes in state
practice need to be explicitly recognised to a much greater extent than has
so far been the case. Only through such explicit recognition can constitutional law ultimately remain capable of influencing state practice. In
essence, this means concentrating on reform measures designed to ensure
the Basic Law's continued effectiveness in its traditional core tasks. By con-

trast, the search for new constitutional purposes should be approached with a healthy degree of scepticism. It might certainly be possible to define new functions for the Basic Law; but before those are stipulated, careful consideration should be given to the question whether constitutional law is really better suited to secure their realisation than ordinary law or political commitment.

NOTES

This article was completed on 30 June 1994, when the Bundestag adopted part of the recommendations of the Joint Constitutional Commission, in some cases with modifications. The subsequent legislative process in the Bundesrat and the judgment of the Federal Constitutional Court on the use of German military forces outside the NATO area of 12 July 1994 could not, therefore, be taken into account.

1.   Peter Häberle, 'Verfassungsentwicklungen in Osteuropa – aus der Sicht der Rechtsphilosophie und der Verfassungslehre', *Archiv des öffentlichen Rechts,* Vol. 117, No. 2 (1992), pp.169–211 (170).
2.   Nevil Johnson, 'Constitutionalism in Europe Since 1945: Reconstruction and Reappraisal', in Douglas Greenberg *et al.* (eds.), *Constitutionalism and Democracy: Transitions in the Contemporary World* (New York: OUP, 1993), pp.26–45.
3.   See, for example, A.E. Dick Howard (ed.), *Constitution-Making in Eastern Europe* (Washington, DC: Woodrow Wilson Centre Press, 1993); Jon Elster, 'Constitutionalism in Eastern Europe', *University of Chicago Law Review,* Vol. 58, No. 2 (1991), pp.447–482; and idem, 'Constitution-Making in Eastern Europe', *Public Administration* Vol. 71, Nos. 1–2 (1993), pp.169-217.
4.   For the discussions on a new GDR Constitution see Uwe Thaysen, *Der Runde Tisch, Oder: Wo blieb das Volk?* (Opladen: Westdeutscher Verlag, 1991); and Klaus Michael Rogner, *Der Verfassungsentwurf des Zentralen Runden Tisches der DDR* (Berlin: Duncker & Humblot, 1993).
5.   Many of the key contributions to the debate are collected in B. Guggenberger and T. Stein (eds.), *Die Verfassungsdiskussion im Jahr der deutschen Einheit. Analysen, Hintergründe, Materialien* (Munich: Hanser, 1991).
6.   Donald P. Kommers, *Judicial Politics in West Germany* (Beverly Hills: Sage, 1976); and Christine Landfried, 'Judicial Policy-Making in Germany: The Federal Constitutional Court', *West European Politics,* Vol. 15, No. 3 (1992), pp.50–67.
7.   Dieter Grimm, 'Die Zukunft der Verfassung', *Staatswissenschaften und Staatspraxis,* Vol. 1, No. 1 (1990), pp.5–33 (28).
8.   Ibid., p.28.
9.   Ingo von Münch (ed.), *Dokumente zur Wiedervereinigung Deutschlands* (Stuttgart: Kröner, 1991), pp.24–6.
10. See Gert-Joachim Glaeßner, *The Unification Process in Germany: From Dictatorship to Democracy* (London: Pinter, 1992), pp.95ff.
11. von Münch, *Dokumente,* pp.122ff.
12. Karl Wilhelm Fricke, 'DDR-Verfassungsrecht und nationale Frage', in Manfred Buchwald (ed.), *In bester Verfassung? Anmerkungen zum 40. Geburtstag des Grundgesetzes* (Gerlingen: Bleicher, 1989), pp.161ff.
13. Glaeßner, *The Unification Process in Germany,* p.95.
14. Wolfgang Schäuble, *Wie ich über die deutsche Einheit verhandelte* (Stuttgart: Deutsche Verlags-Anstalt, 1991), pp.25, 140ff., 158.
15. Ibid.
16. Ibid., pp.55, 65ff.

17. *Bundesverfassungsgericht Entscheidungen* (BVerfGE), Vol. 82, pp.316ff.
18. Schäuble, *Wie ich über*, pp.28ff.
19. Klaus Stern and Bruno Schmidt-Bleibtreu, *Verträge und Rechtsakte zur Deutschen Einheit, Band 2: Einigungsvertrag und Wahlvertrag* (Munich: Beck, 1990), p.43. See also Donald P. Kommers, 'The Basic Law Under Strain: Constitutional Dilemmas and Challenges', in Christopher Anderson *et al.* (eds.), *The Domestic Politics of German Unification* (Boulder: Lynne Rienner Publishers, 1993), pp.135–154.
20. *BVerfGE*, Vol. 88, pp.203ff.
21. Monika Prützel-Thomas, 'The Abortion Issue and the Federal Constitutional Court', *German Politics*, Vol. 2, No. 3 (1993), pp.467–84.
22. *BVerfGE*, Vol. 88, pp.203ff (255).
23. Landfried, 'Judicial Policy-Making', p.56.
24. *BverfGE*, Vol. 84, pp.90ff.
25. Ibid., pp.122–3.
26. *Bericht 'Stärkung des Föderalismus in Deutschland und Europa sowie weitere Vorschläge zur Änderung des Grundgesetzes* (Bundesrats-Drucksache 360/92, 14 May 1992).
27. *Bericht der Gemeinsamen Verfassungskommission* (hereafter *GVK Report*) (Bundestag-Drucksache 12/6000, 5 Nov. 1993), p.6.
28. Arthur Benz, 'A Forum of Constitutional Deliberation? A Critical Analysis of the Joint Constitutional Commission', in this volume.
29. *GVK Report*, p.10.
30. Ibid., p.13.
31. Rudolf Geiger, *Grundgesetz und Völkerrecht* (Munich: Beck, 1985), p.17.
32. Christian Tomuschat, 'A United Germany Within the European Community', *Common Market Law Review*, Vol. 27 (1990), pp.415–36 (418–425); and Robert Lane, 'Scotland in Europe: An Independent Scotland and the European Community', in Wilson Finnie, Christopher Himsworth and Neil Walker (eds.), *Edinburgh Essays in Public Law*, (Edinburgh: Edinburgh University Press, 1991), pp.143–57.
33. Commission of the European Communities, The European Community and German Unification, *Bulletin of the European Communities*, Supplement 4/90, p.27.
34. David Spence, *Enlargement Without Accession: The EC's Response to Germany Unification* (Royal Institute of International Affairs, Discussion Papers No. 36, 1991), p.11.
35. Thomas Giegerich, 'The European Dimension of German Unification: East Germany's Integration into the European Communities', *Zeitschrit für ausländisches öffentliches Recht und Völkerrecht*, Vol. 51 (1991), pp.384–450 (425–43).
36. Siegfried Magiera, 'Grundgesetz und Europäische Integration', in Willi Blümel *et al.*, *Verfassungsprobleme im vereinten Deutschland* (Speyer: Forschungsinstitut für öffentliche Verwaltung an der Hochschule für Verwaltungswissenschaften Speyer, No. 117, 1993), pp.23–46 (29).
37. Sadako Ogata, 'Refugees and Asylum-Seekers: A Challenge to European Immigration Policy', in *Towards a European Immigration Policy* (Brussels: Philip Morris Institute for Public Policy Research, 1993), pp.6–20 (9).
38. Kay Hailbronner, 'Perspectives of a Harmonisation of the Law of Asylum after the Maastricht Summit', *Common Market Law Review*, Vol. 29 (1992), pp.917–39.
39. Sarah Collinson, *Beyond Borders: West European Migration Policy Towards the 21st Century* (London: RIIA/Wyndham Palace Trust, 1993), p.44.
40. Hailbronner, 'Perspectives', pp.923ff.
41. *Bulletin des Presse- und Informationsamts der Bundesregierung*, No. 130, 4 Dec. 1993, p.1192.
42. Everhardt Franßen, 'Der neue Artikel 16a GG als "Grundrechtshinderungsvorschrift"', *Deutsches Verwaltungsblatt*, Vol. 108, No. 6 (1993), pp.301–3.
43. *Gemeinsame Verfassungskommission, Stenographischer Bericht*, 16. Sitzung, 4 Feb. 1992, p.22.
44. Hailbronner, 'Perspectives', p.925.
45. Hans Ulrich Jessurun d'Oliveira, 'Fortress Europe and (Extra-Communitarian) Refugees',

in Schermers *et al.* (eds), *Free Movement of Persons in Europe: Legal Problems and Experiences* (Dordrecht: Nijhoff, 1993), pp.166–82.

46. Klaus Stern and Bruno Schmidt-Bleibtreu, *Verträge und Rechtsakte zur Deutschen Einheit, Band 3: Zwei-plus-Vier-Vertrag* (Munich: Beck), p.21.
47. Reinhard Steiger, 'Relativierte Souveränität – Die Zukunft Deutschlands in einem vereinten Europa', *Frankfurter Allgemeine Zeitung*, 4 Aug. 1993.
48. William Paterson, 'Gulliver Unbound: The Changing Context of Foreign Policy', in Gordon Smith *et al.* (eds.), *Developments in German Politics* (Basingstoke: Macmillan, 1992), pp.137–52 (151).
49. Helmut Kohl, *Our Future in Europe* (Edinburgh: Europa Institute and Konrad Adenauer Foundation, 1991), p.17.
50. Theodor Maunz *et al.* (eds.), *Grundgesetz-Kommentar* (Munich: Beck), Article 87a, pp.12ff.
51. Ibid.
52. Gilbert Gornig, 'Die Verfassungsmäßigkeit der Entsendung von Bundeswehrsoldaten zu "Blauhelm"-Einsätzen', *Juristen-Zeitung*, Vol. 48, No. 3 (1993), pp.123–8.
53. *Der Spiegel*, 25 Jan. 1993, interview with Wolfgang Schäuble, p.21.
54. *BVerfGE*, Vol. 88, pp.173ff.
55. Ibid., p.192.
56. Ibid., p.182.
57. Ibid., pp.182f.
58. Ibid., p.181.
59. Geiger, Grundgesetz, pp.210f.
60. Ibid., p.210.
61. See Stern and Schmidt-Bleibtreu, *Verträge*, p.29.
62. Opinion of the Federal Constitutional Court, 12 Oct. 1993, *Neue Juristische Wochenschrift* (1993), pp.3047–58.
63. Ursula Seiler-Albring, 'Praktische Aspekte der Europapolitik', *Bulletin des Presse- und Informationsamts der Bundesregierung*, No. 89, 20 Oct. 1993, p.1008.
64. Bundestag-Drucksache 12/3338 (2 Oct. 1992), *Gesetzentwurf der Bundesregierung: Entwurf eines Gesetzes zur Änderung des Grundgesetzes*, p.9.
65. Deidre Curtin, 'The Constitutional Structure of the Union: A Europe of Bits and Pieces', *Common Market Law Review*, Vol. 30 (1992), pp.17–69.
66. Dietrich Murswiek, 'Maastricht und der *pouvoir constituant* – Zur Bedeutung der verfassungsgebenden Gewalt im Prozeß der europäischen Integration', *Der Staat*, Vol. 32, No. 2 (1993), pp.161–90; Rupert Scholz, 'Europäische Union und deutscher Bundesstaat', *Neue Zeitschrift für Verwaltungsrecht*, Vol. 12, No. 9 (1993), pp.817–24; see also Thomas Oppermann and Claus-Dieter Classen, 'Die EG vor der Europäischen Union', *Neue Juristische Wochenschrift* (1993), pp.5–12.
67. Murswiek, 'Maastricht', pp.181ff.
68. *Neue Juristische Wochenschrift*, 1993, pp.3050, 3053ff.
69. Ibid., p.3057.
70. Ibid., p.3056.
71. Ibid., p.3048.
72. Ibid., p.3051.
73. See Werner Kaufmann-Bühler, 'Deutsche Europapolitik nach dem Karlsruher Urteil', *Integration*, Vol. 17, No. 1 (1994), pp.1–11, who suggests policy will not change.
74. *Neue Juristische Wochenschrift*, 1993, p.3049.
75. Hans-Werner Rengeling, *Grundrechtschutz in der Europäischen Gemeinschaft* (Munich: Beck, 1993), pp.165–70.
76. Magiera, 'Grundgesetz', p.37.
77. Konrad Hesse, *Grundzüge des Verfassungsrechts der Bundesrepublik Deutschland* (Heidelberg: Müller, 19th ed.), p.117.
78. Ibid., pp.42, 117.
79. *BVerfGE*, Vol. 74, pp.358ff. (370).

80. Ibid.

81. Kristian Köhl, 'Der Einfluβ der Europäischen Menschenrechtskonvention auf das Strafrecht und Strafverfahrensrecht der Bundesrepublik Deutschland (Teil I)', *Zeitschrift für die gesamte Strafrechtswissenschaft*, Vol. 100 (1988), pp.406–43.

82. Ibid., pp.430–31.

83. Hesse, *Grundzüge*, p.118.

84. *BVerfGE*, Vol. 30, pp.1ff.

85. *Klass v. Federal Republic of Germany*, European Court of Human Rights, 2 *European Rights Reports* (1979-80), pp.214–44.

86. Paterson, 'Gulliver Unbound', p.144.

87. Grimm, 'Zukunft', p.24; idem, 'Staat und Gesellschaft', in Thomas Ellwein and Joachim Jens Hesse (eds.), *Staatswissenschaften: Vergessene Disziplin oder neue Herausforderung*, (Baden-Baden: Nomos Verlagsgesellschaft, 1990), pp.13–27.

88. The following draws in part on Klaus H. Goetz, *Public Sector Change in Germany and the UK: Differences, Commonalities, Explanations* (paper presented at the workshop 'German Public Sector Reform in the Light of the British Experience', European Institute, London School of Economics and Political Science, 17–18 Sept. 1993).

89. Patrick Dunleavy and Brendan O'Leary, *Theories of the State* (Basingstoke: Macmillan, 1987), p.2.

90. See, for example, Gunnar Folke Schuppert, *Die Erfüllung öffentlicher Aufgaben durch verselbständigte Verwaltungseinheiten* (Göttingen: Schwartz, 1984); and idem, 'PGOs in the Federal Republic of Germany', in Christopher Hood and Gunnar Folke Schuppert (eds.), *Delivering Public Services in Europe: Sharing Western European Experiences of Para-Government Organization* (London: Sage, 1988), pp.135–50.

91. Klaus H. Goetz, *Intergovernmental Relations and State Government Discretion: The Case of Science and Technology Policy in Germany* (Baden-Baden: Nomos Verlagsgesellschaft, 1992).

92. See, for example, Michael Reidenbach, *Privatisation of Urban Services in Germany* (paper prepared for the conference on 'Privatisation of Urban Services in Europe', 3–5 June 1993, Poitiers).

93. Thus, at the end of 1993, the decision was taken to transform the public railways into a joint stock company which would, however, remain in exclusive public ownership for the time being. See Günter Fromm, 'Die Reorganisation der Deutschen Bahnen', *Deutsches Verwaltungsblatt*, Vol. 109, No. 4 (1994), pp.187–95. Also, for the purpose of project management, the Federation and the five new Länder have set up the German Unity Highway Planning and Construction Company (*Deutsche Einheit Fernstraβenplanungs- und BaugesellschaftGmbh – DEGES*), a private law company to which they have delegated a large part of the management developing road-based transport infrastructures in the new states. Similar private law companies have been set up for managing large-scale railways infrastructure projects. See Rainer Wahl, 'Die Einschaltung privatrechtlich organisierter Verwaltungseinrichtungen in den Straβenbau', *Deutsches Verwaltungsblatt*, Vol. 108, No. 10 (1993), pp.517–27.

94. Frieder Naschold, *Modernisierung des Staates: Zur Ordnungs- und Innovationspolitik des öffentlichen Sektors* (Berlin: Ed. Sigma, 1993).

95. See, for example, Hellmut Wollmann, *Administrative Reform Movements and Developments in Germany* (paper prepared for the workshop on 'State and Administration in Japan and Germany', Kyoto, 1–3 March 1994).

96. Hermann Hill and Helmut Klages (eds.), *Qualitäts- und erfolgsorientiertes Verwaltungsmanagement* (Berlin: Duncker & Humblot, 1993).

97. Grimm, 'Zukunft', p.17.

98. Ibid, p.15.

99. Dieter Grimm, *Die Zukunft der Verfassung* (Chapter 7: 'Verfassungsrechtliche Anmerkungen zum Thema der Prävention') (Frankfurt a.M.: Suhrkamp, 1991), pp.197–220.

100. See, for example, Michael Kloepfer, 'Interdisziplinäre Aspekte des Umweltstaats',

Deutsches Verwaltungsblatt, Vol. 109, No. 1 (1994), pp.12–22 (14).

101. See, for example, Grimm, 'Zukunft', pp.241–97.

102. For a comprehensive discussion see Klaus König and Nicolai Dose (eds.), *Instrumente und Formen staatlichen Handelns* (Cologne: Heymanns, 1993).

103. See, for example, Joachim Jens Hesse, 'The Purpose of a Contemporary Staatslehre', *Yearbook on Government and Public Administration*, Vol. 1 (1989), pp.55–80.

104. Wolfgang Hoffmann-Riem and Irene Lamb, 'Negotiation and Mediation in the Public Sector – the German Experience', *Public Administration* Vol. 72, No. 2 (1994), pp.309–26.

105. See Arthur Benz, *New Forms of Co-operation and Co-ordination in Public Policy-Making: Elements of a Comparison* (paper presented at the workshop 'German Public Sector Reform in the Light of the British Experience', European Institute, London School of Economics and Political Science, 17/18 Sept. 1993).

106. Jürgen Gebhard, 'Verfassungspatriotismus als Identitätskonzept der Nation', *Aus Politik und Zeitgeschichte*, B 14/93 (1993), pp.29–37 (29/30).

107. Useful short surveys of the main issues in the reform debate can be found in Peter Häberle, 'Die Kontroverse um die Reform des deutschen Grundgesetzes', *Zeitschrift für Politik*, Vol. 39, No. 3 (1992), pp.233–63; and Fritz Ossenbühl, 'Probleme der Verfassungsreform in der Bundesrepublik Deutschland', *Deutsches Verwaltungsblatt*, Vol. 107 (1992), pp.468–77.

108. The background materials documenting the Commission's work provide a fairly comprehensive survey of current thinking on the German Constitution. Those publicly available include 26 protocols of its plenary meetings; nine extensive protocols of its public expert hearings; and 119 background papers (*Arbeitsunterlagen*).

109. 'Kritik an der "Eigendynamik" der Verfassungskommission', *Frankfurter Allgemeine Zeitung*, 26 Feb. 1993.

110. See *GVK Report*, p.10.

111. Arnd Uhle, 'Das Staatsziel "Umweltschutz" im System der grundgesetzlichen Ordnung', *Die Öffentliche Verwaltung* Vol. 46, No. 21 (1993), pp.947–54.

112. See, for example, Karl-Peter Sommermann, 'Die Diskussion über die Normierung von Staatszielen', *Der Staat*, Vol. 32, No. 3 (1993), pp.430–47.

113. Friedrich Karl Fromme, 'Als schwerste Brocken liegen die 'Staatszielbestimmungen auf dem Wege', *Frankfurter Allgemeine Zeitung*, 21 Dec. 1992; 'Keine Einigung über ein Staatsziel Umweltschutz in der Verfassung', *Frankfurter Allgemeine Zeitung*, 13 Feb. 1993; and 'Debatte über das Staatsziel Umwelt', *Frankfurter Allgemeine Zeitung*, 15 Feb. 1993.

114. See Peter J. Cullen, 'Constitutional Change in Germany', in William E. Paterson and Charlie Jeffery (eds.), *German Unification* (Oxford: Blackwell, forthcoming).

115. 'Der Staat schützt auch in Verantwortung für die künftigen Generationen die natürlichen Lebensgrundlagen im Rahmen der verfassungsmäßigen Ordnung durch die Gesetzgebung und nach Maßgabe von Gesetz und Recht durch die vollziehende Gewalt und die Rechtsprechung.'

116. In this connection, the proposals of the Bundesrat Commission on Constitutional Reform are of particular significance. See Uwe Leonardy, 'To be Continued: The Constitutional Reform Commissions from a Länder Perspective', in this volume; and Claus Asmussen und Ulrich Eggeling, 'Empfehlungen des Bundesrates zur Stärkung des Föderalismus in Deutschland und Europa', *Verwaltungsarchiv*, Vol. 84, No. 2 (1993), pp.230–59.

117. See Klaus H. Goetz, *German Federalism and European Integration: Compatibility and Adjustment* (paper presented at the ESRC research seminar 'Intergovernmental Relations in the European Union', London School of Economics and Political Science, 16 Dec. 1993).

118. Charlie Jeffery, *Plus ça change. The Non-Reform of the German Federal System after Unification* (Leicester: Leicester University Discussion Papers in Federal Studies, No. FS93/2, 1993).

119. Wolfgang Renzsch, 'Die Finanzverfassungsreform blieb aus', *Das Parlament*, 14 January 1994.

120. See, for example, Scholz, 'Europäische Union'; idem, 'Grundgesetz und europäische

Einigung', *Neue Juristische Wochenschrift*, Vol. 45, No. 41 (1992), pp.2593–601; Ulrich Everling, 'Überlegungen zur Struktur der Europäischen Union und zum neuen Europa-Artikel des Grundgesetzes', *Deutsches Verwaltungsblatt*, Vol. 108, No. 17 (1993), pp.936–47; and Ingolf Pernice, 'Europäische Union: Gefahr oder Chance für den Föderalismus in Deutschland, Österreich und der Schweiz?', *Deutsches Verwaltungsblatt*, Vol. 108, No. 17 (1993), pp.909–24.

121. 'Gesetz über die Zusammenarbeit von Bund und Ländern in Angelegenheiten der Europäischen Union', *Bundesgesetzblatt* (1993), Teil 1, p.313.
122. Scholz, 'Grundgesetz', p.2600.
123. Pernice, 'Europäische Union', p.919.
124. Everling, 'Überlegungen', p.947.
125. See, for example, Henning Voscherau, 'Verfassungsreform und Verfassungsdiskurs', *Aus Politik und Zeitgeschichte*, B 52/53 (1993), pp.5–7; and Hans-Jochen Vogel, 'Die Reform des Grundgesetzes nach der deutschen Einheit', *Deutsches Verwaltungsblatt*, Vol. 109, No. 9 (1994), pp.497–506.
126. Wolfgang Ullmann, 'Ernste Frage der Verfassungsgeschichte', *Das Parlament*, 14 Jan. 1994.
127. See, for example, Hans-Peter Schneider, 'Die Deutschen haben kein Talent zur Verfassungsreform', *Das Parlament*, 14 Jan. 1994.
128. See also Bernd Guggenberger and Andreas Meier (eds.), *Der Souverän auf der Nebenbühne: Essays und Zwischenrufe zur deutschen Verfassungsdiskussion* (Opladen: Westdeutscher Verlag, 1994).
129. Friedrich-Adolf Jahn, 'Empfehlungen der Gemeinsamen Verfassungskommission zur Änderung des Grundgesetzes', *Deutsches Verwaltungsblatt*, Vol. 109, No. 4 (1994), pp.177–87.
130. Detlef Kleinert, 'Manches hätte klarer ausfallen dürfen', *Das Parlament*, 14 Jan. 1994.
131. Josef Isensee, 'Mit blauem Auge davongekommen', *Das Parlament*, 14 Jan. 1994.
132. Joachim Jens Hesse and Klaus H. Goetz, 'Early Administrative Adjustment to the European Communities: The Case of the Federal Republic of Germany', *Jahrbuch für Europäische Verwaltungsgeschichte/Yearbook of European Administrative History*, Vol. 4 (1992), pp.181–205.
133. See, for example, Meinhard Schröder, 'Das Bundesverfassungsgericht als Hüter des Staates im Prozeß der europäischen Integration', *Deutsches Verwaltungsblatt*, Vol. 109, No. 6 (1994), pp.316–25.
134. Klaus Stern, 'General Assessment of the Basic Law – A German View', in Paul Kirchhof and Donald P. Kommers (eds.), *Germany and Its Basic Law* (Baden-Baden: Nomos Verlagsgesellschaft, 1993), pp.17–36 (21).

The Constitution and the Maastricht Treaty: Between Co-operation and Conflict

GEORG RESS

This contribution discusses the new Article 23 of the Basic Law, especially its implications for the Federation–Länder relationship within the European Union (EU). It proves difficult to reconcile Article 23 with fundamental principles of German constitutional law and European Community Law. Questions of compatibility of the Basic Law with European and international legal norms are then examined in the light of the Federal Constitutional Court's Maastricht judgment. The Court's assertion of jurisdiction to review the legality of Community acts, though linked to concerns about democratic accountability, is controversial in terms of international law and may also bring Karlsruhe into conflict with the European Court of Justice.

I. Introduction

As a result of German unification and the continuing process of European integration the possibility of fragmentation of the Basic Law cannot be overlooked.[1] The Basic Law could long be characterised as a coherent and well-balanced constitutional system (*Verfassung 'aus einem Guß'*), which has also proved attractive for those 16 million Germans living under indirect Soviet rule in East Germany. This quality of the Basic Law has been endangered by a number of developments. The amendment to Article 23, which will be discussed in detail below, has given the Länder an extremely strong position in European Union decision-making which will make it increasingly difficult for Germany to act effectively at European level. The acceptance of the Soviet confiscations in former East Germany between 1945 and 1949, that is, the refusal to return expropriated property to the former owners, seemingly for no really compelling reasons, is difficult to accept under a Constitution which claims to protect at least an essential core of property and equality rights. Moreover, some East German conceptions may be finding their way into the Basic Law in other areas. The still unresolved problem of a reform of Section 218 of the German Penal Code, the abortion clause, provides a particular example of the way in which the Constitution is being asked to reconcile divergent East and West German legal approaches, in this instance concerning the question of how far to protect unborn life. Proposals for fundamental social rights or guiding principles or even the proposed stipulation of a citizen's duty to display 'human fellowship and public spiritedness' (*Mitmenschlichkeit und Gemeinsinn*)[2] come very close to the objective character of socialist constitutions. A state which had the power to control whether its citizens' behaviour satisfied such requirements would not be far from an Orwellian type of totalitarianism.

There was and is also no need for the proclamation of new state objective provisions (*Staatszielbestimmungen*); instead the emphasis during the constitutional discussions should have been on improving the protection of individual rights, for example against acts of the EC (see Article 173 (4) EC Treaty[3]), facilitating more effective preparation of European acts by the Bundestag, and providing for the constitutional accommodation of the international responsibility of Germany as one of the major European powers (reform of Articles 87 (2) and 24 (2) of the Basic Law, regulation of German participation in peacekeeping operations and so on). None of this has been achieved; instead the discussion centred around what might be called 'constitutional dreams'. One can only imagine what would have happened had the two German states chosen Article 146 of the Basic Law instead of Article 23 as the constitutional basis for unification.

II. The New 'Article on European Union': Article 23 of the Federal Basic Law

When the new Treaty on European Union (TEU) was signed in Maastricht, the question arose as to whether the German Federal Basic Law needed to be amended.[4] The answer was 'yes' in regard to the new Article 8b TEU under which the citizens of the Union have the right to vote and are eligible for election in municipal elections and elections to the European Parliament, because the Federal Constitutional Court had already held in two earlier decisions that without constitutional changes only German citizens could vote in German elections on every level.[5] Consequently, Article 28 of the Basic Law was amended to accommodate this aspect of the new Union citizenship.[6] It was less evident that an amendment of Article 88 of the Basic Law concerning the Federal Reserve Bank, the Bundesbank, and its new role in the framework of monetary union, would be required. In the end, those arguing in favour of a constitutional clarification prevailed and a new clause was added stipulating that the functions and competences of the Bundesbank may be transferred to an independent European Central Bank,[7] which has the task of securing price stability. The objective of price stability is thus a constitutional prerequisite for the transfer of competences.[8]

Much more significant, however, is the new Article 23, which is often referred to as the 'Article on European Union' of the Basic Law. The old Article 23, originally intended to accommodate the subsequent accession of the Saarland to the Federal Republic and then also used as a constitutional basis for the accession of the five new Länder (former East Germany) had become obsolete after unification had been completed. At the same time, Article 24 (1) of the Basic Law, which had previously served as the constitutional foundation for the process of European integration, that is, for the transfer of competences to Community institutions, was thought to be insufficient to accommodate the new quality of the integrative process instituted by the TEU. That view was not undisputed on the grounds that the European Union is not fundamentally different from the old Communities. Relying on Article 24 of the Basic Law, it has been said, before and after Maastricht, that we are dealing with 'inter-state institutions' (zwischenstaatliche Einrichtungen). This view was indirectly confirmed by the Court's Maastricht decision. Nothing in that decision would have changed had the new Article 23 not been introduced, except that the regulations set out in Article 23 (2) and (3) concerning the participation of the Bundestag in the decision-making process were considered to be essential to fulfil the constitutional requirements derived from the democracy principle.[9]

Be that as it may, a lengthy Article 23 was drafted and incorporated into the Basic Law. The objective of the seven sections of Article 23 is to build a new foundation for the participation of Germany in the development of the European Union and to ensure that the domestic decision-making process in this regard is in line with the principle of democracy on the one hand, and the federal structure of the Republic on the other hand. Article 23 (1) first of all sets out the relationship between Germany and the European Union in broad terms. The constitutional obligation of Germany to participate in the process of European integration in general, and in the development of the European Union as an intermediary step in achieving a united Europe in particular,[10] is transferred from the Preamble into the Constitution proper,[11] but is at the same time tied to the structural quality of the developing entity: the European Union must rest upon democratic, social and federal (in the German sense of the word!) principles, adhere to the rule of law and the principle of subsidiarity, and guarantee fundamental rights and freedoms on a level essentially equivalent to that guaranteed by the Basic Law.[12] The Federation is authorised to transfer powers to that effect, contingent, however, and that is new, upon the consent of the Bundesrat in all cases. The founding of the European Union and any future developments and changes in the treaties constituting the Union are subject to the 'eternity clause' of Article 79 (3) of the Basic Law, which forbids constitutional amendments which would impinge upon the principles contained in Articles 1 and 20 of the Constitution. Those principles are – save the principle of subsidiarity – identical to those mentioned in the first clause of Article 23 (1).

Article 23 (2) provides for the participation of both the Bundestag and the Bundesrat in matters concerning the European Union in general terms. It obliges the Federal Government to inform both chambers of parliament as early and as comprehensively as possible. The participation of the Bundestag is at issue in Article 23 (3). Before taking part in the decision-making process at European level, the Bundestag must be given an opportunity to comment by the Federal Government, which is then obliged duly to consider this comment in the negotiations. These rather nebulous requirements are expanded upon in a separate Federal statute.[13] Paragraph 2 of that statute provides for the institution of a special Committee for matters of the European Union. Paragraphs 3 and 4 provide that the Bundestag must be informed as early as possible, especially about proposed Community legislation (regulations and directives) and about the Government's position on these proposals. Paragraph 5 provides that the Bundestag must be given sufficient time to consider such legislative measures and comment on them before they are actually passed in Brussels.

Even more important, however, are sections 4 to 6 of Article 23, where the problem of the participation of the Länder in the decision-making process at European level is addressed in considerable detail. A statute passed under Article 23 (7), entitled 'Statute on Co-operation between the Federation and the Länder in European Union Matters' (hereafter 'co-operation statute') elaborates further on this matter.[14] The Länder, increasingly suspicious of insidious centralisation and loss of power (developments typical of federally organised states but reinforced in the German case by the process of European integration), seized the opportunity offered in the Maastricht ratification process to reverse that trend with regard to the transfer of powers to the European Communities. Thus, Article 23 (4) lays down the right of the Bundesrat to participate in the formation of the political will of the Federal Republic in regard to the European Union, if and insofar as the measure in question requires its participation in the domestic sphere as well. According to Article 23 (5), if internally the measure falls under an exclusive Federal competence, the Federal Government is obliged to consider the standpoint of the Bundesrat. If the matter mainly concerns competences of the Länder, the standpoint of the Bundesrat will have to be 'considered as definitive' (maßgeblich zu berücksichtigen). According to the co-operation statute, if a consensus cannot be achieved, the standpoint of the Bundesrat will prevail. Finally, Article 23 (6) deals with matters falling under the exclusive jurisdiction of the Länder. In this case, the right to represent the Federal Republic as a member of the European Union shall be transferred to a representative of the Länder, who is to be appointed by the Bundesrat.

III. The Relationship Between the Federation and the Länder in the New European Union

The domestic participation of the Länder in European Union matters

It was the intention of the new Article 23 to resolve the inherent conflicts of the membership of a federally organised member state in a closely integrated supranational organisation. However, the new provision creates more problems than it solves. In fact, parts of the new Article 23 of the Basic Law, especially sections 5 and 6, are questionable from the standpoint of both German constitutional law and European Community law.

The degree of Länder participation in European Union (EU) matters depends on the qualification of the issue in question. Issues which are domestically considered to fall under exclusive Federal jurisdiction and which do not touch the interests of the Länder in any way, require no participation of the Länder at all, which means that the Bundesrat need not – but could – be given an opportunity to comment. If, however, exclusive competences of the Länder are at issue, which could be the case in the fields of education, culture and police, the Federal Republic will not be represented by a member of the Federal Government but by a representative of the Länder appointed by the Bundesrat. In between those two extremes are matters which cannot be qualified as falling either under Federal or under Länder jurisdiction. These will most likely be Community acts of a mixed nature, that is, acts which internally affect Federal as well as Länder competences. If the matter mainly affects the latter, a consent procedure is instituted, in which the Bundesrat has the stronger position because its point of view will in the end prevail (*maßgebliche Berücksichtigung*).

It is evident that these provisions are little more than a recipe for future conflicts, which the Federal Constitutional Court will have to settle. The Court may well be called upon to answer some or all of the following questions:

(i) What is meant by the 'simple' (unqualified) consideration clause of Article 23 (5), sub-section 1, and when does it apply?

Neither Article 23 nor the co-operation statute define what is meant by 'simple' consideration. From a practical point of view, the main question is, who will eventually prevail? Since the second sub-section of Article 23 (5) speaks of 'definitive' consideration, it must be concluded, *e contrario*, that under the circumstances of Article 23 (5), sub-section 1, the Federal Government will prevail. The rights of the Länder are in effect merely procedural: the Bundesrat must be informed and its comments be taken into account without binding the Federal Government. Article 23 and the co-operation statute do not answer the question of what exactly is meant by the Federal Government's obligation to take the Bundesrat's view into account. In my view, one could think of an obligation upon the Federal Government to inform the Bundesrat of its position and to justify it in the light of the Bundesrat's comments. That could also be conceivable after the Federal Government's participation in the decision-making process at European level, notwithstanding the fact that after the decision had been reached in the Council, the legality or illegality of the Federal Government's behaviour towards the Bundesrat could not have any effect on the Community decision.

(ii) What is meant by 'definitive' consideration? (Article 23 (5), sub-sections 2 and 3)

It has been argued above that 'definitive' consideration means that the Bundesrat's view, in the absence of agreement, prevails. This is supported by the terms of paragraph 5, section 2 of the co-operation statute, which provides that 'If no consensus can be reached and if the Bundesrat confirms its position by a two-thirds majority, its position shall be definitive'. This general rule is, however, subject to a major exception, spelt out in the following sentence of section 2: if the decision is one which could lead to increased expenditure or reduced revenues for the Federation, the consent of the Federal Government must be obtained. In other words, consensus must be reached. It is unclear what the consequences are if it is not. The statute does not answer this question, which is, however, likely to be of some importance given, first, that many proposals will have such financial consequences and, second, that it may often be impossible for the Federal Government and Länder, in the time available, to reach agreement. The speed of decision-making at the European level is not and will not in future be determined by German domestic timetables. The logical conclusion must be that, in such circumstances, the Federal Government will prevail.

(iii) When must a Community act be considered to 'mainly' (im Schwerpunkt) affect Länder competences?

The question as to when Länder competences are 'mainly' at issue has also been left unanswered. A clear answer is admittedly hard to find. At this point, the most favoured solution seems to be that Länder competences must form 'the core' of the matter in question. Perhaps it could be useful to describe the term '*im Schwerpunkt*' ('mainly') in a negative way. A proposal touches Länder competences mainly, if the removal of all parts of the proposal which internally would fall under the jurisdiction of the Länder would leave the proposal meaningless or useless, in other words if the Länder competences involved are a *conditio sine qua non* for the proposal.

The same problem arises in the context of Article 23 (6), where representation of the Federal Republic in the Council by an appointee of the Bundesrat is tied to the prerequisite that the issue in question 'mainly' touches exclusive Länder competences. If this issue cannot be resolved, constitutional Federation–Länder disputes are possible, which will have to be decided by preliminary judgments, given the timetable of the deliberations in the Council.

(iv) Is the right of the Bundesrat of 'ultimate prevalence' (*Letztentscheidungsrecht*) constitutional? Is it in conformity with the Community treaties?

The right of the Bundesrat of 'ultimate prevalence' presents problems under both German constitutional norms and provisions of European Community law. Constitutionally, 'ultimate prevalence' of the Bundesrat causes several problems. First, the chain of democratic legitimisation of European decision-making is broken. Normally, the Federal Government is responsible to the directly-elected parliament, the Bundestag, for its behaviour in the European organs, and that responsibility is expressed in the power of the Bundestag to vote the Federal Chancellor out of office. That chain of responsibility is evidently broken if the Bundesrat determines Germany's standpoint in the Council. The Bundesrat is composed of members of the Länder governments and the position of the Bundesrat is determined by a two-thirds majority, so that not even the Länder parliaments are able to guarantee parliamentary responsibility.

Secondly, foreign policy is an exclusive Federal competence and includes the ability to act effectively. The objection that foreign policy is a Federal competence can be overcome by arguing that the Bundesrat is a Federal organ, notwithstanding the fact that it is composed of members of the Länder governments, and by reference to the fact that the Basic Law also guarantees the federal structure of Germany, which may necessitate some kind of Länder participation. However, the ability of the Federal Republic to act effectively at European level is definitely hampered if the German representative in the Council is restricted by an imperative mandate. Will he have to leave the negotiations in Brussels whenever they take an unpredicted turn and ask the Bundesrat for new orders? This difficulty could be overcome by interpreting 'ultimate prevalence' more in terms of a general direction to be given by the Bundesrat, in contrast to a restricted, imperative mandate. However, the more discretion given to the Federal Government's negotiator in the Council, the less will the objective of giving the Länder a decisive say in European matters affecting their sphere of interest be achieved.

Finally, problems concerning the separation of powers must also be taken into account. At Federal level, this part of foreign policy is shifted from the executive branch, the Federal Government, to a legislative organ, the Bundesrat. Again, this could be justified by arguing that in substance this is only the case in matters involving Länder competences. Another problem lies in the necessarily reduced significance of the Bundestag if the final decision lies with the Bundesrat. The Bundestag has also given up substantial competences yet the only compensation it received is the 'simple' participation procedure described in Article 23 (2) and (3).

The main problem from the point of view of Community law is Article 5 EC Treaty, which obliges the member states to take all appropriate measures to facilitate the Community's tasks. That must also be applied to the functioning of the Council as a Community organ, which requires that the member states are flexible enough to enter into *ad hoc* compromises without having to delay negotiations to obtain further directions. If 'ultimate prevalence' of the Bundesrat is construed strictly in terms of an imperative mandate, the Federal Republic will not be able to fulfil its obligation under Article 5 EC Treaty. Thus, the only solution is to define 'ultimate prevalence' less strictly. According to this approach, the Bundesrat would be entitled to determine the basic negotiating position of the Federal Government, but could not hold it to a specific result in the negotiations. The unavoidable result would, of course, be a significant weakening of the Bundesrat's strong position. Not being party to the negotiations in Brussels, it could not know how much compromising was necessary. In effect, the Federal Government would be likely to regain actual 'ultimate prevalence'.

The Participation of the Länder in the Council of Ministers

Representation of the Federal Republic in the Council of Ministers by an appointee of the Bundesrat must answer essentially the same question as raised above in connection with the 'ultimate prevalence' requirement. The chain of democratic legitimisation is broken because it is almost impossible to establish parliamentary responsibility for the Bundesrat representative. One could construe a responsibility to the parliament of the Land of which he is a government member (see Article 146 EC Treaty), but that would mean to limit responsibility to the people of one Land, whereas the actions for which the Bundesrat's representative must answer affect the whole country. The ability of the Federal Republic to act effectively is likewise threatened if its representation in the Council is entrusted to changing appointees of the Bundesrat. It will, in any case, not enhance the stability and reliability of Germany's participation in the Council if the other partners have to deal with a German partner from a different government with different priorities in every round of negotiations.

(v) Is representation of the Federal Republic in the Council by an appointee of the Bundesrat compatible with the Constitution and the European Treaties?

Objections may be raised to Bundesrat represention of the Federal Republic on the basis of the federal principle (*Bundesstaatsprinzip*) and the separation of powers principle (*Gewaltenteilungsprinzip*). For example, can Germany be represented by a Bundesrat appointee in regard to peripheral issues which fall under Federal jurisdiction? Does the Bundesrat appointee represent the Länder as a whole (as distinct from the Federal Republic) and does that imply the creation of a third entity besides the Federation and the (single) Länder? Is foreign policy not a typical power of the Federal executive branch? As already stated, there is also the Community law obstacle, Article 5 EC Treaty. In addition, it will be unclear for the partners in the Community who the representative of Germany in the sense of Article 146 EC Treaty will be, that is, who will act for the Federal Republic.

This leaves only two solutions. Article 23 (6) can either be regarded as 'unconstitutional constitutional law' and, even worse, in the light of the principle of supremacy of Community law, incompatible with the EC Treaty, or one tries to find some interpretation of the clause to avoid this consequence. One possibility would be to give the appointee the right to represent the Federal Republic in the Council only if a member of the Federal Government were also present (if and in what circumstances that might be allowed under Article 146 EC Treaty and the rules of the Council is another question) and if the two agree on the respective issue under negotiation. This is supported by Article 23 (6), sub-section 2, which provides that these rights (of the representative of the Bundesrat) must be exercised with the participation of and in co-ordination with the Federal Government. That would indeed solve the problem raised above, but it would also negate the clear intention of Article 23 (6), because the Bundesrat's right under Article 23 (6) would then be of little practical effect. One might argue that some political formula could be worked out and that one should not attach too much importance to legal technicalities. In Germany, however, such questions tend to become constitutional disputes sooner or later and then fall to the Constitutional Court for resolution on the basis of *legal* rules.

(vi) Will deviation of the Länder representative from instructions of the Bundesrat render Council decisions invalid?

There is another problem which warrants some attention. It relates to the question whether a deviation of the representative of the Länder from the opinion expressed by the Bundesrat can have any effect on the validity of the decision of the Council. The following considerations show that the answer can only be negative. No member state can rely on its own constitution when it comes to fulfilling obligations arising under the EC Treaty. This is not only the position of the European Court of Justice (ECJ), but also of international law in general, as expressed in Article 27 of the Vienna Convention on the Law of Treaties. Even the rule contained in Article 47 of the Vienna Convention, which – *mutatis mutandis* – seems to cover the problem here at issue, cannot change that. According to this rule, a state can only invoke its representative's failure to observe the restrictions under which he was placed if these restrictions were notified to the other member states. But even if Germany or the Bundesrat were to notify such a restriction to the other member states or their representatives in the Council, it could still be argued that the validity of Council decisions cannot depend on the fulfilment of requirements which are based solely on the German Constitution. The decision-making process in the Council would be completely paralysed if every member state were to follow such practices. To hold otherwise would evidently contradict the purpose of the EC Treaty. Therefore, it is my view that the validity of a Council decision does not depend on the fulfilment of the constitutional requirements of Article 23 (6) of the Basic Law.

IV. Is the Maastricht Treaty Compatible with the German Constitution? The Maastricht Decision of 12 October 1993

The Prerequisites of Article 23 Basic Law

The problems raised by the new Article 23 Basic Law do not relate solely to the position of the Länder. As already stated, the European Union of the Maastricht Treaty is not the final step in the process of European integration. Further developments in the political structure and economic coherence of the Union are necessary to set the stage for EMU and its stability objective. Article 23 speaks of German participation 'in the development of the EU', thus making it clear that such a dynamic process is covered by the Basic Law. Article 23 (1) contains very general constitutional prerequisites for the

EU which had to be fulfilled in order to qualify Germany's participation as constitutional. The meaning of those principles, that is democracy (*Demokratieprinzip*), rule of law (*Rechtsstaatsprinzip*), social welfare (*Sozialstaatsprinzip*), federal structure (*Bundesstaatsprinzip*) and principle of subsidiarity is, therefore, very important. The principle of democracy in an international organisation like the EU is not necessarily identical to that in a state[15] or to the concept described in the Basic Law.[16] It is obvious that the federal principle of the German Constitution cannot be the same within the framework of an international organization which is by its very definition composed of 'member states'. It is by no means clear what 'federal' can mean in such a context: must the bulk of legislative power remain with the member states? Would a more general competence (or a *Kompetenz-Kompetenz*) destroy the very structure of a federal conception of the EU? Can it be presumed that the principle of subsidiarity contained in Article B TEU and Article 3b EC Treaty is identical to the principle of subsidiarity contained in Article 23 (1) Basic Law?

An even more striking question arises in the context of Article 23 (1), sub-section 3,[17] which stipulates that

> The establishment of the European Union as well as amendments to its statutory foundations and comparable regulations which amend or supplement the content of this Basic Law or make such amendments or supplements possible shall be subject to the provisions of paragraphs (2) and (3) of Article 79.

This language gives rise to the question whether future regulations passed on the basis of Article 235 EC Treaty might, for example if they affect legislative competences, fall under these provisions, and therefore require the consent of two-thirds majorities in the Bundestag and the Bundesrat.

It is interesting that the German Federal Constitutional Court[18] in its decision of 12 October 1993,[19] which cleared the way for ratification of the Treaty on European Union by Germany as the last of the 12 member states, only answered some of these questions and did not really elaborate on the interpretation of Article 23 (1) Basic Law. The Court concentrated its efforts more on the principle of democracy as expressed in the Basic Law, in particular the question of Bundestag and Bundesrat participation in EU matters (Article 23 (2) and (3) Basic Law), on the rule-of-law principle (*Rechtsstaatsprinzip*), and on related issues such as predictability of law and the principle of limited competences of the EU (including the *Kompetenz-Kompetenz* problem), than on stipulating what 'democratic' or 'federal' prerequisites had to be fulfilled by the EU itself in the light of Article 23. The fact that the Court only reluctantly referred to Article 23 (1) is, however, understandable, given that the Court was looking at the TEU in the framework of the constitutional complaint procedure, not the 'abstract review of norms' procedure (*abstrakte Normenkontrolle*).

The Court dismissed all constitutional complaints which were lodged against the TEU, that is, against the assenting Act of the German Parliament to the TEU,[20] and against the Act of the German Parliament amending the Basic Law.[21] Immediately after the decision the German Federal President as the head of state ratified the TEU. With the documents deposited in Italy, the TEU entered into force on 1 November 1993.[22] The judgment has relevance for a number of questions of public international law: the relationship between international organisations (for example, the European Union and the European Communities) and their member states, the rules of treaty interpretation to be applied by the European Court of Justice, the control of acts of international organisations by constitutional courts in regard to the question whether acts of the former are legally competent or not, the right of a member state to revoke its membership of the EU and, finally, the preservation of essential constitutional structures and principles.[23]

Facts and Procedure

On 7 February 1992, the representatives of the 12 member states of the European Communities signed the Treaty on European Union in Maastricht. According to Article A TEU, a 'European Union' is thereby established which is to mark 'a new stage in the process of creating an ever closer union among the peoples of Europe'. However, before the new European Union could be established, the treaty had to be ratified in all 12 member states. The ratification process nearly went off the rails completely following the negative outcome of the first Danish referendum.[24] The Danish vote precipitated widespread public questioning of the appropriateness of the Maastricht Treaty across the Community. As might have been expected, it offered grist to the mill of Euro-sceptics in the United Kingdom, but it was also followed by critical discussions in member states previously known for their enthusiasm for the cause of European integration. Germany was one such state, where public opinion became increasingly negative, in marked contrast to the opinion expressed by the two chambers of parliament,[25] the Bundestag and the Bundesrat, and in contrast to media opinion, which was heavily pro-Maastricht. However, the country's final stand on this crucially important issue was not to be determined by any of the actors mentioned above but by the Federal Constitutional Court in Karlsruhe, a process which is, of course, not untypical for Germany.[26]

In the Maastricht judgment, the Court had to deal with a number of constitutional complaints with differing underlying motivations. Several were brought jointly by a group of members of the European Parliament (EP), whose efforts were not so much directed against European integration as such but against the perceived lack of democratic legitimisation in the Union. They argued that the new Union's structure violates the principle of democracy because, in comparison to the EP, too much power remains concentrated in the Council and the Commission, neither of which is sufficiently legitimised by the democratic process. In addition, they argued that the creation of the new European Union should be contingent upon a referendum to be held in Germany, a position which was supported by a number of constitutional lawyers.[27]

Another complaint was brought by a former official of the European Commission in Brussels, Brunners, whose opposition to the TEU was more fundamental.[28] His complaint challenged the TEU mainly on the grounds that it constitutes a violation of the principles of democracy and of several basic rights and freedoms guaranteed by the Federal Basic Law which, he alleged, could no longer be guaranteed under the new TEU. He illustrated his claim by referring to European Monetary Union (EMU) as envisaged in the TEU, from which Germany could not withdraw and which would violate property rights guaranteed by the Basic Law by depriving Germans of their currency (the basic foundation of their economic confidence). All of these complaints were brought under provisions of the German Constitution which allow individuals to challenge acts of public authorities, including parliamentary statutes.

The Reasoning of the Court as to Admissibility

In its judgment, the Court dismissed most of the complaints as inadmissible, except that part of Brunner's complaint which dealt with Article 38 of the Basic Law.[29] Article 38 determines the status of the members of the Bundestag, sets out the fundamental electoral principles and defines the electorate.[30] Brunner had argued that Article 38 not only stipulates how the Bundestag must be elected, but that it gives every German citizen the right to democratically legitimised representation in the German Bundestag, thus securing the sovereignty of the citizens in the exercise of public power. To that effect the Bundestag must retain substantial decision-making powers which, according to Brunner,[31] had been eroded by the excessive transfer of competences to the new Union, culminating in Article F (3) TEU[32] which supposedly gives the Union the ultimate competence to procure ever more competences at the expense of the member states (*Kompetenz-Kompetenz*). He also argued that the citizens' right under Article 38 of the Basic Law to elect the true legislative organ is violated by the democratic deficit at Community level which the TEU only partially alleviates. The Council of Ministers, as opposed to the directly elected European Parliament, is and remains the principal legislative organ at Community level. The fact that the Council is composed of members of the executive branches of the member states meant, in the eyes of the complainant, that the executive branch in effect makes the laws which it subsequently executes.

The Court found sufficient substance in Mr Brunner's arguments to support at least the possibility of a violation of Article 38 Basic Law. In order to do so, the Court had to agree with the underlying idea that Article 38 Basic Law goes beyond merely protecting the right to elect the parliamentary assembly; in the words of the Court Article 38 also contains 'the subjective right of all Germans who are entitled to vote to participate in the legitimisation of state power by the people on the federal level and thus influence the exercise of that power'. It is obvious that this participation becomes meaningless if the right to exercise substantial parts of this power is transferred to an international organisation which, by virtue of this transfer, more and more resembles a federal state. The Court concluded that, in the case of a transfer of competences to and subsequent exercise of competences by a supranational organisation, Article 38 must be read in the light of the new Article 23 Basic Law, because Article 23 (1) explicitly authorises such a transfer of competences.[33] Indeed, Article 23 Basic Law was drafted and incorporated into the Constitution for the very purpose of providing a constitutional foundation for the integrative process continued by the TEU.

The Court then defined the right protected under Article 38 in the light of Article 23 and held that

> within the scope of Article 23, Article 38 prevents the legitimisation of state power through elections and popular control of the exercise of power from becoming meaningless owing to the transfer of duties and competences away from the Bundestag. Otherwise, the principle of democracy, rendered inviolable by Article 79 (3), in conjunction with Article 20 (1) and (2) Basic Law, would be violated.[34]

Taking into account the various policy fields in which the Union has been afforded jurisdiction by the TEU,[35] the Court concluded that Article 38 could indeed be violated were the inviolable minimum requirements of Article 79 (3), in conjunction with Article 20 (1) and (2), no longer met as a result of an excessive transfer of powers from the German Bundestag to an organ of the European Union composed of representatives of the governments of the member states.[36]

In deviation from its *Eurocontrol* decisions the Court extended the scope for national (German) control of European legal acts. It held that acts of a public authority distinct from those of the member states may affect the fundamental rights of German citizens and that it is the task of the Federal Constitutional Court, in co-operation with the ECJ, to protect these fundamental rights. Thus, the Court extended the meaning of the term 'public power' (öffentliche Gewalt) in Article 93 (1) and (4a) and broadened the possible access to its review procedures. None the less, the Court's decision does not constitute a step back to the position taken in 'Solange I'.[38]

Having thus declared the complaint admissible in part, the Court then had to review the alleged violation of Article 38 Basic Law in substance, that is, the Court had to decide whether the transfer of powers to the Union in general, and to the Council of Ministers as the Union's main legislative body in particular, indeed rendered the right of German citizens to elect their parliamentary assembly meaningless. This, said the Court, would be the case if the Bundestag were left without any significant powers of autonomous decision-making.

The Problem of Democratic Legitimisation

The Court emphasised that membership in a 'community of states' (Staatengemeinschaft) authorised to exercise governmental powers even by majority vote,[39] is expressly endorsed by the Basic Law (Articles 23, 24).[40] Democratic legitimisation is afforded by national parliamentary assent to the constituting treaties of the respective 'community of states', which also incorporates the granting of authority to decide by majority vote. However, this assessment does not free the 'community of states' itself from securing democratic legitimisation. The Court's answer is dichotomous: democratic legitimisation of the Union's exercise of public power must first and foremost be guaranteed through national parliaments.[41] However, as the Union develops further, the chain of legitimisation must be complemented by parallel institutions at European level. The Court also speaks of the necessity to transfer legislative powers to the EP. Such a development would be regarded by German constitutional law as helping to diminish the democratic deficit in the Community,[42] a deficit which has to date only become more serious as Community competences have expanded. The strengthening of the role of the EP and the creation of European citizenship effected by the Maastricht Treaty are, therefore, important steps in the direction the Court would like the Union to take. The Court identifies language barriers and the lack of a 'political infrastructure' as obstacles to the goals set out in Article 138a of the EC Treaty, that is, the formation of 'European awareness' and the expression of 'political will of the citizens of the Union' (as some sort of collective entity). It may be that such obstacles can be overcome in the course of time and with further integration. Thus, the Court concludes that at the present stage of integration,

> legitimisation through the EP already has a supporting function (stützende Funktion) which could be strengthened if it were elected

under a common election procedure in all member states as envisaged by Article 138 (3) EC Treaty and if its influence on policy and decision-making were to increase.[43]

However, notwithstanding the supporting function of the EP, it is the member states which provide the bulk of the necessary legitimisation. Under these circumstances it is decisive for the Court

> that, with further integration, the democratic foundations of the Union become stronger and that a living democracy in the member states will be preserved as well. A preponderance of tasks and powers in the hands of the European Confederation (*Staatenverbund*) would weaken democracy on the state level considerably, so that the legitimisation of the exercise of these powers could no longer be achieved through the national parliaments.

It follows, therefore, that at the present stage of European integration, where democratic legitimisation is achieved primarily through national parliaments, limits must be set to the transfer of powers to the European Communities, if the democratic principle is not to be breached.[44] On the basis of this analysis the Court infers that the Constitution demands that substantial and substantive competences must remain with the German Bundestag.

The Control of Community Actions

Putting democratic legitimisation mainly in the hands of national parliaments and thus the national constituencies, means that these organs, by way of legislation, must clearly identify the scope, extent and purpose of the integration process in general and the powers transferred in that process in particular. The implementing legislation must make it sufficiently clear what powers have been transferred to the supranational level.[45] The Court went on to state that

> if European institutions or organs were to utilise or develop the Treaty on European Union in a manner not covered by this Treaty and the German implementing legislation based on it, the resulting obligations could not be binding within Germany's sovereign sphere. Accordingly, the German Federal Constitutional Court will examine whether legal acts of the European institutions and organs are within the limits of the competences granted to them or whether they exceed those limits.[46]

The final control of the legality of EU action must, therefore, in the Court's view, lie with it. This is not only true with regard to infringements of fundamental rights but also applies to any *ultra vires* Community or Union act. In the EU, however, it is the European Court of Justice which decides whether an organ has acted illegally. The question, therefore, arises whether the Court henceforth intends to review the relevant judgments of the ECJ.[47] One could well be inclined to think so because the Court reproaches the ECJ for all too frequently having recourse to the ideas of *effet utile* and 'implied powers'. However, the Court also refers to the principle of 'co-operation' between the (constitutional) courts of the member states and the ECJ. Nevertheless, the question remains: does this not in the end amount to a subordination of the ECJ to the final judgment of the constitutional courts of the member states?

Having analysed and identified the exact requirements of the German Basic Law, the Court then had to examine the TEU with respect to these requirements. It started by demonstrating that Article 23 requires the participation of the Bundestag in all important aspects, from membership in the Union to amendments of the constituting treaties and the exercise of German membership rights in the Community organs.[48] Having thus indicated the general scope of parliamentary involvement, the Court turned to the TEU and the powers and competences transferred to the Union, finding that

> the complainant's concern that the European Community could – due to broadly formulated objectives and without further parliamentary assent – develop into a political union with unpredictable powers is unfounded. The TEU adopts and strengthens the principle of enumerated competences which has been effective in the European Communities all along (a); this principle is not jeopardised by Article F (3) TEU which does not constitute an ultimate competence to procure ever more competences at the expense of the member states (*Kompetenz-Kompetenz*) (b); the possibility to assign further tasks and powers to the European Union and the European Communities is limited by sufficiently precise provisions (c); the provisions concerning European Monetary Union also provide for a sufficiently predictable development (d,e,f).[49]

Notwithstanding this clear and unambiguous finding, the Court's subsequent reasoning reveals how seriously the Court took the concerns expressed by the complainants. The Court convincingly demonstrates the TEU's continued adherence to the principle of enumerated powers, notwithstanding the fact that the wording of Article F (3) is far from precise and could be construed as providing a very general competence for the new Union comparable with that provided for in Article 235 EC Treaty.[235] Article F (3) is a

failed attempt to provide the Union, within the framework of the
Community budget, with the financial resources necessary to achieve its
objectives.[51] Thus, the drafters of the provision themselves are to blame for
the Court's threat that, in case Community organs were to construe Article
F (3) in terms of a 'competence-competence' provision, 'the German state
organs would have to deny obedience to legal acts based on such an application ...', because such an interpretation would be outside the scope of reasonable interpretation and therefore also outside the scope of the German
implementing legislation.[52]

Economic and Monetary Union (EMU)

With regard to EMU, the Court assumes that the convergence criteria
spelled out in Article 109j TEU, in conjunction with the respective
Protocol, whose purpose it is to secure the stability of the new currency,
cannot be changed without the consent of the German parliament.[53] As for
the stability risk inherent in the creation of a new currency, the Court con-
cedes that this is too intangible to give rise to legal consequences. However,
the Court adds that

> the Treaty provides for long-range prerequisites, with stability as the
> standard for the currency union, which seek to secure that standard
> through institutional arrangements and which ultimately – as a means
> of last resort – do not prohibit breaking away from the Community
> should the common stability goal not be reached.[54]

The Court admitted, with respect to the European Central Bank, that its
independent status leads, in effect, to a complete lack of democratic accountability in the central field of monetary policy. However, it argued, this is justified because practical experience in Germany implies that monetary policy
will function better if rendered immune from short-term political influence.[55]

The Court finally elaborated on the role of the new principle of subsidiarity (Article 3b (2) TEU) as a means of support for the principle of enumerated competences and as a means to maintain and strengthen the role of
the member states within the Union. The principle of subsidiarity demands
that 'in areas which do not fall within its exclusive competence', the
Community can act 'only if and in so far as the objectives of the proposed
action cannot be sufficiently achieved by the member states' and can, therefore, be better achieved by the Community. The Court emphasises that the
ECJ will have the task of reviewing actions in the light of that principle and
that it will be the duty of the Federal Government to ensure strict observance
of that principle in the Council of Ministers.[56]

Analysis of the Court's Reasoning

The bottom line of the decision of the Federal Constitutional Court is that the TEU is compatible with the German Basic Law. Despite this positive result, it would be wrong to ignore the Court's underlying scepticism.[57] The sheer length of the decision is only one indication; not every constitutional complaint with equally far-fetched allegations will receive such profound scrutiny. More importantly, however, the decision contains some rather questionable passages warranting critical comment.

One principal point raised by the decision concerns the relationship between the legislative branch and constitutional jurisdiction. Even American readers, familiar with the controversy about the Supreme Court overstepping its bounds, might be surprised at a court giving rather detailed instructions as to what is and is not possible in terms of the new European Union. This is especially striking in light of the German parliament's overwhelming endorsement of the new Article 23, which was tailor-made by the Bundestag and Bundesrat constitutionally to accommodate the new Union. Article 23 complements Article 24 of the Basic Law which had served as the constitutional foundation for the European Communities and which some thought was not a sufficient basis for the new Union.[58] Evidently the Court was not among those, because there is no reference to the impact the new Article 23 might have in relation to the old Article 24 Basic Law.[59] The reason lies in the peculiar structure of the German Basic Law: the inviolable 'eternity-clause' of Article 79 (3), which absolutely prohibits amendment of the Basic Law in respect of some fundamental principles, functions as a kind of 'super-constitutional' norm making possible the notion of unconstitutional constitutional provisions. Thus, the Court could perfectly well ignore the obvious will of the elected representatives of the people, as expressed in the new Article 23 Basic Law, by concentrating the debate on the absolute requirements stipulated by Article 79 (3) Basic Law.

From the perspective of international law, the most contentious parts of the decision are the repeated threats of the Court that Community acts not covered by the constituting treaties, that is, *ultra vires* acts, are not binding in Germany, that they must be disregarded by German state organs and that the Court itself will examine Community acts to see if they exceed legal competences.[60] This language expresses a central theme of the decision and, if taken at face value, could wreak havoc on the Union. The first assertion, that *ultra vires* acts are non-binding in Germany, is by itself a correct assumption. Such acts are indeed invalid in the sphere of international law. The question is, however, who is entitled to declare any such act *ultra vires*? Within the European Community, it is the Court of Justice which, under the EC Treaty, is empowered to examine, *inter alia*, whether Community acts have a sufficient legal basis in the constituting treaties.[61] According to the EC Treaty, illegal acts remain valid as long as they have not been nullified by the ECJ (Articles 173, 174 EC Treaty), even if the illegality could also be claimed incidentally (Article 184 EC Treaty). What an international organisation, respectively special types of international organisations like the EU and in particular the EC, can or cannot do, is decided at international level, within the procedures provided for by that organisation, in particular by the rulings of the ECJ and in application of the rules of interpretation which have their well-established place in international law such as the teleological interpretation (*effet utile*) and the relevance of the principle of implied powers.[62] The Court looked at the TEU as if it were more or less an ordinary statute and not an international treaty which is binding on the state regardless of the scope of the implementing statute.

This view of looking at international law merely from the national or state perspective – one is reminded of Hegel's perception of international law as external constitutional law – is not in conformity with the duties of member states of international organisations. The question whether the EU (and the EC) acted *ultra vires* must primarily be answered for all cases by the ECJ. One has to admit that there might be – quite hypothetically – extreme cases where EC organs, including the ECJ, completely misconstrue the treaties in the context of a very important issue. But, with the exception of this rather unlikely situation, all other 'normal' cases of illegal action by organs of the Communities certainly cannot be decided by each individual member of the organisation in question. This is, however, exactly what the Constitutional Court is saying. But not only does the Court reserve the right for itself to decide whether Community acts are within the bounds set by the constituting treaties, it even goes beyond that by advising every state organ to disregard such acts. A brief practical excursion will reveal the untenability of that position. Under Article 189 EC Treaty, regulations are directly applicable within the member states. According to the Court, if such a regulation arrives on the desk of a county official somewhere in Germany, he would have to examine the regulation with respect to its legal basis in the EC Treaty and – if the act is found to be *ultra vires* – deny its application. That goes far beyond domestic practice in Germany, where - unlike in the United States – not even courts are empowered to disregard laws if they find them to be unconstitutional. Only the Constitutional Court itself has that power and all other courts may bring their concerns on the constitutionality of a norm before the Constitutional Court by way of a reference procedure.

It is, therefore, necessary that the Court's nineteenth century perception of international law be put into perspective. In practice, state officials will have to continue to apply Community law as if it were domestic law and courts will first have to resort to the preliminary ruling procedure under

Article 177 EC Treaty before declaring a Community act to be *ultra vires*. Once the European Court of Justice has decided, the question becomes one of acceptance. If the Constitutional Court proves unwilling to accept the European Court's decision there will not only be a European crisis but also a constitutional crisis, probably to be followed by moves to curb the Court's authority. For the time being, there is ample evidence to suggest that the Court wanted to send a warning signal to the European Union to be more careful and stay within the bounds set by the treaties. There are a number of reasons why the adoption of the TEU may encourage the Community institutions, and in particular the European Court of Justice, to exercise such restraint. Maastricht has strengthened the position of the member states in a number of respects, for example by emphasising the role of the European Council in EU policy development. The introduction of the subsidiarity principle and the new limitations on the use of Article 235 EC Treaty represent checks on the exercise and development of Community competences by the Community's political institutions. The ECJ, too, must respect such principles in its interpretation of the treaties. One can also argue that there is little scope left for that court to go much further in the development of Community law than it has already, notably by the elaboration of the principles of direct effect, supremacy of Community law and state liability for failure to transpose directives, now all clearly part of the *acquis communautaire*. It is probably not being too optimistic, therefore, to conclude that the final showdown between the two courts can and will be avoided.

Another weak point of the Federal Constitutional Court's decision is its ambiguous approach to the problem of democratic legitimisation and to the role the state should play within that context. On the one hand, the Court interpreted the German Constitution to the effect that the democratic principle limits the further extension of the tasks and powers of the EC,[63] holding that the Constitution requires that substantial and substantive competences must remain with the German parliament and that it is primarily the peoples of the respective member states who, through their national parliaments, must secure democratic legitimisation of the exercise of Community power.[64] On the other hand, it must be noted that the Court's starting point was that

> the right of the complainant under Article 38 Basic Law can be violated, if the exercise of the powers of the German Bundestag is transferred to an organ of the European Union or the European Communities *formed by the governments* [sic!] to such a degree that ... the minimum requirements of democratic legitimisation of the exercise of public power vis-à-vis the citizen are no longer fulfilled .[65]

The explicit reference to an organ formed by the governments (the Council) could actually be read to imply that the situation would be quite different if competences were transferred to the directly elected EP. If it had been the Court's intention to limit *per se* the transfer of competences away from the Bundestag it could well have done so without the reference to the Council. The Court also tied its requirement of democratic legitimisation through the national parliaments to the present state of integration of the Union[66] and emphasised that democratic legitimisation will increasingly have to be achieved through European organs.[67] Thus, the elimination of the democratic deficit in the Community at some time in the future by giving the EP full parliamentary status, which would result in the democratic legitimisation of Community acts 'primarily' through the EP, would not, *per se*, be precluded by the judgment. The Court expressed the opinion, however, that before that stage could be reached a number of developments would be required at European level. These were stated, rather vaguely, to include the emergence of a 'public opinion, which preshapes the political will' of the EU and of greater transparency in decision-making. The Court also stressed the importance, for the citizen, of being able to communicate with the relevant organs in his or her own language. The Court concluded that, while such conditions may not already exist, they may develop in the course of time within the institutional framework of the European Union.[68]

V. Concluding Remarks

Whether the Federal Constitutional Court has found a just balance between co-operation and conflict is an open question. The Court reserved to itself the last word on the constitutionality of future actions and decisions by the European institutions. To that extent, its proclaimed desire to pursue a policy of 'co-operation' with the ECJ could 'camouflage' an attempt to restrict the jurisdiction of the ECJ by subordinating its decisions to the final judgment of the Federal Constitutional Court.

The decision can be interpreted more optimistically (as Götz[69] did) or more pessimistically (as, for example, Tomuschat[70]). Others will refer to this decision as *'Solange III'*. The limitations set by the Court apply *solange* (as long as) we do not have a European federal state (*Bundesstaat*). Whether a future European federal state (*Bundesstaat*) is compatible at all with the Basic Law is even more controversial.[72]

If one has a high regard for the idea of European integration as it is and has always been embedded in the German Basic Law and wants to retain an optimistic outlook at the same time, it might be best to interpret the Court's decision from a political rather than a legal point of view. The Court put up the warning signs for the new Union in general and for the ECJ in particular. If the signs are received, that is, if the European organs refrain from assuming new powers by according treaty provisions excessively broad interpretations, business will be as usual and the Constitutional Court will refrain from redefining international law in Hegel's tradition. The European organs have that chance because much of what has been or is disputed with regard to the Treaty's interpretation is already part of the *acquis communautaire* The Federal Constitutional Court accepted the *acquis communautaire* without new reservations. It is up to the member states now to reduce further the 'democratic deficit'[73] by giving the European Parliament the full status of a parliament, that is by placing the European Parliament on an equivalent level with the Council of Ministers as the 'chamber of member states'. The revision of the TEU in 1996 is the next opportunity to do so.

The meagre results of the deliberations of the Joint Constitutional Commission have shown that this is not the best time for constitutional reform in Germany. Germany is in the process of mastering the domestic challenges of unification. European integration also needs time to breathe. Consolidation and intensification should be the primary goals. The future enlargement of the EU with the accession of Austria, Finland, Sweden and possibly Norway and the related dispute concerning voting rights of member states in the Council[74] underline the conclusion that the balance between co-operation and conflict of the member states with the EU is a delicate one. The question of sovereignty is still pending.[75]

NOTES

1. Cf. Georg Ress, 'Grundgesetz', in Weidenfeld and Korte (eds.), *Handbuch zur Deutschen Einheit* (1993), p.337 at 348.
2. Cf. Hans-Peter Schneider: 'Das Grundgesetz - auf Grund gesetzt?', *NJW* (1994), p.558 at 559.
3. The improvement of the EC judicial system, especially in regard to protection of the individual, has been the topic of the discussions at the German Jurists Meeting 1994 (*Deutscher Juristentag*), see Manfred Dauses, 'Empfiehlt es sich, das System des Rechtsschutzes und der Gerichtsbarkeit in der Europäischen Gemeinschaft weiterzuentwickeln?' Gutachten D zum 6. Deutschen Juristentag (1994); under the same title Eberhard Schmidt-Aßmann, *Juristen-Zeitung* (JZ) (1994), p.832; Thomas Oppermann, 'Die Dritte Gewalt in der Europäischen Union', *Deutsches Verwaltungsblatt* (1994), p.901.
4. For general background information on the revision of the Federal Basic Law by the Joint Constitutional Commission (*Gemeinsame Verfassungskommission*) see Friedrich-Adolf Jahn, 'Empfehlungen der Gemeinsamen Verfassungskommission zur Änderung und Ergänzung des Grundgesetzes', *Deutsches Verwaltungsblatt* (1994), p.177.
5. *Reports of the Decisions of the German Federal Constitutional Court (BVerfGE)* 83, p.37 (Schleswig-Holstein) and BVerfGE 83, p.60 et seq. (Hamburg), where the Court had held that the sovereignty of the people relates to German nationals. The question whether an *exception* might be possible on the level of local governments for citizens of other member

states in the process of European integration is left open in those decisions. The right of Union citizens to vote in elections for the European Parliament is not dealt with in the Basic Law and will be realised by amending the Statute on the Elections of the Deputies to the European Parliament from the Federal Republic of Germany (*Europawahlgesetz*) of 16 June 1978, BGBl. I, p.709.

6. Act to Amend the Basic Law of 21 Dec. 1992, *Official Journal of the Federal Republic of Germany*, Part I *(Bundesgesetzblatt (BGBl.)* Teil I), p.2086.

7. Ibid.

8. The Court concluded in its Maastricht judgment that if during the third stage of EMU price stability could no longer be realised, the FRG would be under a constitutional obligation to end its participation unilaterally, which could only be possible under the circumstances provided for in Article 62 of the Vienna Convention on the Law of Treaties (*clausula rebus sic stantibus*). However, Kokott has correctly explained that Article 62 VCLT is interpreted very restrictively and that it is, therefore, questionable whether it could be applied in regard to the EMU, if only because the objective of price stability cannot be defined and is subject to the current economic situation; see Juliane Kokott, 'Deutschland im Rahmen der Europäischen Union – zum Vertrag von Maastricht', *Archiv des öffentlichen Rechts*, Vol. 119 (1994), p.207 at 231.

9. The newly created term *Staatenverbund* which is used to describe the 'ever closer union' of the Maastricht Treaty and which goes back to the seminal article of Paul Kirchhof, 'Der deutsche Staat im Prozeß der Europäischen Integration', *Handbuch des Staatsrechts der Bundesrepublik Deutschland*, Vol. VII, No. 183, does not denote a new legal type of international organisation. The Union, though perhaps more in the usual sense, remains a *Staatenbund* in the legal sense of the word; cf. Kirchhof's definition id. at marginal No. 68 and Bruno Kahl, 'Europäische Union: Bundesstaat – Staatenbund – Staatenverbund, Zum Urteil des BVerfG vom 12. Oktober 1993', *Der Staat*, Vol. 33 (1994), p.241 at 257, so that a new constitutional basis for the Union was not mandatory.

10. The constitutional objective of a united Europe goes beyond the European Union now established.

11. So-called 'state-function' or 'state-objective' clause (*Staatszielbestimmung*).

12. So-called 'structural protection' clause (*Struktursicherungsklausel*).

13. 'Statute on Co-operation between the Federal Government and the Bundestag in European Union Matters' ('Gesetz über die Zusammenarbeit von Bundesregierung und Deutschem Bundestag in Angelegenheiten der Europäischen Union)' of 12 March 1993, *BGBl.* Teil I, p.311.

14. 'Gesetz über die Zusammenarbeit von Bund und Länder in Angelegenheiten der Europäischen Union' of 12 March 1993, *BGBl.* Teil I, p.313.

15. Georg Ress, 'Democratic Decision-Making in the European Union and the Role of the European Parliament', *Festschrift Schermers*, Vol. II, (1994), p.151.

16. See Albrecht Randelzhofer, 'Zum behaupteten Demokratiedefizit der Europäischen Gemeinschaft', in Hommelhoff and Kirchhof (eds.), *Der Staatenbund der Europäischen Union* (1994), p.39. See also my remarks as discussant in *Veröffentlichungen der Vereinigung der deutschen Staatsrechtslehrer*, Vol. 53 (1994), p.124.

17. For a complete translation of Article 23 (1) see the Appendix to this volume.

18. Hereinafter referred to as the Court.

19. *Bundesverfassungsgericht (BVerfG)*, 12 Oct. 1993 - 2 BvR 2134/92 und 2159/92, not officially published at the time of writing, reproduced in *Europäische Grundrechtezeitschrift (EuGRZ)* (1993), p.429; *Juristen-Zeitung (JZ)* (1993), p.1100; *Neue Juristische Wochenschrift (NJW)* (1993), p.3047. The citations in this paper refer to the decision as published in the *EuGRZ*. The translations of the excerpts from the Court's opinion which appear in the paper are my own. See also my commentary in 88 *American Journal of International Law (AJIL)* (1994), p.539.

20. Act of 28 Dec. 1992 concerning the Treaty on European Union of 7 Feb. 1992, *BGBl.* Teil II, p.1251. Statutory approval was required under Article R(1) TEU as well as under Article 59(2) of the Basic Law.

21. Act amending the Basic Law of 21 Dec. 1992, Part I *BGBl.* Teil I, p.2086.
22. See Article R(1) and (2) TEU; Treaty on European Union of 7 Feb. 1992, *Official Journal of the European Communities (OJ)*, C 224/1 (1992)
23. The judgment has received praise for its 'very restrictive and stringent' interpretation of the Maastricht Treaty 'in order to find the provisions on monetary union compatible with the concept that the German parliament still controls the major decisions', see Kokott, 'Deutschland im Rahmen', p.237.
24. Of 2 June, 1992 (50.3% voted against the TEU).
25. The Act of 28 Dec. 1992 concerning the Treaty on European Union of 7 Feb. 1992 was passed in the Bundestag on 2 Dec. 1992 by the impressive majority of 543 to 25. Consent in the Bundesrat – the representative body of the German Länder – was unanimous. See Decision of the Federal German Constitutional Court (hereinafter referred to as 'decision'), *EuGRZ* (1993), p.429 at 431.
26. As has been demonstrated again recently in the Constitutional Court's judgment of 12 July 1994 (joined cases 2 BvE 3/92; 5,7,8/93) concerning the military engagement of Germany in Bosnia and Somalia.
27. See for example Dietrich Murswiek, 'Maastricht und der *pouvoir constituant*', *Der Staat* (1993), p.161; Hans Stöcker, 'Die Unvereinbarkeit der Währungsunion mit der Selbstbestbestimmungsgarantie in Art. 1 Abs. 2 GG', *Der Staat* (1992), p.495.; Hans-Heinrich Rupp, 'Muß das Volk über den Vertrag von Maastricht entscheiden?' *NJW* (1993), p.38.
28. Manfred Brunner was *chef de cabinet* of the German Commissioner Manfred Bangemann. Like Bangemann, Brunner was active in the Free Democratic Party (FDP) and at one time headed the organisation in Bavaria. Commissioner Bangemann fired Brunner after he began publicly to criticise the TEU. Brunner recently left the FDP, founded his own party and intends to run on a mainly, anti-European Union platform in at least some of the many elections of this year in Germany, notably in the state elections of Bavaria.
29. Brunner's complaint had been based on the alleged violation of a myriad of constitutional norms and whereas some of those allegations gave ample evidence of his legal imagination they were nevertheless close to absurdity. For example, Brunner claimed a violation of Article 5 of the Basic Law (freedom of speech, expression, press etc.) on the grounds that the TEU changes the conditions of communication, in that henceforth European [political] organs must be influenced instead of German ones. Likewise he saw the freedom of association in political parties (Article 9 in conjunction with Article 21) jeopardised because Article 138a TEU supposedly orders parties to work towards a European identity.
30. Article 38 of the Basic Law reads as follows:
    (1) The Members of the German Bundestag shall be elected in general, direct, free, equal and secret elections. They shall be representatives of the whole people; they shall not be bound by any instructions, only by their conscience.
    (2) Anybody who has reached the age of eighteen is entitled to vote; anybody of majority age is eligible for election.
    (3) Details shall be the subject of a federal law.
    [Official translation by Press and Information Office of the Federal Government, Revised and Updated Edition, August 1993]
31. Referring to a speech of the President of the European Commission, Jacques Delors, and of Commissioner Bangemann according to which even before the TEU some 80% of laws and regulations in the field of economic law and some 50% of all German legislation is caused by Community law, see Decision, *EuGRZ* 429 at 434. This comes, in fact, close to the truth.
32. Article F (3) TEU: The Union shall provide itself with the means necessary to attain its objectives and carry through its policies.
33. The so-called 'Article on the European Union' (new Article 23) was incorporated into the Basic Law by the Act amending the Basic Law of 21 Dec. 1992, see supra note 21. The text of Article 23 appears in the Appendix to this volume. Article 79 (2) of the Basic Law makes amendments of the Basic Law contingent on a two-thirds majority in both the Bundestag and the Bundesrat and Art. 79 (3) proscribes any amendment of the Basic Law aimed at revising the principles set forth in Articles 1 and 20 Basic Law which are in essence those already

mentioned in Article 23 (1) (principles of democracy, federalism, social welfare, rule of law, protection of human rights, with the exception of the principle of subsidiarity).

34. Decision, p.434.
35. E.g. economic and monetary union; education and training; culture; public health; consumer protection; trans-European networks (transport, telecommunications, energy infrastructures).
36. Decision, p.434.
37. *BVerfGE* 58, p.1 and 59, p.63.
38. *BVerfGE* 37, p.271.
39. The Court underlined that majority voting in the Council does not break the chain of democratic legitimisation without hinting what kind of majority is acceptable. However, if democratic legitimisation can only be achieved through the national parliaments, does that not necessitate the consent of the national representative?
40. Later in the judgment the Court analysed the status of the Union and came to the conclusion that the European Union is not a state and that the member states are still sovereign entities, because the Union is mainly an economic community (internal market, monetary union etc.) and because co-operation in the fields of justice and home affairs and the common foreign and security policy is structured intergovernmentally. Thus, the Court concluded that Germany is one of the 'masters of the treaty' which, having expressed their will for long-term or unlimited membership could also revoke that intention. In Germany that passage of the decision was widely misinterpreted as stipulating Germany's right to withdraw from the Union unilaterally. The Court's use of the plural, however, demonstrates that no such blatantly unlawful holding was intended. The Court consequently made it quite clear that the question whether the Basic Law allows or precludes German membership in a European state did not arise under the given circumstances (Decision, p.439).
41. For a similar view see Kokott, 'Deutschland im Rahmen', p.214.
42. Cf. Georg Ress, 'Über die Notwendigkeit der parlamentarischen Legitimierung der Rechtsetzung der Europäischen Gemeinschaften – Überlegungen zum europäischen Gemeinschaftsrecht und deutschen Verfassungsrecht', in Fiedler and Ress (eds.), *Verfassungsrecht und Völkerrecht, Gedächtnisschrift für Wilhelm Karl Geck* (1989), p.625 at 628; But see Albrecht Randelzhofer, 'Zum behaupteten Demokratiedefizit der Europäischen Gemeinschaft', in Hommelhoff and Kirchhof (eds.), *Der Staatenbund der Europäischen Union* (1994), pp.54-5.
43. Decision, p.438.
44. Decision, p.438.
45. The question of how much control can or must be exercised by a national parliament gives rise to problems similar to those which have been addressed above in regard to the restrictions imposed on the respresentation of Länder in the Council.
46. Decision , p.439.
47. Cf. Helmut Steinberger and Eckart Klein, 'Der Verfassungsstaat als Glied einer europäischen Gemeinschaft', *Veröffentlichungen der Vereinigung der Deutschen Staatsrechtslehrer (VVDStRL)*, Vol. 50 (1991), pp.17, 66 and my remarks as discussant on p.172.
48. Decision, p.439.
49. Ibid, p.440.
50. For the text of Article F (3) see supra note 32. Cf. Georg Ress, 'Die Europäische Union und die neue juristische Qualität der Beziehungen zu den Europäischen Gemeinschaften', *Juristische Schulung* (1992), p.987. Article 235 reads as follows:If action by the Community should prove necessary to attain, in the course of the operation of the common market, one of the objectives of the Community and this Treaty has not provided the necessary powers, the Council shall, acting unanimously on a proposal from the Commission and after consulting the European Parliament, take the appropriate measures.
51. Beutler, Bieber, Pipkorn and Streil, *Die Europäische Union – Rechtsordnung und Politik* (4th ed. 1993), p.74. However, there are also indications of profound confusion as to the purpose of Article F (3). The Court cites statements of German government officials in the proceedings and of the German Bundestag in which the provision is qualified as 'a

programmatic principle' without specifying the contents, see decision at p.441.
52. Decision, p.440.
53. Ibid, p.443.
54. Ibid.
55. Ibid, p.445.
56. Ibid. Whether acts can be found to be *ultra vires* on the grounds of non-compliance with this principle of subsidiarity and whether this question is under the control of the courts of the member states is a crucial question. An affirmative answer would bring complete legal instability into the relationship between the EU and its member states.
57. A first draft of the judgment was even more critical and leaned towards declaring the TEU unconstitutional.
58. Rupert Scholz, 'Europäische Union und deutscher Bundesstaat', *Neue Zeitschrift für Verwaltungsrecht* (1993), p.817 at 819; see also Ulrich Everling, 'Überlegungen zur Struktur der Europäischen Union und zum neuen Europa-Artikel des Grundgesetzes', *Deutsches Verwultungs blatt* (1993), pp.936.
59. See Christian Tomuschat, 'Die Europäische Union unter Aufsicht des Bundesverfassungsgerichts', *EuGRZ* (1993), p.489 at 492-3.
60. See supra n.46 and accompanying text. Decision at pp.438-9, 440, 445.
61. See Articles 164 ff., EC Treaty. For a discussion of this position see Klein, 'Der Verafassungsstaat', pp.66.
62. Cf. Georg Ress, 'Die Bedeutung der Rechtsvergleichung für das Recht internationaler Organisationen', *Zeitschrift für ausländisches öffentliches Recht und Völkerrecht*, Vol. 36, 1976, pp.420 ff.; Id., 'Wechselwirkungen zwischen Verfassung und Völkerrecht bei der Auslegung völkerrechtlicher Verträge', *Heft 23 der Berichte der Deutschen Gesellschaft für Völkerrecht* (1982), pp.7 ff.
63. Decision, pp.429, 438.
64. Ibid, p.437.
65. Ibid, p.434.
66. Ibid, p.438: 'as is presently the case'. At present it is obviously not so much the concern for democratic, i.e. parliamentary legitimisation, as concern for the influence of the member states as such (here: Germany) on the decision-making process of the Union. Member states see their position better protected by the currently strong position of the Council and the Commission's monopoly of legislative initiative than by a diffuse participation of elected representatives of their peoples in the Ep. The smaller a member state is, the stronger the weight of this argument. The Court argued that
    notwithstanding the necessity of democratic control of the governments, the enactment of European legal norms may rest in the hands of an organ composed of representatives of the governments of the member states, i.e. in a governmentally determined organ, to a larger degree than could be constitutionally tolerated within the national sphere.
   See Decision , p.438.
67. Decision, pp.437-38.
68. Ibid; see also Tomuschat, 'Die Europäische Union', p.494, who is slightly more pessimistic and sees the Union being manoeuvered into an 'insoluble situation'.
69. Volkmar Götz, 'Das Maastricht-Urteil des Bundesverfassungsgerichts', *Juristen-Zeitung* (1993), pp.1081ff.
70. Christian Tomuschat, 'Die Europäische Union unter der Aufsicht des Bundesverfassungsgerichts', *EuGRZ* (1993), pp.489ff.
71. Cf. Bruno Kahl.
72. It is interesting that Hans Hugo Klein, one of the judges of the Second Chamber (*Zweiter Senat*) of the Court which decided the case, did not preclude the possibility that, despite Article 79 (3), the Basic Law is open for such reform. See 'Maastrichter Vertrag und Nationale Verfassungsrechtsprechung', VI. Europäische Rechtskonferenz der Konrad-Adenauer-Stiftung, Luxembourg, 18 Nov. 1993. Cf. also Kahl, 'Europäische Union' p.242.
73. The notion of the 'democratic deficit' is often misunderstood. It is a deficit from the point of view of *constitutional* requirements in the member states, in particular the German Basic

Law, which arises in the process of the transfer of powers. It is not a deficit from the perspective of the law of international organisations, such as Randelzhofer seems to believe (Randelzhofer, 'Zum behaupteten Demokratiedefizit'; p.39 ff.). See Georg Ress, 'Über die Notwendigkeit der parlamentarischen Legitimierung der Rechtssetzung der Europäischen Gemeinschaften', in Wilfried Fiedler and Georg Ress, (eds.), *Verfassungsrecht und Völkerrecht – Gedächtnisschrift für Wilhelm Karl Geck* (1989), p.625 at 681-4.

74. See Council Decision of 29 March 1994, OJ C 105/01 (1994).
75. Cf. Helmut Steinberger, 'Anmerkungen zum Maastricht-Urteil des Bundesverfassungsgerichtes', in Hommelhoff and Kirchhof (eds.), *Der Staatenbund der Europäischen Union* (1994), p.25 at 33.

To be Continued: The Constitutional Reform Commissions from a Länder Perspective

UWE LEONARDY

This article summarises and compares the recommendations on Federal–Länder relations of the Bundesrat Commission on Constitutional Reform and the Joint Constitutional Commission. It also points to areas where further constitutional reform is required, including intergovernmental fiscal relations, territorial organisation and a state objective relating to the equivalence of living conditions throughout the country. Whilst the scope for large-scale constitutional reform is limited, incremental change needs to be continued, in particular in view of the implications of European integration.

I. Introduction

Federalism, as a form of political organisation of the German state, was not 'invented' with the Basic Law of 1949. Throughout much her constitutional history, Germany was either a confederation or a federation of states located within changing territorial boundaries. There have been only two major deviations from that tradition.[1] The first was the period between the dissolution of the Holy Roman Empire of the German Nation in 1806 and the Imperial Constitution on 1871, which was marked by the existence of numerous monarchies and republics of a sovereign character. Even these, however, displayed confederal, quasi-federal or, ultimately, fully-fledged federal characteristics. One need only mention here the German Confederation of 1815 to 1866, the German Customs Association of 1833 to 1871 and the North German Federation of 1867 to 1871. The second exception to the federal tradition was Hitler's centralist dictatorship from 1933 to 1945, though it could be argued that it represented an interruption rather than an exception to constitutional history, since not just federalism, but any form of constitutional government had ceased to exist.

The Basic Law of 1949 thus re-established federalism as a constitutional pattern which had undergone many profound changes during a century-long tradition. Against this background, it can occasion no surprise that since the adoption of the Basic Law, the federal system has been one of the central topics in all attempts at major constitutional reform. For example, very soon after the establishment of Federal Republic, the Luther Commission[2] (1951–55) produced numerous recommendations on territorial reform.

These, however, were partly contradictory and, not least for that reason, were not implemented. Similarly, although the Ernst-Commission[3] (1970–72), which dealt with the same subject, avoided that mistake by submitting a comprehensive and consistent scheme for reducing the number of the Länder from the then 11 to five or six, none of its recommendations achieved any greater success. This was due to the opposition of 'unholy alliances' between the SPD–governed city states (which were to be abolished), leading Social Democrats and Liberals in the social-liberal Federal Government, and the then Minister-President of Rhineland-Palatinate, Helmut Kohl, whose state was threatened by the proposed reforms. As a result, the only successful measure of territorial reform so far, the creation of Baden-Württemberg from its three predecessor states in 1951, was accomplished on the basis of a constitutional provision in the original Basic Law (Article 118), referring specifically to this case. As regards financial reform, the Troeger-Commission[4] (1964–66) was markedly more successful, as its suggestions, directed chiefly at the creation of the joint tasks (*Gemeinschaftsaufgaben*), did find their way into the Constitution. This was, however, very much the exception. Thus, the Bundestag Commission of Inquiry on Constitutional Reform[5] (1970–76) produced suggestions for new schemes for joint intergovernmental planning and co-financing, none of which were adopted. Nonetheless, its recommendations concerning the Länder's international relations within the federal structure were a valuable basis for the deliberations in the two most recent constitutional commissions.

In spite of the obvious failure to secure comprehensive constitutional reform in the federal field, no less than 22 of the 36 acts of amendment to the Basic Law passed before 1990 had brought about piecemeal reforms to the federal system. Of these, only the changes following the report of the Troeger-Commission could be said to have resulted from an at least partially comprehensive approach. It is against this background of continuous gradual change that the work of the Bundesrat Commission on Constitutional Reform (1991–92)[6] and the Joint Constitutional Commission of the Bundestag and the Bundesrat (1992–94)[7] needs to be considered.

The following will present the main substance of the recommendations of the two Commissions in so far as they relate to the federal system and highlight the central controversies surrounding their proposals. In this context, special emphasis is given to the differences of substance between the proposals of the two Commissions (II). This is followed by an evaluation of the results from a Länder perspective, which serves to highlight the need for further debate (III). Finally, the paper assesses the prospects for incremental constitutional adaptation compared to large-scale reform (IV).

II. The Commissions and Their Proposals

Federation and Länder in the European Union and International Relations

Building on the 'Cornerstones of the Länder for Federalism in a Unified Germany', a document adopted by the Minister-Presidents' Conference on 5 July 1990[8], the Bundesrat Commission on Constitutional Reform was established in April 1991 and concluded its work in May 1992. It consisted of two members from each of the 16 post-unification Länder, of which each had one vote. The two-thirds majority necessary for passing Commission recommendations, therefore, totalled 11 votes.[9] By contrast, all of the 64 members of the Joint Constitutional Commission (again two representatives from each Land and 32 members of the Bundestag) voted individually, so that the two-thirds majority, which was again required to adopt a recommendation, totalled 43.[10] Both Commissions were established on the basis of Article 5 of the Unification Treaty, which directed them to take into account any changes necessitated by the simultaneous processes of German unification and European integration. Due to the pressure on the Federal Government to secure the ratification of the Maastricht Treaty, the latter field became the first priority of the Joint Commission early in 1992, by which time the Bundesrat Commission had already begun to work on other aspects of constitutional reform.

With the ratification of the founding Treaty of the European Union rapidly approaching, both Commissions had to consider the implications for the federal system of a new – and yet to be adequately defined – constitutional or quasi-constitutional institution, the European Union, which would act as the recipient of both past and future transfers of sovereign rights.[11] Its significance for the relations between the Federation and the Länder had to be evaluated and, where necessary, addressed in amendments to the Basic Law. The Bundesrat Commission had unnecessarily narrowed its own horizons in this field by concentrating entirely on securing provisions for Bundesrat consent to transfers of sovereign powers, alongside new conditions and procedures for stronger Länder participation in European affairs. It had, in effect, limited itself to constitutionalising concessions won on ratification of the SEA. In so doing, the Commission was largely blind to the more far-reaching political and legal problems raised by the new level of integration inherent in the Maastricht Treaty.

In an attempt to carry this decisive new dimension into the deliberations of the Joint Constitutional Commission, Lower Saxony had, however, launched an initiative in the Minister-Presidents' Conference to the effect that two-thirds majorities in both the Bundestag and the Bundesrat should be necessary for any future transfers of sovereign powers to the European

Community or Union. The rationale behind this move[12] was the fact that the sum-total of the past and ongoing transfers of sovereign rights to the EC/EU had begun to encroach progressively upon the triad of basic constitutional values – democracy, federalism and human rights protection – enshrined in Article 79 (3) of the Basic Law.

Building on Lower-Saxony's initiative, the Joint Commission made these central issues its first priority. Not surprisingly, there was, initially, little concensus on how the Constitution should be changed to accommodate the Länder's concerns. Whilst the Social Democratic members of the Commission and also increasingly the parliamentary and the Länder representatives of the CDU and CSU demanded substantial amendments, the Federal Government and, in particular, the Liberal members of the Commission, backing the line of the FDP-controlled Foreign Ministry, wanted to agree to only minimal changes. After long and sometimes heated disputes, the Joint Commission ended up with a whole package of 'European Amendments' to the Basic Law.[13] Amongst these, the new Article 23 emerged as the centre-piece. It

- takes account of the fact that the European Union has begun to assume 'statelike' qualities;

- declares European integration to be a state objective;

- safeguards the Basic Law's central values, as specified in Article 79, in the process of further integration (*Struktursicherung-sklausel*);

- establishes the right of the Länder to the final say in European affairs which impinge upon their exclusive competences through the means of 'decisive comments' on draft secondary European legislation; and

- confirms the Länder's right to represent the Federal Republic in the European Council of Ministers in such matters (for this the way had been opened by the Maastricht Treaty amending Article 146 of the EEC Treaty).

Article 23 was complemented by amendments to several other articles of the Basic Law, such as those on the Bundesrat's basic constitutional role (Article 50), the constitutionalisation of the European Chamber of the Bundesrat (Article 52), and the establishment of a Bundestag Committee on Matters of the European Union (Article 45). In addition, the European Amendments included several other matters not directly relevant to inter-governmental relations.[14] Of all the recommendations of the Joint Commission, the European Amendments were the first to be passed into law prior to the Act of Ratification to the Treaty on European Union in December 1992.[15]

The tough political struggle, in particular for the new Article 23, did, however, have its effects on other fields relevant to federal issues in the Joint Commission's deliberations. The European policy achievements for the Länder and the Bundesrat produced strong pressure for compromise, compelling the Länder to sacrifice, in part, some of their other aims, especially in the areas of international relations[16] – as distinct from European affairs – and the Federation's powers of concurrent and framework legislation. As regards the first of these two areas, the Länder failed to constitutionalise the so-called Lindau Agreement. Under this 'gentlemen's agreement', concluded in 1957, the Federation respects the need for the unanimous consent of the Länder for foreign treaties signed by the Federation in fields of exclusive Länder competences and informs the Länder on the negotiation of such treaties. The Bundesrat Commission had recommended an amendment to Article 32 of the Basic Law, which would have constitutionalised this practice. The Federation, however, which had had to give much ground on the European Amendments, refused to accept this demand, a position for which it also enjoyed support from amongst representatives of the Bundestag opposition parties.

The Länder also failed to secure a recommendation which would have provided for a strengthening of the Bundesrat's rights in transfers of sovereign powers to institutions other than the European Union. The Länder, particularly in the Social Democratic Working Group of the Joint Commission, had been pressing for an extension of the Bundesrat veto on such transfers with a view to the potential future transfer of sovereign powers to international organisations such as the CSCE and institutions designed to bring the countries of central and eastern Europe closer to the European Union. They based their argument on the fact that the lack of obligatory Bundesrat consent to the transfers of sovereign powers within the process of European integration under Article 24 had created an 'open flank of the federal order',[17] through the intrusion of Federal power into areas of Länder competences. However, given their success with the new Article 23, they failed to carry their view. Nevertheless, in a third field, the Länder did achieve success. This concerned the possibility of transfers of Länder sovereign rights to 'transfrontier institutions in neighbourhood regions'. By placing this demand in the European Amendments package, the Länder secured a new Section 1a in Article 24 to make such transfers possible.

Legislative Powers

The Joint Commission, despite demands made in the 'Cornerstones' of the

Minister-Presidents' Conference, failed to recommend substantial changes in the federal distribution of legislative powers set out in the catalogues of the Basic Law. It did, however, recommend some significant other amendments in this area. The first concerned the preconditions for Federal concurrent and framework legislation. Article 72 of the Basic Law sets out the conditions under which the Federation can enact laws of concurrent legislation with regard to the subject matters enumerated in Article 74, and these criteria also apply to Federal framework legislation under Article 75. In essence, the Commission recommended that more stringent criteria be applied in this area. Thus, the maintenance of 'economic unity' is to be deleted as a precondition for Federal legislation, since this is already implied in the notion of 'legal unity'. It also suggested the replacement of the misconceived notion of a 'uniformity of living conditions' by the 'equivalence' of living conditions. The Joint Commission further recommended that concurrent legislative powers should be returned to the Länder by Federal Act, if the need to regulate such matters at the Federal level had be come obsolete. Finally, it proposed that the power of the Länder to pass laws in a particular field of concurrent legislation should no longer be barred merely because federal legislative proceedings making use of that concurrent power had been set it train.

Perhaps most importantly, the Joint Commission recommended that through an amendment to Article 93 (1, No. 2a) of the Basic Law, the Federal Constitutional Court would, in effect, be forced to renounce its present interpretation which holds that the clause on the need for Federal legislation (*Bedürfnisklausel*) for these two types of legislation is to be assessed by the legislature rather than by the Court.[18] By contrast, the Bundesrat Commission favoured a political solution to this problem. Thus, it recommended that any Federal Act making use of a concurrent or framework power should contain a statement to the effect that the invocation of those powers would be in line with the *Bedürfnisklausel* and, moreover, this statement should in all cases be subject to the consent of the Bundesrat.

As regards the rules governing framework legislation, both Commissions stressed that the definition of framework legislation needs to make it clear that framework rules relate to matters of Länder power. Regarding the degree of detail in framework legislation, there was, however, a difference between the two. While the Bundesrat Commission demanded that there should be neither detailed nor exhaustive regulations in these fields,[19] the Joint Commission (again under pressure from the Bundestag and the Federal Government side) suggested that regulations of this type should only be adopted 'in exceptional cases'.

If we turn to the actual distribution of legislative powers, the recommendations of the Joint Constitutional Commission did not amount to much.

Specifically, they envisaged that

- measures to prevent the transfer of German cultural property abroad should fall under framework legislation rather than concurrent legislation;

- the Federation be given a new concurrent power in matters affecting state liability for wrongful administrative acts, provided that such legislation is subject to Bundesrat consent;

- framework legislation regarding the principles of higher education be narrowed by excluding university constitutional law from Federal power;

- legislation on the general legal status of the film industry be removed from the framework catalogue;

- regulations regarding artificial insemination and related topics be added to the catalogue of concurrent powers;

- the law of citizenship in the Länder be removed from the concurrent catalogue, since this was considered an obsolete regulation; and

- the law on development contributions following measures of town and country planning be taken out of the concurrent list.

It is, then, clear that as far as legislative powers are concerned, the most important issues for the federal system were clearly those concerning the need for concurrent and framework legislation in Articles 72 and 75 of the Basic Law. However, the effectiveness of the judicial solution favoured by the Joint Constitutional Commission would seem to be doubtful, since it assumes that the Federal Constitutional Court would be willing to judge upon matters which imply political decisions rather than judicial ones. If the Court is not to be forced to stage hearings on issues which would better be dealt with in a parliamentary or Bundesrat committee, then it cannot be expected to deviate from its present line of jurisdiction. To try to force the Court to do so means a replacement of legislative decisions by judicial ones. That would add further weight to the increasing criticism of an over-reliance on judicial arbitration for the solution of essentially political conflicts. The political solution favoured by the Bundesrat Commission, which would subject such decisions to the Bundesrat's consent, would, therefore, appear to be more appropriate, as it leaves the solution of conflict in the political arena of negotiation and potential compromise.

Legislative Procedures

Although procedural rules may, at first, appear a rather technical subject, they are of essential importance in a federal state. This applies all the more

FIGURE 1

PROCEDURAL SCHEME FOR "CONSENT BILLS"

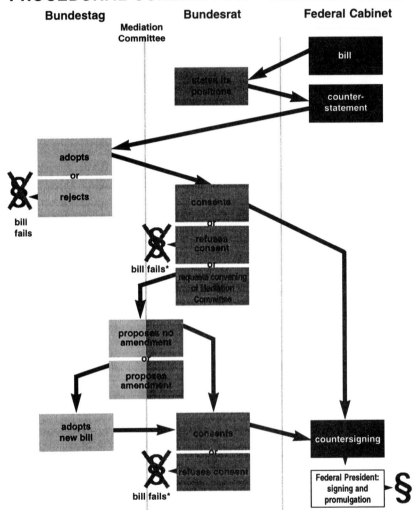

* unless the Federal Cabinet or the Bundestag request the convening of the Mediation Committee

Notes: This scheme shows the route taken by a Cabinet-introduced bill (the most frequent source of legilsation). Bundersrat bills must first be submitted to the Cabinet. Bills from the political parties represented in the Bundestag are submitted directly to the Bundestag.

Source: Bundesrat (ed.), *The Germans Bundesrat–Second Legislative Body* (2nd edition, Bonn, 1992) p.25.

when one takes into account the position and relative strength of the Bundesrat in the German legislative process (Figure 1). The report of the Bundestag Inquiry Commission on Constitutional Reform of 1976 had already contained substantial recommendations in this area[20], and the 1990 'Cornerstones' document of the Minister-Presidents also included this subject in their demands for constitutional amendments. It was, therefore, only to be expected that both the Bundesrat Commission and the Joint Commission should formulate proposals regarding legislative procedures.

A first set of proposals concerned the time limits imposed on the Bundesrat in commenting on Federal Government bills. Under Article 76 of the Basic Law, the Bundesrat is, at present, generally obliged to comment on a Government Bill within six weeks. The Joint Constitutional Commission recommended that, if particularly voluminous or legally complex bills are involved, this period should be extended to up to nine weeks on demand of the Bundesrat, unless the Federal Government can claim a special and substantiated need for speeding up the procedure. However, the Joint Commission did not follow the Bundesrat Commission's suggestion that a similar extension should also be granted for the second stage in the parliamentary legislative process, that is after a bill is returned from the Bundestag to the Bundesrat. Both Commissions were agreed in recommending a general extension of the Bundesrat's consideration period on all bills containing constitutional amendments and transfers of sovereign rights under Articles 23 and 24 of the Basic Law. One of the main aims behind these proposals was to give the Länder parliaments a better chance of influencing the position taken by Länder governments in the Bundesrat in these matters. In close connection to these proposed changes, both Commissions also recommended that the time accorded to the Federal Government to respond to bills originating from the Bundesrat be shortened to six weeks, or nine weeks in exceptional circumstances, which would result in a harmonisation of practices for Federal Government and Bundesrat-sponsored bills. This should also apply to Bundesrat initiatives relating to constitutional amendments and transfers of sovereign rights, where the Federal Government was to be given nine weeks to comment.

As regards the interplay between Bundestag and Bundesrat, the Commissions proposed to constitutionalise the requirement that both houses consider, and decide on, legislative initiatives 'within adequate time'. At present, there is no time limit for either the Bundestag with regard to Bundesrat initiatives or the Bundesrat to decide on its consent to bills. The Commissions also agreed that the Bundesrat should have the right to draft delegated legislation and to pass such drafts on to the Federal Government. Up to now, there has been no such right. Finally, the two Commissions recommended the establishment of a Länder right to regulate details of federal-delegated legislation by Acts of their state parliaments rather than by further delegated legislation adopted by Länder executives, if Federal Acts permit such Länder-delegated legislation.

However, whilst both Commissions agreed on a number of constitutional amendments in matters of legislative procedure, several proposals by the Bundesrat Commission did not find sufficient support in the Joint Commission. For example, the Bundesrat Commission had recommended that, as on Government bills, there should be a first stage in the Bundesrat for bills originating in the Bundestag. The reason for this recommendation is to be found in the fact that the Federal Government increasingly introduces bills through its parliamentary groups and, thereby, deprives the Bundesrat of an early opportunity to consider proposed bills.[21] The Bundesrat Commission also proposed that for bills not requiring Bundesrat consent, a full two-thirds majority in the Bundestag should be necessary to overturn an objection (*Einspruch*) that had been supported by a two-thirds majority in the Bundesrat. At the same time, the Bundesrat should be given more time – six instead of three weeks – to demand that the Mediation Committee be convened and for deciding on an objection. Moreover, the Bundesrat Commission had argued that all Federal Acts administered by the Länder should require Bundesrat consent.

Finally, one further proposal concerning legislative procedures ought to be mentioned. This concerns the participation of Länder legislatures in constitutional changes regarding legislative powers. Here, the SPD introduced an amendment in parliament which would make it mandatory for a majority of the Länder parliaments to consent to changes in the Federal–Länder distribution of legislative powers; this consent would be deemed to be given unless explicitly refused within three months.

Territorial Reform

There has been a long history of failure in the Federal Republic not only to achieve territorial reform, but also to shape adequately the rules concerning procedures for territorial reorganisation. The present text of Article 29 of the Basic Law, which contains these rules, represents already the third version since 1949, following an alteration in 1969 and a complete but rather badly distorted redrafting in 1976.[22] The present version is commonly, and rightly, regarded as a means of preventing rather than enabling territorial reform, since it provides for a system of consecutive referenda in the territories concerned, through which any reform scheme would be hard put to survive.

The Bundesrat Commission did not dare to tackle the subject at all, and the Joint Commission also failed to recommend a more workable scheme for overall territorial reform. However, the Joint Commission did initiate a new approach to the problem. Through a new section 8 in Article 29, it provides for a step by step process of territorial reform by way of agreements between neighbouring Länder either on total amalgamation or partial territorial alterations. These agreements should be subject, first, to obligatory popular referenda, which in cases of partial alterations could be restricted to the areas concerned and, second, to the 'consent of the Bundestag', to be expressed through a resolution rather than an Act of Parliament (a device which would constitute a novelty in German constitutional law). In addition to the amendment to Article 29, both Commissions recommended a special Article 118a in the Basic Law for the amalgamation of the City State of Berlin with the surrounding State of Brandenburg, a process which had already been initiated by the Unification Treaty.

It could be argued that these recommendations are once again only cosmetic changes doing little to tackle a problem which has persisted since 1949. However, this would seem to be a precipitate judgment. A remarkable feature behind the emergence of the new approach toward reform by Länder agreement is that it was initiated by the City State of Hamburg, which, up to the 1980s, had been strongly opposed to any attempt at territorial reform at all. But with the economic expansion following the disappearance of the Iron Curtain, which had, up to 1990, cut off Hamburg's economic artery, the Elbe, Hamburg suddenly found itself in a situation in which the shortage of space for further economic development became painfully obvious. History has thus changed traditional attitudes and produced new constitutional energies.

Moreover, there may also be a chance of initiating territorial reform through a combination of the existing and new procedural elements in Article 29. The present section 4, which is to be left unchanged, provides for a right to a popular referendum in densely urbanised areas divided by Länder boundaries in order to achieve improved territorial organisation. If this device were to be used successfully, this could provide encouragement for those Länder governments which are in favour of achieving agreements with their neighbours under the new procedural rules, while at the same time propelling more reluctant Länder governments to do the same. In fact, even the threat of using the possibilities offered by section 4 may provide a powerful incentive for negotiating intergovernmental agreements in this new manner. Viewing the innovative potential of the new section 8 from this perspective suggests that it might emerge as having more political and constitutional significance than it would appear at first sight. For the sake of completeness, it should also be mentioned that the Joint Commission recommended that lesser measures of territorial reorganisation through simple intergovernmental agreement should be facilitated. Whereas so far, this route to reorganisation is only open if the territory which is the subject of a boundary modification has less than 10,000 inhabitants, the threshold should, in the Joint Commission's view, be increased to 50,000.

Administrative Structures

A further topic which received considerable attention in the report groups of the Joint Commission concerned the Federal–Länder distribution of organisational and supervisory powers in relation to administrative authorities; but major changes in this area were the subject of specific Federal Government and coalition bills formulated outside the Joint Commission. This applies to the privatisation of air traffic control[23], of the railways system[24] and also of the postal and telecommunications services.[25] By contrast, the Joint Commission itself developed and recommended only a relatively minor innovation, when it suggested that agencies administering social insurance should in future only be Federal ones if their responsibility covers the area of more than three Länder.

Other Topics of Relevance to the Federal System

Apart from the aforementioned areas, the recent constitutional reform discussion has brought up a number of other topics which are of relevance to the federal system. For example, the Joint Commission recommended that the institutional guarantee extended to local government under Article 28 of the Basic Law be explicitly extended to cover its financial bases. Also of note were the attempts in the Bundesrat Commission to restrict Länder elections to one, two or three specific dates within a four-year period, which did not find the Länder's approval and were also dismissed by the Joint Commission, which argued that to include such a provision into the Basic Law would represent a violation of the constitutional autonomy of the Länder.

The Joint Commission's Recommendations in the Legislative Process

As has been noted above, the European Amendments to the Basic Law, with the new Article 23 at their centre-piece, were already passed into legislation in December 1992, when the Joint Commission was still working on the other parts of its agenda. These amendments had been introduced as a Government Bill, together with two other bills, regulating the co-operation of the Federal Government in European affairs with the Bundestag and with the Bundesrat and the Länder respectively. Although the latter two bills had to be referred to the Mediation Committee, compromise was finally reached in February 1993.

Legislation was, accordingly, still needed for the implementation of the Joint Commission's other recommendations. At the time of writing (June

1994), the final results of this legislation cannot be fully foreseen, since the proceedings in both houses are still in progress. However, the following seeks to outline the most likely outcome.

The legislative process relating to the Joint Commission's recommendations started in the Bundesrat, which introduced all of the Commission's recommendations (except, of course, the European ones) in a Bill forwarded to the Federal Government as early as 17 December 1993.[26] The Bundestag took considerably longer to stage its First Reading on an identical, joint Bill of the CDU/CSU, the SPD and the FDP[27] on 4 February 1994, following efforts to secure consensus in the coalition parties on a number of matters mainly unrelated to the federal system. At the same time, the Social Democrats introduced a Bill of their own[28], which contained their more far-reaching demands for constitutional reform; however, they only impinged marginally on the federal system. Both Bills were referred to a number of Bundestag committees, with the Legal Committee in overall charge.

The Federal Government eventually submitted its comments[29] on the Bills on 17 March 1994, that is the latest date permissible under the Constitution. As to the federally relevant recommendations, the Government raised objections in six fields:

1. The judicial solution for safeguarding the *Bedürfnisklausel* in concurrent and framework legislation as suggested by the Joint Commission would not be workable in practice.

2. The criterion of 'economic unity' within the *Bedürfnisklausel* should not be deleted, mainly because this would endanger federal concurrent powers in matters of vocational training.

3. The proposal to return to Länder law on the basis of a Federal Act in the area of concurrent legislation, if Federal regulation of a particular subject-matter had become obsolete, was declared unacceptable.

4. The law on development contributions following measures of town and country planning should stay within concurrent powers, and framework powers regarding the principles of higher education should not be restricted.

5. The Federal Government rejected almost all of the proposals relating to legislative procedures and, in particular, to the harmonisation of time limits for the consideration of bills by the Bundesrat and the Bundestag. The only exception conceded was the prolongation of the time limit from six to nine weeks relating to bills on constitutional amendments and the transfer of sovereign rights.

6. Finally, the Federal Government did not go along with the suggestion that

the Bundesrat should have a right of initiative relating to delegated Federal legislation.

To this list, other objections were added in the non-federal fields. Since the coalition parties were at loggerheads about several reform issues, it proved impossible to take votes in two meetings of the Legal Committee on 3 March and 21 April 1994, or on 25 May 1994, when the Legal Committee had initially intended to finalise the project. Since then, however, negotiations within the coalition and with the Social Democrats have been taking place, with the following probable results:

- The judicial solution for the *Bedürfnisklausel* will remain as recom mended.

- The criterion of 'economic unity' within that clause will not be deleted, but it will be qualified by reference to the 'interest of the whole state', which must exist for the Federation to lay claim to the legislative power in question.

- The possibility of returning to regulation by the Länder in case of obsolescence will, in principle, remain as recommended.

- With the exception of university constitutional law (see above), the alterations in the subject-matter catalogues will also remain as suggested.

- The same applies to the recommendations of the Commission on legislative procedure.

The crucial controversy within the federal area has, thus, boiled down to the issue of removing university constitutional law from the catalogue of federal framework legislation, and it remains to be seen how this matter will be resolved in the further course of Federal–Länder negotiations.

III. The Reform Commissions Assessed: Missed Opportunities, Failures and the Need for Further Debate

It was noted at the outset that attempts at comprehensive constitutional reform have, until now, hardly been successful in the Federal Republic. The Finance Reform of 1969 and the European Amendments of 1992 could be considered as the only exceptions.[30] Looking at the record of both the Bundesrat Commission and the Joint Commission, one could justifiably argue that such a goal, if advisable, has again been missed. Certainly, in view of both the achievement of German unity and the increasingly statelike structure of the European Union, many had harboured high hopes. However, if constitutional reform is to be conceived of as an ongoing process, then it is necessary to identify the issues and lines on which future constitutional change should take place. In so far as the federal system is concerned, there are three fields in particular which merit further attention[31]: intergovernmental fiscal relations; territorial organisation; and 'the equivalence of living conditions' as a state objective.

Reform of the Financial Constitution

In a federal system, the distribution of legislative powers, territorial organisation and administrative structures cannot be separated from the financial constitution. In Germany, with a relatively high number of constituent units in a small, densely populated and partly highly urbanised territory, such interdependencies deserve particular attention.

Nevertheless, the Bundesrat Commission was excluded from deliberating on the issue of financial reform by its own terms of reference,[32] which provided for an inclusion of that field on the basis of a later Bundesrat resolution. Such a resolution was, however, never introduced and attempts at legislative initiatives in this area by the City State of Hamburg,[33] did not survive the committee stage. The most important reason for this failure to address the financial constitution was the tendency of the Länder finance ministers to count in budgetary terms rather than to think in constitutional categories. Due to the powerful position which the Conference of Finance Ministers has even *vis-à-vis* the Conference of Minister-Presidents, this tendency again predominated in the Länder camp. The same influence also made itself felt in the Joint Commission. Although not barred from considering financial reform by its terms of reference,[34] it abandoned discussions on this matter towards the end of its procedures 'for reasons of time'. The real reason was, however, to be found in a strong reluctance to tackle the numerous and complex problems in the financial field in the face of a 'do not touch attitude' held by the Federal and the Länder finance ministers and the Minister-Presidents.

Financial reform is too broad a subject to be discussed here in detail.[35] Nonetheless, two problems which call for the attention of the constitutional legislator are worth highlighting. First, unification has further strengthened the rule of the 'golden lead', by which the Federation takes advantage of the economic and financial disparities amongst the Länder to 'divide and rule'. Second, the consent of the Bundesrat is, at present, not required for expenditure-relevant legislation (*Geldleistungsgesetze*) to be administered by the Länder, if less than one-quarter of those costs falls upon the Länder according to the rules of Article 104a (3) of the Basic Law. The Federation is, consequently, able to legislate at the cost of the Länder. As long as these two basic problems, to which many others could be added, are not addressed, a reform of the financial constitution will prove elusive.

The present state of affairs in the distribution of financial resources is well illustrated by the Solidarity Pact of 1993. With this agreement, the Länder succeeded in securing a substantially improved quota of 56 per cent (Federation) to 44 per cent (Länder) in the sharing of value-added tax as the most important of the shared taxes. However, they could achieve this only by forming a common front *vis-à-vis* the Federation and after abandoning any plans to tackle the problem of the 'golden lead', particularly in the field of joint tasks (*Gemeinschaftsaufgaben*). The second, no less important, political factor which made the Solidarity Pact possible was the willingness of the Federation to take responsibility for a large share of the financial burdens of the new Länder, thus securing the consent of the old Länder to the entire package. In so doing, the Federation achieved a long-lasting influence on the policies of the new Länder, which, as a result, will remain in danger of sinking to the status of provinces of the Federation rather than become autonomous constituent parts of it.

Territorial Organisation

The pressures for territorial reorganisation have been increased by the effects of unification, with no less than 16 Länder on a comparatively small, but very densely populated territory. Many of the borders of these Länder cut right across heavily industrialised and urbanised parts of the country, such as those surrounding the city states in the north, the Rhine-Main and the Rhine-Neckar areas in the south-west or Dresden-Halle in the east. In a federal system which has turned more and more into a federalism by participation, the problems of co-ordination amongst the constituent parts, and also between them and the Federation, are becoming more and more difficult in view of the number of participants involved. Moreover, the social and economic disparities amongst the Länder have greatly increased by the addition of the five new and much weaker parts to the federal system. Unification has, therefore, brought about extreme imbalances which increase the dangers of playing off the weaker against the stronger members of the Federation.

Moreover, the shortcomings of the territorial structure prejudice the chances of the Länder to live up to their claims in the process of further European integration. It is here that problems of inter-Länder co-ordination are felt most acutely. The rights of participation under the new Article 23 will make those problems even more visible, since many Länder lack the administrative and personnel capacities to cope with the volume and complexity of European business. With the present territorial structure left unchanged, Article 23 could, thus, turn out to have been a Pyrrhic victory, not only for those Länder immediately affected by a deficient territorial structure, but for the Länder community as a whole. On the European level itself, the dangers to effective co-ordination due to the number of Länder involved, inter-Länder disparities and playing off tactics are likely to damage the Länder's role in the new Regional Committee of the European Union perhaps even more than in the domestic context.

Against this background, territorial reorganisation needs to remain firmly on the constitutional reform agenda. It has already been mentioned that the procedure for territorial reform specified in Article 29 of the Basic Law was left unchanged, because attempts at a comprehensive reform failed to win sufficient support. Since this procedure strangulates itself in an almost unworkable network of partial and locally bound referenda, the largest part of Article 29 will remain a dead letter. The need for a general revision of this procedure, therefore, continues. In order to give life to this part of the Constitution, which is, after all, concerned with a vital task, it might make sense to re-consider a proposal originally discussed in 1976, when the present version of Article 29 was adopted. Its central idea was to start the procedure with a nation-wide referendum on the principle of territorial reform based on concrete reform proposals, which after a probable success in the initial referendum would have to be subjected to referenda in the area concerned.[36]

'Equivalence of Living Conditions' as a State Objective

As has been pointed out above, the Joint Commission recommended the replacement of the notion of 'uniformity of living conditions' with the more appropriate 'equivalence' of living conditions in the wording of Article 72 of the Basic Law. However, not only did the Commission leave the notion unchanged in Article 106 (3) of the Basic Law, but, more importantly, that proposal in no way does justice to the importance of this genuinely federal directive principle in the structure of the Constitution. The impact of the demand for 'equivalence of living conditions' on the German federal system can hardly be overestimated. It is one of its leading values, incorporating not only the constitutional need for solidarity amongst the Länder and between the latter and Federation, but it is also a standard for an equal distribution of wealth, both collectively and individually, throughout the whole of the Republic.

Yet, in its debates on the desirability and feasibility of enshrining state objectives in the Constitution, the Joint Commission failed to recognise that the 'equivalence of living conditions' has extensive implications for many of the objectives which were discussed. In fact, one could argue that an overall state objective to secure such an equivalence would have implied objectives such as the ones on employment, housing, education and vocational training, none of which gained sufficient support for inclusion in the Joint Commission's recommendations. Also, the close relation of 'equivalence' to financial and terriorial reform would appear to be obvious, since the achievement of equivalent living conditions has always been the leading aim in all discussions on fiscal equalisation schemes. Concerning territorial reform, the ability of the Länder 'by their size and capacity ... to fulfil the functions incumbent upon them' (Article 29 of the Basic Law) is, after all, the leading criterion for the adequate demarcation of their boundaries with regard to the paramount purpose of securing the 'equivalence of living conditions'.

It barely needs emphasising that this subject has particular relevance for the completion of internal German unity. Unless the wide differences in the living conditions of east and west are successfully reduced in the not too distant future, that internal completion will be jeopardised. It was on these grounds that the SPD in the Joint Commission argued, unsuccessfully, for an amendment to the Preamble of the Basic Law, which would have explicitly mentioned this goal ('die innere Einheit Deutschlands zu vollenden'). In pursuing, at the same time, its detailed and rather too extensive catalogue of state objectives, the SPD failed to see that many of them could have been combined under the common denominator of the 'equivalence of living conditions'. Suggestions in that direction were made by the Party of Democratic Socialism (PDS), especially in the hearing of the Joint Commission on state objectives, but the PDS made the mistake of demanding equivalence as an additional state objective alongside those already fought for.

In sum, the demand for equivalence should be upgraded in the Constitution in order to make it a leading state objective. A possible way to achieve this could be by amending Article 20 (1) of the Basic Law to read:

> The Federal Republic of Germany shall be a democratic and social federal state that aims, through the efforts of the Federation and the Länder, at ensuring the equivalence of living conditions throughout the country.

The European Dimension

In addition to the need for further constitutional debate on domestic matters, European integration, both in and outside the European Union, poses strong challenges to the adaptive capacity of the Basic Law. Although, in most of the affected areas of constitutional law, textual drafts of amendments are, at the present stage, hardly feasible, the implications, particularly for the federal system, need to be identified and possible adaptive strategies be considered. Already, there is a working group of the Conference of Länder

Ministers of European Affairs charged with preparing the Länder's response in the forthcoming negotiations on the revision of the Maastricht Treaty. Amongst the constitutional issues raised in this connection, possible future transfers of sovereign rights to institutions such as the CSCE and international organisations which link the European Union to the countries of central and eastern Europe are of special significance. If such transfers are not to create another 'open flank of the federal system', as did Article 24 in relation to European integration, there is clearly a growing constitutional need for the consent of the Bundesrat to such transfers, such as exists now in relation to the European Union in the new Article 23.

Some of the problems posed by the upcoming accession of new member states to the European Union in 1995 and the start of the negotiations on the revision of the Maastricht Treaty in 1996 have already been foreshadowed in the recent disputes on the size of the blocking minority in the Council of Ministers. These problems will inevitably focus on a new debate on federalism between the member states in the European Union. In order to ensure a more rational debate on this key topic, legal and political sciences need to identify and define the extent to which the existing structures of the European Union already contain elements of a federal organisation. These elements need to be made more widely understood and adequately developed. Misunderstandings in this area may be especially problematic in the UK, but also elsewhere in the Union.

For federal countries such as Germany, the concept of regionalism within a European federal system will also have to be shaped into a workable concept. Here, the new Committee of the Regions of the European Union will be of particular significance. Attention needs to be given to the working and legal relations between the Länder governments and the Länder legislatures regarding their participation in the Regional Committee; the duration of the Committee's members' mandates in view of the fact that Article 198a in Article G of the Union Treaty fixes a term of office of four years, whilst it could be argued that their mandates should end with the termination of their democratic legitimation 'back home'; and the conflict that can arise when Länder ministers participate in the Council of Ministers on the basis of the new versions of Article 146 of the EEC-Treaty and Article 23 of the Basic Law, simultaneously scrutinising their own decisions in the Council in their additional function as members of the Committee of the Regions.

One problem, which is more political than legal, is posed by the question of whether the concept of a 'Europe *of* the Regions' should not be replaced by one of a 'Europe *with* the Regions'. Any such concept should certainly not encourage secessionist movements in any of the member states. The idea that the members states should in the course of time be dissolved in favour of their regions, as clearly favoured by some regionalist movements, ignores that instead of promoting regionalism, the realisation of such an idea would lead to extreme centralisation at the European level, as the European institutions would find it easy to 'divide and rule' under such circumstances. The emphasis in the regional idea should, therefore, be on partnership and not on conflict. It should aim at regionalism within and not without federalism in Europe. Taking all this into account, a 'Europe *with* the Regions' would surely be the more feasible and more realistic idea.

The issue of subsidiarity is closely related to the latter point. If subsidiarity, understood in relation to the member states and to the European Union's regions, is to mean anything of substance and not just of procedure at the European level, then a clear allocation of powers defined by subject matter must replace the present attribution of aims as defined by the legal bases of the European Union. If that cannot be achieved by the revision of the Maastricht Treaty, the politically defined aims of the Union will continue to absorb the legislative powers of its national and its subnational units. As a result, subsidiarity will have no chance to unfold. A clear allocation of powers should, accordingly, be a high priority – and not only for the German Länder – in the process of revising the Treaty on European Union. Unless the Treaty is revised in this way, internal federalism in the German domestic context is increasingly unviable.

IV. Incremental Reform versus Macro Constitutional Change

Both the sum-total of the Joint Commission's recommendations[37] and, even more, its probable final results in legislation are facing widespread criticism for falling far short of what could rightly be termed a comprehensive constitutional reform.[38] In particular, the SPD correctly claims that more should have been done in order to take account of the political and social changes accompanying the German unificiation process[39], though it should be emphasised that these claims refer mainly to issues not directly related to the federal system.

In trying to assess the constitutional reform debate since unification, it is first worth noting that public involvement was not very strong. It was, of course, debated at length in the Joint Commission whether or not Article 146 of the Basic Law, in its new version following unification, should be applied with its ruling that the Basic Law 'shall cease to have effect on the day on which a constitution adopted by a free decision of the German people enters into force'. It was widely acknowledged that this act of the *pouvoir constituant* replacing the Basic Law by a Constitution considered to be a new one would have required a popular referendum. So, what would or could have happened if the Basic Law as amended by the recommendations of the Joint Commission had been subjected to such a referendum? Provided such a referendum had been successful (if not, what then?), the path to further amendments in the future would, in political terms, have been barred for a long time. Not only in the face of the fairly minor adjustments of the Joint Commission, but even more so with a view to the constitutional implications of European developments, such a premature confirmation of the *pouvoir constituant* would have been a severe risk. The dangers of such referenda were illustrated in Canada by the consultative referendum of October 1992 which followed the Charlottetown Accord. When a package of constitutional reform legislation containing a multitude of different, and frequently controversial, proposals is presented for public approval, it becomes exposed to the scrutiny of pressure groups and minority interests who have a tendency to focus on particular issues within the package. Their representations tend to ignore the fact that such packages are usually the result of carefully drafted compromises and trade-offs, and can, therefore, easily unravel if the precarious balance between their different elements is upset. For the wider public, the importance of the individual items bound together in the package may, on the other hand, be obscured. This risk was exposed in the public debate on the recommendations of the Joint Constitutional Commission, particularly in relation to the discussion of the proposals in the federal field. A step-by-step approach to constitutional reform offers a better prospect of the individual issues receiving the close public attention they deserve.

Second, the history of German constitutional reform has proven up to now that it has, on the whole, only been successful if taken step by step. In light of this, the Joint Commission should not be criticised too severely for deciding to keep to that road. As long as the awareness of the need for further steps is kept alive and strengthened in the political parties and the general public, there is nothing fundamentally wrong with the present results. However, such an awareness cannot be taken for granted. Preferring incremental to comprehensive constitutional reform implies that one does not allow pressures for reform steps to accumulate to such an extent that neglected issues create a constitutional bottleneck. The vicious circle implied by such a course of (in)action is all too often overlooked or pushed aside by conservative opposition to constitutional reform. Federal structures, with their delicate balances of powers, are in particular danger of becoming caught up in such a dilemma.

Constitutional reform in Germany needs, therefore, to be continued on an evolutionary, incrementalist path. In this respect, it should be noted that federal constitutions, in particular, are not only further developed by amending their texts, but also by judicial review, financial accords, intergovernmental agreements, and by conventions and accepted practices. However, these forms of constitutional adjustment do not render formal constitutional amendments unnecessary, especially in view of the fact that Article 79 (1) of the Basic Law stresses that the Basic Law 'may be amended only by a law expressly modifying or supplementing its text'.

Yet, this is no proof of the advisability of premature macro-constitutional change. Both from the German and from comparative international experience,[40] such changes have hitherto only been successful in post-revolutionary situations where no existing legal framework was available and and a new one was, therefore, obviously needed. This is evidently not the case in Germany. Although the Peaceful Revolution in the German Democratic Republic successfully initiated unification, it did not produce a situation without a legal framework. Paradoxically, however, a potentially unsuccessful referendum following a premature effort at large-scale constitutional change could result in just such a situation. Incremental reform will, therefore, have to be continued for a longer time before the sum-total of its results can be consolidated and decided upon in a new and final Constitution.

If by that time the Basic Law had proved equal to the demands placed upon it, in particular those addressed to the federal structure, then it could even be accepted as the final Constitution itself by general consensus and, thus, without a referendum. The meaning and function of its concluding Article 146 would then change into that of a safeguard against any undemocratic or anti-federal overthrow. More than most other living constitutions, the Basic Law does, however, have to be kept amendable not only legally but also politically in a process of step-by-step reform.

NOTES

This article reflects the personal views of the author and it should thus in no way be identifie with the institution or the Land to which he is affiliated.

1. For details see Konrad Reuter, *Praxishandbuch Bundesrat* (Heidelberg: C. F. Müller Juristischer Verlag, 1991), pp.51–60.
2. Report: *Die Neugliederung des Bundesgebietes*, published by the Federal Minister of the Interior (Bonn 1955).
3. Report by Sachverständigenkommission für die Neugliederung des Bundesgebiets, *Vorschläge zur Neugliederung des Bundesgebiets gemäß Art. 29 des Grundgesetzes* (Bonn 1972). The author served as the liaison officer for the Federal Chancellor's Office on this Commission.
4. Report by Kommission für die Finanzreform, *Gutachten über die Finanzreform in der Bundesrepublik Deutschland* (Stuttgart/Berlin/Köln/Mainz, 1966).
5. Report Bundestags-Drucksache 7/5924, *Schlußbericht der Enquête-Kommission Verfassungsreform* (also published by Deutscher Bundestag, Bonn, 1976; Zur Sache 3/76 and Bonn, 1977; Zur Sache 2/77). The Federal Chancellor's Office followed the deliberations of this Commission through its Planning Division, in which the author had responsibility for this field between 1971–73.
6. Report Bundesrats-Drucksache 360/92, *Bericht der Verfassungskommission des Bundesrates – Stärkung des Föderalismus in Deutschland und Europa sowie weitere Vorschläge zur Änderung des Grundgesetzes* (also published by the Bundesrat, Bonn 1992).

In order to minimise the number of notes, references to the report mentioned here and the report in note 7 have not been identified in detail in the remaining text.

7. Report Bundestags-Drucksache 12/6000 and Bundesrats-Drucksache 800/93, *Bericht der Gemeinsamen Verfassungskommission* (also published by Deutscher Bundestag, Bonn, 1993; Zur Sache No. 5/93).

8. Published in *Zeitschrift für Parlamentsfragen*, Vol. 21, No. 3 (1990), pp.461–3. For an English translation and commentary see Charlie Jeffrey and John Yates, 'Unification and Maastricht: The Response of the Länder Governments', in Charlie Jeffery and Roland Sturm (eds.), *Federalism, Unification and European Integration* (London: Frank Cass, 1993), pp. 58–81.

9. *Bundesrats-Drucksache 103/91* (Beschluß).

10. *Bundestags-Drucksachen 12/1590; 12/1670* and *Bundesrats-Drucksache 741/91* (Beschluß).

11. For further details and references see Uwe Leonardy, 'Federation and Länder in German Foreign Relations: Power-Sharing in Treaty-Making and European Affairs', *German Politics*, Vol. 1, No. 3 (1992), pp.119–35; and in Brian Hocking (ed.), *Foreign Relations and Federal States* (London/New York: Leicester University Press, 1993), pp.236–51. See also idem, 'Regionalism within Federalism: The German Constitution Prepared for European Union', in Bertus de Villiers (ed.), *Evaluating Federal Systems* (Cape Town: Juta, 1994), with an English translation of the European Amendments and a selected bibliography in the annex.

12. Within Lower Saxony, this proposal was initiated by the author.

13. See the contribution by Georg Ress in this volume.

14. Ibid.

15. Act to amend the Basic Law of 21 Dec. 1992, *Federal Law Gazette Part I* (BGBl. I), 1992, pp.2086–7.

16. See note 11.

17. Reuter, *Praxishandbuch Bundesrat*, p.635.

18. This was first formulated by the Court in 1954 (BVerfGE 2, 224) and followed by further decisions to the same effect in 1954, 1959, 1961, 1969, 1972, 1974, 1983, 1984 and 1988.

19. This has been acknowledged in rulings by the Federal Constitutional Court of 1954, 1958, 1973, 1974, 1977, 1983 and 1984.

20. Report *Bundestags-Drucksache 7/5924*, pp.80–88.

21. See Reuter, *Praxishandbuch Bundesrat*, p.150.

22. An English translation of all three texts, along with an evaluation can be found in Uwe Leonardy, 'Demarcation of Regions: International Perceptions', in Bertus de Villiers and Jabu Sindane (eds.), *Regionalism: Problems and Prospects* (Pretoria: Human Sciences Research Council, 1993), pp.1–31.

23. *Bundestags-Drucksachen 12/1800, 2450*; BGBl I 1992, p.1254.

24. *Bundestags-Drucksachen 12/4610, 5015*; BGBl I 1993, p.2089.

25. *Bundesrats-Drucksachen 12/6717, 7269.*

26. *Bundesrats-Drucksachen 886/93* (Beschluß); Plen Prot BR 664. Sitzung, pp. 623ff.

27. *Bundesrats-Drucksachen 12/663*; Plen Prot BT 209. Sitzung, pp.18087ff.

28. *Bundesrats-Drucksachen 12/6323.*

29. *Bundestags-Drucksachen 12/7109*, pp.13–18.

30. The Amendment Acts of 1956 and 1968 relating to defence and to the state of emergency have to be considered as supplements to the original Basic Law, in which these areas could not be regulated due to lack of the necessary sovereign powers under occupation.

31. See Uwe Leonardy, *Working Structures of Federalism in Germany: Crossroads German and European Unification* (Leicester: Centre for Federal Studies, Discussion Paper 1/1992).

32. See report *Bundesrats-Drucksache 360/92.*

33. *Bundesrats-Drucksache 240/93.*

34. See report by Bundestags-Drucksache 12/6000.

35. See instead Wolfgang Renzsch, 'Föderative Problembewältigung; Zur Einbeziehung der neuen Länder in einen gesamtdeutschen Finanzausgleich ab 1995', *Zeitschrift für*

Parlamentsfragen, Vol. 25, No. 1 (1994), pp.116–38.

36. For details see Leonardy, 'Demarcation of Regions...'
37. Summed up in *Aus Politik und Zeitgeschichte (Beilage zur Wochenzeitung Das Parlament)* No. 52–53/93. See also Stephan Rohn and Rüdiger Sannwald, 'Die Ergebnisse der Gemeinsamen Verfassungskommission', *Zeitschrift für Rechtspolitik* (1992), pp.65–73.
38. See, for example, Charlie Jeffrey, *Plus ça Change ... The Non-Reform of the German Federal System after Unification* (Leicester: Centre for Federal Studies, Discussion Paper 2/1993); Hans-Peter Schneider, 'Das Grundgesetz – auf Sand gesetzt', *Neue Juristische Wochenschrift* (1994), pp.558–61.
39. Hans-Jochen Vogel, 'Die Reform des Grundgesetzes nach der deutschen Einheit', *Deutsches Verwaltungsblatt* (1994), pp.497–506; idem, in Plen Prot BT 209. Sitzung, pp. 18090 B – 18098 C.
40. See Peter H. Russell, 'Attempting Macro-Constitutional Change in Australia and Canada: The Politics of Frustration', *International Journal of Canadian Studies* (1993), pp.41–61 (with bibliography).

A Forum of Constitutional Deliberation? A Critical Analysis of the Joint Constitutional Commission

ARTHUR BENZ

The Joint Constitutional Commission of the Bundestag and the Bundesrat submitted the Basic Law to a wide-ranging review, but its recommendations are characterised by minor adaptations and a lack of innovative and forward-looking proposals. This outcome can be explained by reference to the institutional features of the Joint Commission and, in particular, the predominance of bargaining behaviour as opposed to rational arguing in the Commission's negotiations. Instead of providing for the open deliberation of constitutional issues, the Commission largely reproduced the established political framework, and, thus, encouraged bargaining processes amongst the political elite. Althoug alternative institutional structures cannot guarantee an improvement in the quality of constitutional policy, they can at least provide opportunities for more open and rational arguing to emerge.

I. The Constitutional Problem: Reform or Adaptation of the Basic Law?

The unification of Germany gave rise to intensive debates on the Constitution. Initially, they focused on the question of whether the new German state needed a new Constitution or whether the Basic Law of the West German Federal Republic should be retained and thus provide for constitutional stability. Given the time pressures of the unification process, this problem was solved by a pragmatic political compromise. The new Länder which were created in the former GDR acceded to the Federal Republic and accepted the Basic Law in its existing version. The Unification Treaty, however, stipulated that the German Constitution was to be reviewed during the following two years.

This decision had two important consequences for the subsequent processes of constitutional policy. On the one hand, the substance and objectives of revision were left unclear. Both alternatives – to create a new Constitution or to merely adapt the existing one – remained on the agenda. On the other, the Basic Law defined not only the point of departure for substantial discussions, but also the 'default condition'[1] of constitutional policy-making. Thus those who were interested in preserving the *status quo* could rely on a powerful veto position.

Nevertheless, German unification and continuing European integration seemed to provide a 'window to reform',[2] which justified hopes for comprehensive constitutional change. For this reason, some observers feared the emergence of a 'totally different republic'.[3] Now, after the Joint Constitutional Commission has submitted its recommendations,[4] conservatives are more or less satisfied,[5] while those who expected a thorough reform of the Basic Law openly express their disappointment.[6] Although at the time of writing (June 1994), the reform process has not yet reached its final stage and although additional proposals for amendments have been introduced in the parliamentary process, we can conclude that the 'modernisation' of the German Constitution has failed. In a nutshell, one can observe more adaptation of constitutional law to political change than innovations or forward-looking decisions.

In the following sections, I try to explain this result. In order to understand the outcome of constitutional debate, it is important to analyse constitutional policy-making as a negotiation process (II). This process is, to a considerable degree, influenced by the institutional arrangements for preparing reform proposals. Therefore, after describing the agenda of constitutional policy in the wake of German unification (III), the analysis focuses on the structure and the institutional embeddedness of the Joint Constitutional Commission (IV) and on the negotiation processes (V). I argue that the institutional arrangements chosen for preparing the reform of the Basic Law and the predominance of bargaining amongst a political elite largely explain the outcome (VI). In the final section, I sketch an alternative form of constitutional policy-making, which may promise a more rational deliberation of constitutional problems that goes beyond the bargaining routines of the political elite (VII).

II. Constitutional Policy-Making as a Negotiation Process

In the Federal Republic of Germany, constitutional amendments require a majority of two-thirds of the votes in both the Bundesrat and the Bundestag (Article 79, 2) and thus they need the approval of the leading parties and a majority of the Länder governments. This rule intends to ensure that constitutional norms are based on a broad societal consensus, and, as such, corresponds to a fundamental demand which is widely accepted in the theory and practice of constitution-making.[7] Therefore, constitutional policy does not follow the normal rules of parliamentary democracy. It is based on negotiation processes, in which participating actors have to find broadly based agreement.

In principle, this is not an unusual practice for policy-making in the German federal system. About two-thirds of all Federal laws can only be passed with the consent of the Bundesrat, in which the majority of the Länder governments often belongs to a different political party than the majority coalition in the Bundestag. So it is particularly true in the Federal Republic that 'constitution-making [. . .] involves not a radical break but an extension and often intensification of normal processes.'[8]

However, as the experiences of 40 years of West German history show, political decisions dealing with constitutional amendments provoke, as a rule, severe party political conflict. Most of the changes to the Basic Law proposed or passed before 1989 caused intense controversy among the parties or between the Federal and Länder governments.[9] The Mediation Committee of the Bundesrat and the Bundestag was brought into the parliamentary process more often than in the course of normal legislation. On average, decision-making took more time and proposals were more often rejected.[10] The difference between ordinary legislation and constitution-making can be explained by the substance of constitutional norms. They refer to the fundamental values or principles of a social order or of public policy, and they constitute institutions and rules which guide the decisions of the political actors. Thus, they constrain the behaviour of politicians by commitments which cannot easily and quickly be revised.[11] Whereas the decision rules of constitutional policies require that amendments must find 'approval by a majority, which is so qualified that it indicates a basic consensus of all relevant political groups',[12] the substance of constitutional rules suggests that constitutional politics is accompanied by intensified conflicts which make agreements between negotiating parties difficult. Nevertheless, negotiation processes can end in acceptable decisions if all actors in constitutional policy-making abstain from striving for individual goals or competitive claims and try to argue about the normative reasons of their interests. Negotiations then shift from a bargaining mode, which is characterised by strategies and tactics of participants pushing through their own interests, to processes of 'problem-solving' or 'rational arguing'.

When we look at the real political world, it seems at first glance unrealistic to hope for an argumentative search for consensus. However, studies on constitution-making suggest that this mode of negotiation is not unlikely to emerge.[13] They reveal an oscillation between bargaining and rational arguing during the deliberation of different constitutional questions. Negotiation theories stress this assumption by emphasising the dynamics of communication processes. Direct communication fosters the development of mutual trust, the growing convergence of knowledge and assessments as well as the strengthening of co-operative behaviour, all of which contribute to changing strategic bargaining behaviour into communicative behaviour aiming at a discussion-induced consent.[14]

Even if this is not the case, bargaining processes do not necessarily end in stalemate and produce an outcome which is appreciated only by those interested in preserving the existing law. As long as actors in constitutional policy negotiate strategically, reforms can find agreement if the divergent interests of parties and societal groups can be linked in such a way that vetoes can be overcome. This requires that different constitutional issues, which affect different interests, are discussed at the same time and combined into package deals. Taken as a whole, such deals can be positively evaluated by the participants even if they disagree on individual parts. They concur on contractual agreements, which balance their interests. It is this mode of finding agreement which underlies the concept of constitution-making formulated by the theory of social contract. Although it is doubtful whether this theory can explain the creation of a new constitutional order,[15] it may provide some insights into particular ways of reforming constitutional law. As a rule, changes to an existing constitution lead to controversies over political goals or over the allocation of power. In comprehensive revisions of constitutional law, these conflicts can be resolved if parties or groups enter into pragmatic exchange procedures, in which each gains agreement to its most favoured proposal by giving up its resistance to issues which others regard as most important.[16]

Both types of negotiation can be identified in real policy-making by some indicators that can be derived from studies on negotiation. Table 1 gives an overview of some indicators which may clarify the difference between rational arguing and bargaining.[17]

TABLE 1
TYPES OF NEGOTIATION

	rational arguing	**bargaining**
goals of participants	• problem-solving	• individual gain
negotiation behaviour	• communicative • search for agreement • co-operative	• strategic • power orientated • competitive
way of argumentation	• flexible positions • changing proposals • questions/reasons • formulating ideas • search for common interests	• fixed positions • static proposals • propositions • conditional concessions • stressing divergence • threatening
outcome	• innovative solution • integrative consensus	• no agreement • package deals

Bargaining and exchange processes do not by themselves lead to more problematic outcomes than rational arguing. Furthermore, it is hardly realistic to take the 'ideal discourse' as a standard for evaluation. In practical politics, we must (as even Jürgen Habermas conceded[18]) always expect actors to behave strategically and to strive for optimal 'bargains'. However, in processes of reforming constitutional law, a pure bargaining behaviour can lead to problematic outcomes and, therefore, has to be viewed critically. Firstly, political package deals are made as a rule among short-term orientated actors, whereas constitutions create commitments and constraints, 'by which members of a polity can incorporate long-term considerations into current-period decisions'.[19] Secondly, such solutions only guarantee decisions in accordance with public interests, if exchange processes include all affected individuals, groups or organisations. Finally, outcomes of bargaining processes are influenced by the bargaining power of the participating actors. Among them, those interested in defending the *status quo* can profit from their veto-position. Hence, bargaining processes and political exchange reveal the asymmetries of the decision structures. They are only acceptable as modes of constitution-making, if all important parties in negotiations accept reforms in principle and merely disagree on the substance. For this reason, elements of rational arguing should counterbalance pure strategic bargaining. Since it is evidently not very probable that they completely replace the bargaining behaviour of politicians, they can at least fulfil a regulative function by compelling actors to review their strategies with regard to long-term consequences and general norms.

Whether constitutional policies are founded on strategic bargaining or on rational arguing depends, above all, on the agenda and on the institutional structures. Package deals are in the offing, if the reform agenda includes a wide range of issues. Other circumstances being equal, they are more likely in comprehensive revisions of a Constitution than in amendments of single norms. Institutional arrangements often support rather than lessen adversary politics, but they can also be designed so that they constrain power and bargaining strategies and promote open communication.

As I show in the following sections, constitutional policy after German unification has been characterised by a most problematic combination of agenda setting and institutional arrangements. The agenda was not clearly defined and, therefore, open to encompass nearly all aspects of constitutional law. At the same time, policy processes were organised in a way which led to a predominance of political strategies and bargaining tactics of parties and governments at the Federal and the Länder levels.

III. The Agenda of Constitutional Reform

The agenda of constitutional policy after German unification was never precisely defined. Soon after the collapse of the Communist regime in the GDR, public discussions emerged in East and West Germany on whether a united nation needed a new Constitution or whether the jurisdiction of the West German Basic Law should simply be extended to the new Länder. Even when this question was answered by the rapid unification process, the necessity and scope of a revision of the Basic Law were debated. The Unification Treaty mentioned some specific issues which should be considered in a future reform (Article 5). However, it opened debates on the scope and the objectives of the reform by bringing in Article 146 of the Basic Law and the question of a referendum on the revised Constitution. In its current version, Article 146 refers to the opportunity for the German people to create a new Constitution. Thus, the formulations of the Unification Treaty left room both for necessary adaptations and a comprehensive revision of the Constitution.

As a consequence, disagreements between political parties on the objectives of constitutional reform persisted after unification. In the Federal parliament, the Social Democrats and Bündnis 90 pleaded for an extensive deliberation and a complete revision of the Constitution. Representatives of the Christian Democrats and the Liberal Party argued that the Basic Law had proved worthwhile and that there was no need for far-reaching reform. When on 28 and 29 November 1991 both houses of parliament decided on establishing a Joint Constitutional Commission, the dispute over the agenda was still unresolved. The Commission was instructed to deal 'in particular with the amendments of the Basic Law mentioned in Article 5 of the Unification Treaty and with amendments which are required by the realisation of the European Union'.[20] This formulation hardly provided a clear definition of the remit of the Joint Commission and failed to set a precise agenda.

In fact, the Joint Commission defined its task extensively. Thus, it acted in accordance with a policy style which developed in the Federal Republic of Germany after 1949, and was diagnosed by Wilhelm Hennis as 'the tendency to lay down all law in the Constitution',[21] which he saw as a typical German problem. Although this statement may be exaggerated, it is true that government and opposition tend to justify their political positions with reasons ostensibly derived from the Constitution, which give them the appearance of irrefutability.[22] As a result, the Basic Law has become the object of permanent debates amongst the political parties.[23] If political controversies emerge, then they are often discussed as constitutional problems, and this is exactly what one can also observe after unification. Nearly all important issues in unified Germany were defined as problems of the Constitution, which were then introduced in the process of constitutional reform. Therefore, the fact that the Joint Commission extended its agenda does not indicate so much an enthusiasm for constitutional reform; rather this tendency can be traced back to a specific element of the German political culture.

IV. The Institutional Framework of Constitution-Making

The formal rules for constitution-making and amendments, as they are established by the Basic Law, lead to constitutional policy being characterised by negotiation processes. How these negotiations take place and which mode of negotiation behaviour becomes predominant mainly depends on the organisational framework structuring the processes in which proposals are developed and drafts prepared. While the constitutional rules definitely fix the proceedings in the parliamentary arena, the structure in the preliminary stage of constitutional policy-making is open to definition. It is this stage which is the most important in constitutional policy-making.[24] Hence, in evaluating the current constitutional reform we must focus our analysis on the structures and procedures which guided the negotiations that took place prior to debates and decisions in parliament.

Here, discursive elements of deliberation can be fostered either by pluralistic procedures[25] or by establishing an independent expert commission. Pluralistic procedures develop if constitutional questions are dealt with in a complex network of arenas, which may exist in different territories, concentrate on different issues, or vary in their organisational form.[26] Such arenas emerged immediately after German unification, when groups and forums were organised in order to stimulate and influence constitutional reform, when conferences of experts discussed the Constitution, when the parliaments of the Länder installed commissions to scrutinise the organisation of the federal system[27] or decided on amendments of the Land constitution (Lower Saxony, Schleswig-Holstein), and when the new Länder had to pass constitutional charters. Taken as a whole, the deliberations in these different arenas contributed to an unusually open, stimulating and creative discussion on constitutional policies.

Commissions of experts can elaborate reform proposals at some distance from the normal political disputes. In the Federal Republic, all important amendments to the Basic Law were prepared by such commissions. Thus, policy-making could be objectified at least in the preliminary stage. The strategic behaviour of parties and bargaining tactics could be limited. On the other hand, deliberations on constitutional questions became the business of experts, in particular of professors of law.[28] This resulted in academic or

technocratic discourses producing proposals which were difficult to imple-
ment in party politics and in parliament. As experiences in other countries
show, constitutional reform 'has tended to remain under the firm control of
the political decision-makers and so the possibility of their being over-
whelmed by the experts' opinions has never been substantial, even assuming the experts have wanted to play such a role'.[29]

After German unification, both of these institutional designs were ruled
out by the decision of the Bundesrat and the Bundestag to set up a Joint
Constitutional Commission. This decision was mainly a reflection of public
discussions on the Constitution which developed in a dynamic way. This
was suspiciously observed by conservatives, while others saw the chance for
an innovative constitutional reform. Under these conditions, an unpolitical
expert commission seemed unsuitable to prepare amendments. The opposition parties in the Bundestag proposed a Constitutional Council, which
would be responsible for a comprehensive revision of the Basic Law and
bring together citizens representing different societal groups and interests.
After controversial debates, the parties in the Bundestag and the representatives of the Länder governments came to a compromise on a Joint
Constitutional Commission. Of its 64 members, half were appointed by the
Bundestag and the other half by the Bundesrat. Thus, the Joint Commission
was, in fact, a Federal–Länder committee, which reflected both the relative
strength of the political parties and the balance of power between the Federal
and the Länder governments.[30]

It was the intention of this institutional design to control the dynamics of
the constitutional debate. The Joint Commission should identify proposals
for amendments of the Constitution that were likely to find a two-thirds
majority in parliament. The structure and decision rules of the Commission
should make sure that only those solutions which had passed the test of compromise between parties and governments entered the formal legislation
process.[31] This was the reason why decisions required the consent of two-
thirds of the Commission's members, that is the same qualified majority
necessary to achieve constitutional amendments in parliament.

However, the composition of the Joint Commission and its internal deci-
sion-rules were not the decisive structural element of constitutional policy
after German unification. Of course, public discussion on the Constitution
took place in the various arenas mentioned above. Constitution-making is
always a multi-level process, the outcome of which is mainly influenced by
the linkage of the different arenas. In this context, a constitutional assembly
or committee could work as a linking pin, collecting information, arguments
and proposals, stimulating public discussions and mediating between conflicting interests.

The Joint Constitutional Commission, which from January 1992 to

October 1993 held 23 sessions, was, however, unable to fulfil such a nodal function. Although it was independent according to formal institutional rules, its discussions were not free from external influences and pressures by political parties and governments. Members of the Joint Commission acted as representatives of their parties and governments and tried to realise their specific positions, which were formulated inside the party organisations and the Federal and Länder governments. Feedback from these arenas to the members of the Joint Commission was effected through working groups of members of the same party. In order to guarantee that representatives of the Joint Commission followed the party line, the party whip of the CDU resorted at some stage even to open pressure.[32] The Länder governments had elaborated and co-ordinated their proposals for a reform of the Basic Law in the Constitutional Commission of the Bundesrat,[33] which had completed its work before the Joint Commission met for the first time. Although the Länder governments did not agree on all issues, their position was mainly fixed and clearly stated. Therefore, members of the Joint Commission were subject to commitments and expectations, which – according to negotiation research findings – cause strategic bargaining behaviour and the confrontation of positions instead of open deliberation on norms and interests.[34] This mode of negotiation makes agreement on far-reaching reforms less likely. This is even more the case as the set of possible solutions which the Joint Commission could negotiate was narrowly constrained by premises formulated by political parties and governments. Although the Commission should elaborate proposals for constitutional reform, the scope of innovation was restricted at the outset.

However, these structures did not contribute to limiting the agenda of the Joint Commission. In fact, it discussed a wide range of topics including nearly all issues of constitutional law which had been of some importance in the past. From this point of view, Wilhelm Hennis correctly stated that the Joint Commission changed into a constitutional council which placed all constitutional norms at its disposal,[35] with the exception of the principles laid down in Article 79 (3) of the Basic Law. However, as regards its internal structure and institutional embeddedness, the Joint Commission resembled a committee of both houses of the Federal parliament and not a constitutional council. This institutional framework, instead of creating the necessary conditions for an effective reform policy, reproduced the combination of competition between political parties and intergovernmental bargaining between the Federal and Länder governments which is often said to cause political immobilism.[36] It explains why constitutional policy-making was from the beginning characterised by a mode of negotiation which left no room for reform-orientated policies based on rational arguing. More likely were agreements by political exchange or decisions based on the lowest common denominator. Indeed, this is what we find when we look at the negotiation processes.

V. Processes of Negotiation and Decision-Making

The contradiction between a broad agenda and a constraining institutional structure had two important consequences for the negotiation processes and the course of constitutional reform. On the one hand, innovative reform proposals failed to find consent; on the other hand, those amendments which were recommended by the Joint Commission showed all the signs of compromise by exchange and bargaining routines.

The Joint Commission started with an ambitious programme, but was finally unable to achieve its original high goals. This is, above all, explained by the fact that it subordinated itself, to a large extent, to the premises set in meetings between party leaders and by agreements between the Federal and the Länder governments. Moreover, the Joint Commission's discussions followed the routines and constraints typical of parliamentary committees. They were never open to rational arguing, not to mention creative deliberations. Hans-Peter Bull, who as a Land minister was a member of the Joint Commission, found that it was 'tremendously scared to include new ideas as if there was a steady threat that the whole Constitution could be overturned'.[37]

A clear indicator for this assessment can be found in the way the Joint Commission operated. Discussions were introduced by statements from the spokesperson of each party or the Länder governments. As a rule, they reported elaborated positions, sometimes even referring to drafts proposed as motions in parliament. Time for speaking was regulated to the advantage of the large parliamentary groups, regardless of the substance of their arguments. The ensuing discussions seldom went outside the parameters set by the opening statements. Mostly, they reflected debates on well-known positions, which remained unchanged. Strategic behaviour predominated both in negotiations and in voting. The members of the Joint Commission were more inclined to consider the interests of parties, coalitions and governments than to examine substantial argument.

In the first meeting of the Joint Commission, Hans-Jochen Vogel, the spokesman for the SPD parliamentary party, expressed his hope, 'that the Commission will not work as a closed circle of experts, but will be accompanied by broad public discussions'.[38] This hope was to be disappointed. The Joint Commission was no forum of public deliberation. According to the parliamentary resolution which set up the Joint Commission, the standing orders of the Bundesrat should regulate its work. These rules normally exclude the public from meetings of the committees. In its first session, the

Joint Commission voted on a proposal to alter this rule, but the necessary majority of two-thirds of the votes was not achieved. Only in its fourth meeting, after informal negotiations between the spokesmen, did the Joint Commission decide to make the discussions public. However, given the unsuccessful start, the Commission found no effective ways of transferring its discussions and arguments into public arenas. The press, for example, did not report in detail until the Commission met with a severe crisis in February 1993, when Rupert Scholz, one of the two co-chairmen of the Commission, temporarily resigned from his post after conflicts with the whip of his own party.

Public involvement in the meetings of the Joint Commission was constrained, with interested citizens being assigned the role of a passive audience. Despite this, their engagement in the constitutional reform debate was astonishing. More than 800,000 petitions were sent to the Joint Commission, which mainly concerned basic rights and citizens' participation. Several associations and groups formulated proposals, suggestions and recommendations. Their effect on the discussions and decisions of the Joint Commission was, however, very limited. In fact, it is doubtful whether the Commission even seriously considered these petitions. Most were answered by the secretary of the Joint Commission, whilst its members did not gain knowledge of their content. Even letters addressed directly to the members of the Commission evidently did not induce any dialogue between politicians and citizens.

The same has to be said of the influence of the constitutional policies of the Länder where a multitude of draft constitutions and proposals, containing innovative ideas, were formulated. The minutes of the Joint Commission reveal that they played only a minor role in the constitutional reform process at the Federal level. Here, the discussions remained largely within the confines of well-known controversies. Most members of the Joint Commission who came from the eastern Länder adapted to this practice; thus, they hardly put forward innovative arguments, something which might have been expected in view of the discussions on constitution-making in the new Länder. Wolfgang Ullman, a former participant in the civil rights movements in the GDR and the representative of Bündnis 90 on the Joint Commission, resigned his position in April 1993, as he saw no chance to create a constitution which would take up impulses from movements concerned with constitutional reform in East Germany.

During the discussion of important issues, the Joint Commission organised several hearings with experts, most of whom were professors of public law. A further hearing gave the presidents of the Länder parliaments the opportunity to bring forward their specific interests, which differed in several respects from those of the Länder goverments represented in the

Commission. The substantial relevance of these hearings is difficult to assess, but in general, they did little to push back bargaining behaviour. They could hardly shatter the fixed positions of the parties or resolve conflicts between them.

Thus, the Joint Commission never developed into the centre of a public discussion on the Constitution. Instead, it became a closed circle of a political elite. This tendency was aggravated by the fact that negotiations on the details of amendments took place among a small group of the spokesmen of the parties and the governments. It was not only that the basis for negotiations was formulated in the established political organisations, but also that important aspects of future constitutional law were elaborated in exclusive negotiations. Neither parliament nor the public had much chance of controlling these processes or of comprehending the reasons which led to the final compromises. As a consequence, there was no corrective against a pure bargaining mode of policy-making. The regulative function of rational arguing, which could have been fulfilled by the public deliberations of the Constitutional Council or Assembly, before the policy process entered the stage of party politics and 'typical' intergovernmental bargaining, did not become effective.

VI. Constitutional Policy between Political Exchange and Non-Decision

In October 1993, the Joint Commission submitted its recommendations for a reform of the Basic Law,[39] which were then introduced into the legislative process. Although it cannot be taken as the final result of the current constitutional reform process, the report of the Joint Commission follows the expected path of decision-making. Despite the fact that the Basic Law was subjected to a comprehensive review, it is evident that the reform process will not eventuate in a new Constitution for the united Germany; rather it will, for the most part, merely result in quite limited adaptations of the existing Constitution to current challenges of national and international political developments.

The results of the processes described above show all the signs of the bargaining mode of policy-making. They can be divided into three groups of issues. Among the first group, there are problems which were dealt with as a matter of routine. One example was the privatisation of air traffic control. The Joint Commission decided on it after two short statements which referred to existing bills and the discussions in the responsible Bundestag committee. The problem of the financial structure of the federal system was treated in a similar way, but with a quite different result. The Joint Commission decided in its 23rd meeting to exclude this topic from the agenda, because the Länder ministers of finance, who had set up a working group to formulate proposals for a reform of the financial system, had not yet elaborated a position that was ready for public discussion. This non-decision on an important aspect of the Federal Constitution shows the dependence of the Joint Commission on other arenas, in which institutional interests of the Federal and Länder governments predominate. As a consequence, the Commission's recommendations for a reform of the federal system lack a decisive element and leave essential problems untackled.

The second group of issues included those which caused controversial and open discussions at the outset. This was the case for proposals to introduce direct citizens' participation with the possibility of a referendum on the Federal Constitution and to strengthen the role of the Bundestag. The members of the Joint Commission started by clearing the relevant positions and by assessing the scope of negotiable solutions. In these areas, the minutes of the Commission reveal elements of rational arguing and problem-solving behaviour as several participants advanced remarkable arguments in support of the suggested reforms. However, this was merely part of the picture, since these discussions were particularly susceptible to interventions from outside. Therefore, the Joint Commission was either finally unable to find a consensus on those issues or it decided on a weak compromise. It did not provide any recommendations for improving citizens' participation or the parliamentary process, and formulated proposals for basic rights and state objectives which are not entirely convincing. These proposals might be criticised for their substance. What is more, however, is that issues which did not fit into the patterns of interests of the leading parties and of governments in the federal system were filtered out even in the preliminary stage of the policy process – in part as a result of negotiations behind the scenes and without the public taking notice. In the institutional framework of constitutional reform described above, this was a likely outcome.

A third group of topics required decisions in the face of challenges which are associated with German unification, European integration and international developments, and had to be dealt with under the pressure of time. Examples were the constitutional questions raised by the Maastricht Treaty and the asylum problem. The latter was discussed in the Joint Commission after the formal amendment procedure had already commenced. Therefore, the Joint Commission did not make any recommendations. The reform of Article 16 of the Basic Law followed negotiations between the leaders of the main parties, who narrowed the set of alternatives to the short-term strategy of restricting immigration with or without the abolition of the right to asylum. In fact, the same holds true for the adjustment of the Basic Law to the process of European integration. This was the first issue which the Joint Commission took up. However, it was obvious that the positions of the Länder governments, which they had formulated in prior meetings, constrained the scope of a possible solution. Moreover, the Länder openly threatened to vote against the ratification of the Maastricht Treaty if the Basic Law would not be altered according to their interests. By this strategy, they achieved a decision which represents a typical package deal. Whereas the Länder governments finally approved the Maastricht Treaty, the Federal Government conceded far-reaching rights to the Länder to participate in EU-related policy-making. Thus, the Länder governments, by using their bargaining power that accrued to them in a specific situation, induced a significant change in the federal system, which will have long-term consequences. Instead of seeking an adequate solution for integrating European and national decision procedures, the Federal and Länder governments traded positions. The result was a new Article 23 which requires complicated intergovernmental co-operation.[40]

Solutions by exchange processes can also be observed in other fields concerning the reform of intergovernmental relations. The Länder governments waived their claims for decentralisation in order to gain improved veto-rights over Federal legislation. Here, however, the bargaining strategies were not too successful, at least from the Länder governments' point of view. After informal intergovernmental negotiations led to a compromise, representatives of Federal and Länder interests in the Joint Commission agreed on only minor changes, which would prevent an increasing influence for the Länder governments via the Bundesrat and result in only a marginal reallocation of responsibilities to the state legislatures. Nevertheless, the Federal Government complained about the concessions the Länder had achieved, while the Länder governments announced that they would push for further decentralisation in parliamentary processes.[41] This shows that the recommendations of the Joint Commission represent an agreement governed by the lowest common denominator, which, in addition, is unstable.

More problematic package deals were in the offing during constitutional reform. After the CDU/CSU members of the Joint Commission voted against the introduction of a constitutional commitment to environmental protection, the SPD announced that it would refuse any changes of the constitutional norms regulating the deployment of the armed forces. Indeed, it was not willing to compromise until the Federal Government appealed to the Constitutional Court. Finally, the CDU/CSU accepted a compromise solution on a norm laying down a rather weak commitment for governments to preserve the environment (see the new Article 20a).

That such problematic issue linkages were realised merely in a limited number of cases is due to the fact that *do-ut-des* strategies of the parties worked more towards impeding reform proposals than generating amendments. The recommendations of the Joint Commission are, accordingly, not characterised by important innovations. While necessary amendments of the

Basic Law required by international developments are already in force, real reforms had no chance in the bargaining processes between the Federal and Länder governments and between political parties. In these processes, the comprehensive revision of the Constitution was step by step reduced to minor adaptations. The main reason for this result was that in the institutional framework established by the parties, constitutional norms were treated as bargaining chips instead of being subjected to rational arguing.

In sum, the preliminary results of the constitutional reform process must be interpreted as the outcome of the strategic bargaining of parties and governments. This mode of policy-making will persist in the parliamentary stage. In December 1993, the parties of the governing coalition and the SPD jointly introduced the proposals of the Joint Commission as a bill in the Bundestag without undoing the 'package'.[42] However, the ensuing discussions showed the fragility of this consensus. Representatives of the CDU and the CSU raised objections against changes to the basic rights catalogue and state objectives. As a consequence, members of the opposition felt compelled to bring forward proposals which had not found the necessary majority in the Joint Commission. Finally, the Federal Government called into question the compromise over changes to the federal system.[43] These events help to elucidate the character of current constitutional policy as a process of mutual give and take among members of the political elite, which is marked by power and exchange strategies and often ends in disagreement.

If the package deal developed in the Joint Commission is unravelled in parliament, new subjects and proposals can come onto the agenda. However, even in this case, there is no better chance for a more far-reaching reform of the Constitution. The probability that new proposals will be implemented would only increase if the mode of negotiation and decision-making changed. But the parliamentary arena consists of more than just committees or commissions influenced by confrontation between opposing parties.[44] Therefore, it is to be feared that constitutional policy will be blocked rather than promoted by new opportunities for reform, should the agreements reached by the Joint Commission be broken.

VII. Conclusion

During the constitutional reform process after German unification, the Basic Law was subject to a comprehensive review. However, the institutional structures in which this review took place were ill-suited to the task. The Joint Commission on the Constitution was not a forum for open deliberation, which could, by reasoned argument on constitutional principles, lead to new solutions and find broad societal consensus for them. Instead, its discussions were marked by the 'blindness' of the political elite to problems outside their own world.[45] Moreover, the relevance of the Commission for the elaboration of reform proposals was limited compared to the effects of established political structures. As a consequence, constitutional reform ended in bargaining processes amongst the political elite which reduced the scope of possible changes and made constitutional norms a matter of political deals. Even if one accepts the result of a mere adaptation of the Basic Law, the way of treating constitutional issues in the current political process must be criticised.

This critical assessment of constitutional reform in unified Germany gives cause to think about more adequate structures for constitutional policy. They should contribute to strengthening the elements of rational arguing in the deliberations on constitutional norms against strategic bargaining. Constitution-making is an outstanding political function which is to be fulfilled beyond the routines of ordinary policy-making and the bargaining routines between the leaders of political parties and governments. Any structure which merely reproduces the established political framework when it creates forums for considering constitutional issues and for negotiating politically acceptable proposals is intrinsically problematic.

Alternative institutional structures do not, of course, guarantee an improvement in the quality of constitutional policy: 'No amount of institutional design can produce a reliable tendency for speakers to become genuinely motivated by the common good'.[46] Nevertheless, institutions which reduce the selectivity of existing political structures constitute necessary prerequisites for opportunities for open and rational arguing to emerge. This becomes more probable if the multitude of arenas, which invariably exist in a differentiated federal system and in a pluralistic society, are taken as an advantage for constitutional policy-making.

The chance for a far-reaching constitutional reform after German unification was not founded on the accumulation of urgent problems, as is often argued. Rather it was raised by the fact that forums for constitutional deliberation formed simultaneously in different societal arenas and at the Federal and Länder tiers. In each of these arenas, that is in parliaments at both levels of the federal system, in parties, associations and *ad hoc* groups, different constitutional issues could be discussed from different points of view. A Constitutional Council can co-ordinate these diversified discussion processes if it includes representatives of those arenas and is independent from immediate control of the ruling political elite. Thus, it can constitute the core of a network of various arenas. While negotiating processes in these arenas should take place independently from one another, they should be integrated by a second level of negotiations in a Constitutional Council comprising representatives of interests and independent experts.

Such an organisation, which combines and integrates different arenas, has at least two advantages compared to the institutional design of the recent reform process. On the one hand, it may prevent the negotiation processes from ending in a blind alley too quickly. By shifting discussions between arenas and between levels of policy-making, new opportunities for agreement can reopen in the case of looming stalemate. On the other hand, decisions based on pure strategic bargaining and on problematic political package deals may become less likely. If proposals had to be justified in different arenas, they could no longer be supported by referring to the balance of exchanges between limited interests alone. Instead, participants in the constitutional policy process are forced to find reasons which gain general acceptance in different arenas; they also have to declare their definition of the situation, their perception of problems and their evaluations and expose them to critical discussion. Integrative negotiation processes are then promoted, in which ideological or distributive conflicts are superseded by orientations which emphasise common grounds of interest or at least accept the standpoint of the other side as worthy of consideration.[47] From this it follows that such a form of constitutional policy does not only increase the chances that real reforms will be implemented but also serves to legitimise outcomes and to provide for a stable societal consensus on the Constitution.

These are merely brief hints which require further elaboration. It should be taken as an important task of political science to contribute to the search for adequate structures and procedures for constitutional policy, a demand which Klaus von Beyme put forward in 1968. Today, it is no less relevant, and just as important, as a discussion on the substance of the Constitution. As von Beyme formulated, it is necessary 'to work on a procedure which allows the creation of a broad consensus on the Constitution and in which the people – or better its parts in organisations and forums of public opinion – are not restricted to mere acclamation'.[48]

NOTES

1. Elinor Ostrom, 'An Agenda for the Study of Institutions', *Public Choice*, Vol. 48 (1986), pp.3–25.
2. John Keeler, 'Opening the Window to Reform', *Comparative Political Studies*, Vol. 25 (1993), pp.433–86.
3. Wilhelm Hennis, 'Auf dem Weg in eine ganz andere Republik', *Frankfurter Allgemeine Zeitung*, 26 Feb. 1993.
4. BT-Drucksache 12/6000.
5. Josef Isensee, 'Mit blauem Auge davongekommen – das Grundgesetz', *Juristische Wochenschrift*, Vol. 46 (1993), pp.2583–7; F.-A. Jahn, 'Stabilität und Kontinuität nicht angetastet: Unser Grundgesetz hat sich bewährt', *Das Parlament*, 14 Jan. 1994.
6. Ernst Lieberman and Uwe-Jons Heuer, 'Die Arbeit der Gemeinsamen Verfassungkommission: Gute Debatten, schlechte Ergebnisse', *Demokratie und Recht*, Vol. 21 (1993), pp.118–33; Hans-Jochen Vogel, 'Plädoyer für eine wirkliche Verfassungsreform: Beharren oder erneuern?', *Das Parlament*, 14 Jan. 1994.

116   CONSTITUTIONAL POLICY IN UNIFIED GERMANY

7. Edward McWhinney, *Constitution-making: Principles, Process, Practice* (Toronto: University of Toronto Press, 1991), pp.16–21.
8. Keith G. Banting and Richard Simeon, 'Introduction: The Politics of Constitutional Change', in Keith G. Banting and Richard Simeon (eds.), *Redesigning the State* (Toronto, Buffalo: University of Toronto Press, 1985), pp.1–29 (17).
9. Brun-Otto Bryde, *Verfassungsentwicklung, Stabilität und Dynamik im Verfassungsrecht der Bundesrepublik Deutschland* (Baden-Baden: Nomos, 1982), pp.124–33.
10. Stefan Schaub, *Der verfassungsändernde Gesetzgeber 1949-1980* (Berlin: Duncker & Humblot, 1984), p.127.
11. Geoffrey Brennan and James M. Buchanan, *The Reason of Rules* (Cambridge: Cambridge University Press, 1986), pp.67–81; and Jon Elster, 'Constitution-making in Eastern Europe: Rebuilding the Boat in the Open Sea', *Public Administration*, Vol. 71, Nos. 1–2 (1993), p.175.
12. Helmut Quaritsch, 'Eigenarten und Rechtsfragen der DDR-Revolution', *Verwaltungsarchiv*, Vol. 83 (1992), p.323 (author's translation).
13. Jon Elster, 'Constitutional Bootstrapping in Philadelphia and Paris', *Cardozo Law Review*, Vol. 14 (1994), p.563; and Calvin Jillson and Cecil Eubanks, 'The Political Structure of Constitution-Making: The Federal Convention of 1987', *American Journal of Political Science*, Vol. 28, No. 3 (1984), pp.435–8.
14. Arthur Benz, *Kooperative Verwaltung. Funktionen, Voraussetzungen und Folgen* (Baden-Baden: Nomos, 1994), pp.127–35.
15. Douglas D. Heckathorn and Steven M. Maser, 'Bargaining and Constitutional Contracts', *American Journal of Political Science*, Vol. 31, No. 1 (1987), pp.142–68; and Reinhard Zintl, *Individualistische Theorien und die Ordnung der Gesellschaft* (Berlin: Duncker & Humblot, 1983).
16. Fritz W. Scharpf, 'Koordination durch Verhandlungssysteme. Analytische Konzepte und institutionelle Lösungen', in Arthur Benz, Fritz W. Scharpf and Reinhard Zintl, *Horizontale Politikverflechtung* (Frankfurt/M., New York: Campus, 1992), pp.51–96.
17. Besides the elaboration of a conceptual framework, the empirical study of negotiation processes raises questions of research methods. On the one hand, the modes of negotiation cannot easily be distinguished in reality as they appear in mixed forms. On the other, researchers are mostly not able to gain immediate access to negotiation processes in order to observe the negotiation behaviour of participants at first hand. The following findings are based on the minutes of the Joint Constitutional Commission, which reveal the course of the negotiations and the arguments used by participants. Moreover, we can conclude from the results of negotiations whether participants resorted to strategic bargaining behaviour or principled negotiation. The former is the case if agreements fail due to continuing confrontation, if they are achieved by give-and-take processes or if they reflect the bargaining power of the negotiating parties.
18. Jürgen Habermas, *Faktizität und Geltung* (Frankfurt: Suhrkamp, 1992).
19. Brennan and Buchanan, *The Reason of Rules*, p.81.
20. Bundesrats-Drucksache 741/91 (author's translation).
21. Wilhelm Hennis, *Verfassung und Verfassungswirklichkeit* (Tübingen: Mohr, 1968), p.21 (author's translation).
22. Bryde, *Verfassungsentwicklung*, p.124 and Schaub, *Der verfassungsändernde*, p.76.
23. Martin Kriele, 'Das Grundgesetz im Parteienkampf', *Zeitschrift für Rechtspolitik*, (1973), p.129.
24. Klaus von Beyme, *Die verfassungsgebende Gewalt des Volkes* (Tübingen: Mohr, 1968).
25. Ibid, p.63.
26. Habermas, *Faktizität und Geltung*.
27. Landtag Nordrhein-Westfalen, *Bericht der Kommission 'Erhaltung und Fortentwicklung der bundesstaatlichen Ordnung innerhalb der Bundesrepublik Deutschland – auch in einem vereinten Europa'* (Düsseldorf: Landtag NRW, 1990).
28. Gerhard Lehmbruch, 'Verfassungspolitische Alternativen der Politikverflechtung. Bemerkungen zur Strategie der Verfassungsreform', *Zeitschrift für Parlamentsfragen*, Vol. 8 (1977), pp.461–74; and R. Steinberg, 'Verfassungspolitik und offene Verfassung',

Juristenzeitung, Vol. 35 (1980), pp.385–92.

29. McWhinney, *Constitution-making*, p.28.

30. Peter Häberle, 'Die Kontroverse um die Reform des deutschen Grundgesetzes (1991/2)', *Zeitschrift für Politik*, Vol. 39 (1992), pp.233–63 (238).

31. Hartmut Klatt, 'Verfassung und Verfassungsreform: Das einzig Beständige ist der dauernde Wandel', *Das Parlament*, 14 Jan. 1994.

32. In February 1993, the speakers of the SPD and the CDU in the Commission had found a compromise on the formulation of the constitutional amendment concerning the state objective of environmental protection. To prevent a positive decision on this norm, the whip of the CDU in the Bundestag called on the members of the CDU/CSU group in the Commission to vote otherwise (*Süddeutsche Zeitung*, 13 Feb. 1993).

33. Bundesrat, *Stärkung des Föderalismus in Deutschland und Europe sowie weitere Vorschläge zur Änderung des Grundgesetzes, Bericht der Kommission Verfassungsreform des Bundesrates* (Bonn: Bundesrat, 1992).

34. For a summary of findings see Benz, *Kooperative Verwaltung*.

35. Hennis, *Verfassung*, p.35.

36. Gerhard Lehmbruch, *Parteienwettbewerb im Bundesstaat* (Stuttgart: Kohlhammer, 1976); and Fritz W. Scharpf, 'Der Bundesrat und die Kooperation auf der dritten Ebene', in Bundesrat (ed.), *Vierzig Jahre Bundesrat*, (Baden-Baden: Nomos, 1989), pp.121–62.

37. Cited by Gunter Hoffmann, 'Eine Chance wird vertan', *Die Zeit*, 19 Feb. 1993 (author's translation).

38. Record of the first meeting of the Joint Commission on the Constitution, 16 Jan. 1992, p.8.

39. Bundestags-Drucksache 12/6000.

40. For a critical evaluation see Fritz W. Scharpf, 'Europäisches Demokratiedefizit und deutscher Föderalismus', *Staatswissenschaften und Staatspraxis*, Vol. 3 (1992), pp. 293–306.

41. Günther Hartwig, 'Stärkung des Föderalismus beabsichtigt. Nicht alle Blütenträume der Länder werden reifen,' *Das Parlament*, 14 Jan. 1994.

42. Klatt, *Verfassung*.

43. Günter Bannas, 'Der Bund möchte nicht zum abgenagten Knochen werden', *Frankfurter Allgemeine Zeitung*, 22 April 1994.

44. Renate Mayntz and Friedhelm Neidhardt, 'Parlamentarische Handlungsorientierungen von Bundestagsabgeordneten – eine empirisch explorative Studie', *Zeitschrift für Parlamentsfragen*, Vol. 20 (1989), pp.370–87.

45. Heribert Prantl, 'Wieder eine der verpaßten Gelegenheiten – Aus dem Mut der Bürgerrechtler keine Konsequenzen gezogen', *Das Parlament*, 14 Jan. 1994.

46. Elster, 'Constitutional Bootstrapping'.

47. Fritz W. Scharpf, 'Versuch über Demokratie im verhandelnden Staat', in Roland Czada and M. Schmidt (eds.), *Verhandlungsdemokratie, Interessenvermittlung, Regierbarkeit* (Opladen: Westdeutscher Verlag, 1993), pp.25–50 (43).

48. Klaus von Beyme, *Die Verfassungsgebende Gewalt*, p.67 (author's translation).

The Constitutionalisation Process of the New Länder: A Source of Inspiration for the Basic Law?

CHRISTIAN STARCK

The five new German Länder enjoy constitutional autonomy under the Basic Law, and since unification all of the new Länder have used this autonomy in adopting their own constitutions. Compared to the Basic Law and also to most of the constitutions of the old Länder, the new documents contain a number of significant innovations, concerning the parliamentary form of government, plebescites, basic rights, and social rights and state objectives. Many of these innovations seem, however, problematic; with some significant exceptions, they provide little positive inspiration for a reform of the Basic Law.

I. Introduction

This paper[1] is concerned with the constitutionalisation process in the new German Länder and its impact on the reform of the Basic Law. After reunification, constitutions were adopted in each of the five new Länder. Between January 1991 and September 1993, committees in all five state parliaments approved a final text. These texts were the result of numerous proposals, and they exerted a degree of influence on each other. Saxony was the first state to adopt a constitution on 26 May 1992,[2] followed by Brandenburg (by plebiscite, after adoption by the Landtag, on 14 June 1992),[3] Saxony-Anhalt (16 July 1992),[4] Mecklenburg-Western Pomerania (23 May 1993),[5] and, finally, Thuringia (25 October 1993).[6]

To set this constitutionalisation process in context, it is important to realise that, as states, the new German Länder enjoy constitutional autonomy within the framework of Article 28 of the Basic Law. Section 1 of this article reads:

> The constitutional order in the Länder shall conform to the principles of the republican, democratic and social state under the rule of law, within the meaning of this Basic Law. In each of the Länder, counties and municipalities, the people shall be represented by a body chosen in general, direct, free, equal and secret elections. In the municipalities the local assembly may take the place of an elected body.

The following two sections of Article 28 guarantee self-government and the duty of the Federation to ensure that the constitutional order in the Länder conforms to the basic rights enshrined in the Basic Law. According to Article 1 (3) of the Basic Law, the basic rights bind the legislature, executive and judiciary, both of the Federation and of the Länder, as directly enforceable law. This means that the basic rights of the Federal Constitution are part of the constitutional order of the Länder.

Section 16 of the French declaration of the Rights of Man and the Citizen states that 'Any society in which the guarantee of rights is not secured, or the separation of powers not determined, has not constitution at all'. According to this definition of a western-style constitution,[7] and in view of the fact that the Federal basic rights are valid within the Länder, the new Länder constitutions could conceivably have been limited to the organisation of the state organs, the division of their jurisdiction and fundamental procedures. However, all the new constitutions go beyond this. Thus, they include classic basic rights and general objectives concerning welfare, environmental protection and cultural issues. In addition, some contain social rights. In the following, we will discuss constitutional innovations in the new Länder regarding the parliamentary form of government (II); plebiscites (III); new formulations of classic basic rights (IV); and, finally, social rights and state objectives (V).

II. The Parliamentary Form of Government

Parliamentary Groups

All five constitutions refer to the parliamentary groups (*Fraktionen*) as associations of members of the Landtag. The Constitution of Saxony is unique in deferring the regulation of parliamentary groups to the Code of Procedure of the Landtag, while protecting the rights of unassociated members. The other constitutions contain more detailed provisions about the formation and minimum size of parliamentary groups, their legal status as independent entities in the Landtag, their role in the formulation of policy and their claim to adequate material support. The Brandenburg Constitution goes so far as to ban explicitly the possibility of enforced party discipline. To maintain free representation, it is not permissible to force a member of parliament to act against his or her conscience or conviction. The other constitutions guarantee free representation in the better known formulation of Artice 38 (1) of the Basic Law, which states that members of parliament 'shall be representatives of the whole people, not bound by orders and instructions, and shall be subject only to their conscience'. The stronger wording of the Brandenburg Constitution can, however, have no greater legal effect than the classical guarantee.

Parliamentary groups, as sub-divisions of parliament, are not mentioned in the Basic Law. The necessary regulations can be found in the Code of Procedure of the Bundestag. A provision concerning the formation and size of parliamentary groups, their legal status and their role in the formulation of policy, as well as their claim to adequate material support, should, however, be adopted into the Basic Law, since parliamentary groups are indispensable organs within the system of parliamentary government. Yet, the Joint Constitutional Commission, whilst considering this view, did not include a recommendation on this matter in its report.

Members' Remuneration

To protect the independence of members of parliament, all five constitutions guarantee the right to adequate remuneration. In Saxony-Anhalt, the President of the Landtag must consult an independent commission, the advice of which forms the basis of a statutory grant or alteration of salary, whilst the final word on renumeration rests with the Landtag, whose members are, inevitably, the beneficiaries of their own legislation. Nevertheless, adopting the advice of an independent commission means that the assembly takes its decision on the basis of proposals agreed on at some distance. By contrast, the Constitution of Thuringia goes further in attempting to create an objective means of setting the levels of renumeration. It seeks to avoid the charge of self-service by providing for salaries to be altered (that is, raised) in line with the general level of income. This indexing of remuneration is, however, constitutionally and politically dangerous and could form an unwelcome precedent. In order to protect themselves from the criticism of self-interest, MPs could be tempted to adopt indexing as a solution in other areas of legislation. It is, therefore, undesirable that the Thuringian example be followed in the Basic Law or, indeed, any Federal statute. By contrast, the idea of an independent commission at the Federal level, which would make suggestions on the renumeration of Federal MPs, is rather attractive.

The Opposition

All five new constitutions follow a recent trend[8] in referring explicitly to the parliamentary opposition. Parliamentary opposition groups have a right to equality of opportunity, and in Saxony-Anhalt 'a right to those facilities necessary to fulfil their special duties'. Indeed, in the constitutions of Brandenburg and Thuringia, the opposition is described as a fundamental and significant part of parliamentary democracy. This formula suits a Westminster-style parliament, but it does not really fit the German system of government, principally because of the different electoral system. To characterise the opposition as a fundamental part of parliamentary democracy would seem to exclude an all-party coalition government, which is entirely plausible in times of emergency or given a particular distribution of seats. This has to be constitutionally permissible. It would have been sufficient to describe the opposition as a *normal* part of parliamentary democracy, and this would also have implied that it would be unnecessary to regulate it. It is, therefore, not without good reason that Saxony has done without provisions concerning the opposition altogether. For the parliamentary opposition, simply as a real entity, can act within the framework of constitutional and other law without specific functions being defined. In short, it is unnecessary to describe the role of the opposition in a constitution. Moreover, to assign specifically to the opposition the function of controlling government could be misunderstood to imply that those parliamentary groups supporting the Government have no such function. Accordingly, it would be unwise to adopt into the Basic Law a description of the role and functions of the parliamentary opposition.

Parliamentary Control of Government

The Brandenburg Constitution is characterised by extremely far-reaching and incisive minority rights in trying to ensure governmental accountability to parliament. Thus, every member of the Landtag must be granted access to public employees and state civil servants, be allowed to consult their files and documents, and must be granted any information requested. The Government may only refuse such a request if it is outweighed by a strong public or private interest in confidentiality. This decision must be communicated and justified to the member concerned. By contrast, in Saxony-Anhalt the right to see files and the right of access to public offices can only be exercised by a quarter of the members of a Landtag committee in connection with a committee deliberation. The government can refuse such a request not only on the grounds given in the Brandenburg Constitution, but also when the efficiency or responsibility of the Government or civil service would be seriously affected.

Rights of control are even weaker in the other three constitutions. Either they refer to information from the Government, which every member has a right to, or the right to consult files is made dependent on the demand of the majority of a committee. It does, however, seem worth considering whether the provisions of the Constitution of Saxony-Anhalt could be adopted into the Basic Law in order to strengthen the controlling function of parliamentary minorities. Finally, the establishment of a commission of enquiry and its gathering of evidence are also protected as a minority right, in that a fifth or a quarter of Landtag members can demand this. Against this background,

Article 44 of the Basic Law on commissions of enquiry should, indeed, be altered to the extent that the vote of a quarter of the committee representatives should suffice to force a hearing of evidence.

Governmental Duties to Inform

The new constitutions all make provision for the government to inform parliament about its activities to the extent that this is necessary for it to fulfil its duties. The duty to inform is made more specific in four of the constitutions in that various spheres of activity which must be reported on are individually listed. In particular, they include the preparation of legislation, regional planning, participation in the Bundesrat, co-operation with the Federation, the Länder, other countries and the European Union. This duty to inform is subject to the exception for the efficient and responsible functioning of government already referred to.

It would seem that this novel regulation, which first appeared in Article 22 of the new Constitution of Schleswig-Holstein, adopted in 1990, is well-suited to the changed relationship between parliament and government. In fact, such procedures have been generally adopted in the old German Länder, though without a corresponding constitutional obligation. As regards the affairs of the European Union, the Basic Law was amended following the conclusion of the Maastricht Treaty. The Federal Government is now obliged to keep both houses of parliament fully informed about European affairs at the earliest opportunity (Article 23 (2), sub-section 2 of the Basic Law). According to Article 53, sub-section 3, the Bundesrat is to be kept continually informed about government business. In addition, whilst a corresponding duty to the lower house is not explicit in the Basic Law, in practice it, too, is continuously kept up to date with relevant developments.

III. The Plebiscite

The plebiscite, which complements the normal means of legislation through representative democracy in almost all the west German Länder constitutions, except Hamburg and Berlin, has also found its way into the new east German constitutions. But compared with the western Länder, the quotas for initiating referendums are lower. All five rule out direct legislation in the areas of taxation, official remuneration and the budget. As regards the budget law, this follows automatically from the requirement that income and expenditure be balanced, and it is for this reason that the Government has a constitutional duty to table the budget bill. In addition to this, the fact that statutes concerning public sector salaries and taxation may not be passed by plebiscite shows – perhaps unintentionally – the higher quality of legislation by a representative parliament. The constitutional legislators in the new

Länder obviously fear that the voters might relieve themselves both of their tax burden and the remuneration of state officials. However, since almost all responsibility in this area belongs to the Federation[9] rather than the Länder, caution seems unnecessary.

In principle, there can be no objection to legislation by plebiscite at state level. It all depends on the precise constitutional formulation. By contrast, the introduction of plebiscitary legislation at Federal level seems problematic, in particular as far as Federal jurisdiction for foreign policy and defence is concerned. Clearly, these areas would have to be removed from the scope of the plebiscite in order to protect the Federation from becoming immobilised in its foreign affairs. Plebiscitary legislation at Federal level raises a host of often difficult questions. For example, how would one secure the federal participation of the upper house? Moreover, the reductionist yes or no decision-taking of a plebiscite irrationalises the process of legislation and weakens the responsibility of the appropriate representative bodies, which can always fall back on a referendum for politically difficult issues. Over time, it would also be difficult to maintain the constitutional review of plebiscitary legislation, which, after all, benefits from direct democratic legitimation.

IV. New Formulations of Basic Rights

During the process of framing the new constitutions, it was widely considered appropriate to equip them with their own basic rights catalogue and institutional guarantees. Four of the constitutions have complete catalogues of rights, and two of these do not distinguish clearly between basic rights and state objectives. Only the Constitution of Mecklenburg-Western Pomerania restricts itself to a declaration that the fundamental rights of the Basic Law are part of the Land Constitution and a more detailed statement of a small number of rights contained in five articles. Reasons why the new Länder have opted for extensive rights catalogues are not hard to find. An attempt was made to produce definitive statements in the belief that this was necessary to clarify or even extend the formulations of the Basic Law. The history of the German Democratic Republic certainly also played a role. On the one hand, the ineffective declaration of classic basic rights under the Communist regime meant that this matter was to be accorded prominence in the new democratic constitutions. On the other, however, there was a tendency for the promises of the old GDR Constitution, which were partly formulated as social rights, to be carried over into the new constitutions.

When one considers the classic basic rights and the most significant institutional guarantees contained in the catalogues of the four constitutions, along with the supplementary rights of the Constitution of Mecklenburg-Western Pomerania, one finds various novelties compared to the basic rights of the Federal Constitution. However, only rarely have new rights as such been created. Generally speaking, the fundamental rights of the Basic Law have been reformulated in line with judgments of the Federal Constitutional Court. Some civil rights, which are enjoyed solely by German nationals under the Basic Law, have been protected as universal rights, and there are also some innovations with regard to the limitation of basic rights which are worth considering.

New Fundamental Rights

In various terms, the new constitutions guarantee to everyone the protection of personal data, and a right to information about such data held by public authorities. These rights may only be limited by statute. This is in line with recent developments, which for a number of years have led to adjustments to West German Länder constitutions.[10] In 1983, the Federal Constitutional Court derived a right of privacy from Articles 2 (1) and 1 (1) of the Basic Law,[11] which protects the individual from the uncontrolled accumulation, processing, use and transmission of personal information, and includes the right to be informed of the existence of personal information held by public authorities. Consequently, the protection of personal information through a new Federal basic right does not seem necessary, since it is already adequately protected. By contrast, the protection of the Basic Law would be extended by a right to environmental information concerning one's own area. Here, we are concerned with a genuine claim-right, which would apply with the proviso that it does not conflict with the legally protected interests of third parties, such as rights to confidentiality, or with more significant general requirements. Before such an amendment is considered at the Federal level, the effect of a right to environmental information should, however, first be tested at state level.

Some constitutions clarify the right to physical integrity in the context of police powers, punishment and scientific experiments. In Saxony-Anhalt, mental integrity is protected alongside physical integrity, although this is arguably covered by the general personality right of Article 2 (1) in connection with Article 1 (1) of the Basic Law. The constitutions of Brandenburg and Thuringia extend the fundamental dignity of humanity (Article 1 (1)) specifically to the dying; and the Constitution of Brandenburg emphasises the third-party effect of this right, which is also included in the Basic Law. Also, all five constitutions extend the right of petition to include the duty of public authorities to give a justified response within a reasonable time.

After guaranteeing freedom of association in the words of the Basic Law, the Brandenburg Constitution goes on to protect freedom of collective bargaining, the access of unions to industry and the right to strike. Silence on the issue of lock-out, however, makes the issue unclear; the lock-out is also a legitimate part of freedom of association, even if it is, like the right to strike, subject to certain restrictions.[12]

In line with Article 6 (1) of the Basic Law, three constitutions place marriage and the family under the particular protection of the state. By contrast, in Brandenburg, we find merely that 'marriage and the family are to be protected and supported by the community'. In addition, this Constitution explicitly recognises the need to protect other permanent personal relationships. This gives rise to the problem of the registration, and with that the institutionalisation, of such relationships. So long as they are functioning well, registering is generally perceived as an unacceptable attack on freedom. Legal regulation is extremely difficult in this area. For this reason alone, one would be ill-advised to adopt such a protection for alternative long-term relationships alongside the protection of marriage and the family in the Basic Law.

Four of the constitutions protect equality of opportunity in education with remarkable textual variations. These rights have been introduced into the constitutions of the Länder because of their far-reaching legislative jurisdiction over education. They need not be inserted into the Basic Law, not least because equality of opportunity in general follows from Article 3 (1) of the Basic Law, together with the principle of the social state, with this, of course, applying to education.[13] Finally, all five constitutions guarantee the independent administration of universities within the law which the Federal Constitutional Court derives from Article 5 (3) of the Basic Law.[14] In three of the constitutions, the right of independent administration is attached in different way to rights of participation by various university interest groups. These represent real constitutional restrictions, since according to the judgments of the Federal Constitutional Court, Article 5 (3) of the Basic Law does not require a university to take this form.[15] It would certainly not be advisable to include any of these provisions in the Basic Law, as this would unnecessarily restrict the legislative powers of the Länder in regulating their higher education systems.

The Extension of German Civil Rights into Universal Rights

Freedom of assembly is protected by the majority of the new constitutions as a universal right in the sense of paragraph 1 of the Federal Act of Assembly; thus, they go beyond the formulation of Article 8 of the Basic Law. Professional freedom is also protected as a universal right in Saxony and Brandenburg. The latter Land has also reaffirmed the other two rights of the Basic Law guaranteed only to Germans, freedom of movement (Article 11) and freedom of association (Article 9 (1)), as universal rights. Freedom of association is already protected as a universal right by Federal statute, but one must warn against adopting professional freedom and freedom of movement as universal rights at the Federal level. If this were done, the tide of asylum seekers could, obviously, not be stemmed effectively.

Novel Limitations to Fundamental Rights

To the extent that constitutional innovations seek to define limitations on basic rights more narrowly than the Federal Constitution, they can result in a larger degree of freedom, as the powers of the state are more restricted than under the Basic Law. Such innovations would reduce the possibility of the state justifiably encroaching upon basic rights, and so long as no duties of protection towards third parties flow from the Federal rights and require stronger intervention,[16] limitations on the state's rights to intervene appear unproblematic.

By contrast greater limitations on basic rights in the catalogues of the Länder cannot be reconciled with the Basic Law. Before one reaches this conclusion, one must obviously try to interpret the new limitations in accordance with the Basic Law. The 'additional' limits are often derived from the judgments of the Federal Constitutional Court; they transform judgments into constitutional text and enshrine the limitations at the Länder level. This must inevitably lead to the premature ageing of the Länder constitutions, as the case law of the Federal Constitutional Court continues to develop.

If one takes a look at the limitations to basic rights, three constitutions provide limits to the freedom of research by deference to the protection of human dignity and the preservation of the natural environment. These are probably implicit limitations that also apply to the equivalent Federal right in Article 5 (3) of the Basic Law.[17] Of course, the legal interest in maintaining the 'natural environment' must be narrowly interpreted, otherwise the constitutional limitations on freedom of research within the Länder could come into conflict with the parallel Federal basic right. In this connection, it should also be mentioned that the 'public interest' limitation to the right to private property has been extended in two constitutions by the duty to enhance the natural environment. This duty is already encompassed by the public interest clause of Article 14 (2) of the Basic Law, which reads as follows: 'Property imposes duties. Its use should also serve the public weal.' Finally, two of the new constitutions contain special guarantees for the existence and development of the public broadcasting corporations. In this way, they adopt and consolidate the recent judgments of the Federal Constitutional Court,[18] while the Court itself remains unbound by its previous judgments.

The main problem with the new limitations of basic rights outlined above lies in the fact that the judgments of the Federal Constitutional Court are being solidified at the Länder level. Real innovations in these provisions which would be of interest in reforming the Basic Law are not obvious, since the extensions are, on the whole, too trifling. If the limits of our basic rights are to be revised at all, then total revision is necessary. Moreover, up to now the limitation of basic rights has been satisfactorily performed by the Federal Constitutional Court.

In connection with the limitation of basic rights, some new fundamental obligations must also be mentioned. Occasional examples can be found in the new constitutions, but a particularly rich mine for such obligations is the Brandenburg Constitution. All constitutions refer to the obligation of every citizen to protect the environment, with a particular application to those in agriculture, forestry and the water industry. However, the Brandenburg Constitution goes far beyond this by stipulating that animals are to be respected as fellow creatures; each person must recognise the dignity of the other; the abuse of economic power is forbidden; and, finally, each person is obliged to render assistance as may be required by statute in the case of accident, catastrophe or special situations of emergency. This last clause makes quite clear the need for statutory regulation if the obligations of a citizen are to be effectively enforced. To a certain extent, this area is already covered by Federal or Land statute, but it would not be advisable to incorporate such basic duties into the Basic Law. Rather, it is the job of the ordinary legislator to impose precisely formulated obligations on the citizen, whilst having regard for his fundamental rights.

V. Social Rights and State Objectives

The constitutions of Brandenburg and Thuringia do not establish a clear division between basic rights, social rights and state objectives. In this, both constitutions appear to cling somewhat to the textual form of the old GDR Constitution. It seemed more important to those forming the constitutions that they adopt the popular division according to the particular aspect of life involved, with all relevant rights and objectives lumped together, rather than making a clear division between the classic basic rights that are directly binding on the state, on the one hand, and state objectives and social rights, on the other. But this division is of prime importance for the jurisdiction of Länder constitutional courts over constitutional claims, since these must be based on the vitiation of a basic right.

Thus, the rights catalogue of the Brandenburg Constitution fails to reflect the level of understanding that currently exists concerning the different structure of basic rights and social rights. This distinction between classic basic rights, which directly bind the organs of the state, and programmatic social and cultural rights is one that is, for example, very clearly expressed in the modern constitutions of Portugal and Spain.[19] The distinction secures that essential division in a constitutional state between the political function of parliament and the legal function of the courts. The latter can only lay down the framework of politics under the guidance of the constitution, and must not enter politics on the basis of soft constitutional provisions. For this reason, one can find no model for the reform of the Basic Law in this *mélange* of fundamental rights, social rights and state objectives.

A proposal was put before the Joint Constitutional Commission that state objectives should also be included in the Basic Law. Therefore, the state objectives of the Länder are of special interest. The state objectives oblige the new states to promote factual equality for women and men; equality of value in the living conditions of old and handicapped people; the mental, spiritual and physical development of children; work, accommodation, and a minimum standard of living for everyone; cultural, artistic and scientific creativity and sporting activity; national and ethnic minorities of German nationality; and environmental protection. For the most part, the state objectives are phrased using vague provisions, according to which the state must 'work towards', 'promote' and so on. This makes it obvious that state objectives do not enshrine individual basic rights which could become the foundation of a constitutional claim. But there are also general procedures of statutory review before the constitutional courts,[20] in which all constitutional law constitutes the relevant standard. In addition to this, there is an obvious temptation to realise state objectives in the course of litigation, for example by using them as an aid to the interpretation of statute, thereby reading more into the statute than the legislator intended, or made provision for in the budget.

However, even if the judges are disciplined enough not to use state objectives to 'improve' legislation, such objectives are still problematic. Citizens will look towards state objectives, which, after all, sound good and contain promises of various kinds; but, for the most part, there is insufficient money to realise the far-reaching constitutional programmes represented by these state objectives. It is easy to envisage that one will start to hear complaints supported in the mass media that reality does not match up to the constitution, that statutes which restrict social benefits depart from the constitution and so on. In that case, the constitution could be in danger of forfeiting its authority, something which might spill over to other constitutional provisions. A constitution that is laden with far-reaching and detailed objectives demands a high level of public action from its public servants. Reference must continually be made to the economic conditions, the division of jurisdiction between the Federation and the Länder, and the competing duties of the state. The opposition, which wants to win the next election, will accuse the Government of failing to 'realise' the constitution. As a consequence, even elections will be fought with legal rather than political arguments.

In the light of these comments, it is generally advisable not to incorporate further state objectives into the Basic Law. One exception, however, must be made to this rule. Just as the goal of the social state describes the character of the state in general terms, as an attribute of the *Rechtsstaat* (see Article 28 (2) of the Basic Law), so the protection of the natural environment could be included in the same clause. This task of the state is of equal importance to the task of achieving social justice. If one limited oneself by simply placing the ecological objective next to the social objective, the overriding importance of the objective, as against any particular social rights or promises would be clearly expressed. Apart from that, the ecological objective limits the variety of means available to achieving the social objective. Giving the protection of the environment a place in the Basic Law would restore an obvious imbalance. The Joint Constitutional Commission has, accordingly, proposed a new Article 20a to be adopted into the Basic Law, which stipulates that:[21]

> In responsibility also towards future generations, the state protects the natural environment within the framework of the constitutional order, through legislation and through the executive and the judiciary, in accordance with statute and law.

It is certainly possible to question the wisdom of this particular way of trying to give environmental protection the status of a state objective. The adoption of environmental protection has, it seems, been more successful in Lower Saxony. According to Article 1 (2) its new Constitution, adopted in 1993, Lower Saxony is, among other things, a 'social *Rechtsstaat* committed to the protection of the natural environment'.

In sum, the sources of inspiration from the constitutions of the new Länder for the Basic Law are not numerous. Some new provisions that concern the system of parliamentary government are, however, worth considering, notably the role of parliamentary groups, improved minority rights in the control of government, and governmental duties of information. As regards basic rights and their limits, the new constitutions are living off the Basic Law and its interpretation by the Federal Constitutional Court, and it does not appear advisable to match the text of our Federal basic rights to the judgments of the Federal Constitutional Court. Finally, as far as state objectives are concerned, ecological responsibility should be given an equal place alongside the principle of the social state, but it does not seem necessary or desirable to include further state objectives into the Basic Law.

NOTES

1. Translated by Julian Rivers BA, LLM, M.iur, Lecturer in Law, University of Bristol. For broader elaboration see Christian Starck, *Die Verfassungen der neuen deutschen Länder* (1994).

2. *Law Gazette of Saxony* (1992), p.243.
3. *Law Gazette of Brandenburg* (1992), p.298.
4. *Law Gazette of Saxony-Anhalt* (1992), p. 600.
5. *Law Gazette of Mecklenburg-Western Pomerania* (1993), p.372.
6. *Law Gazette of Thuringia* (1993), p.625.
7. See also Georg Jellinek, *Allgemeine Staatslehre* (3rd ed. 1914), p.505.
8. See the Constitution of Hamburg (Article 23a) and the Constitution of Schleswig-Holstein (Article 12).
9. See Article 105 of the Basic Law and, in connection with the Federal Salary Act, Article 74a.
10. See the Constitution of Berlin (Article 21b), the Constitution of Nordrhein-Westphalia (Article 4 (2)), and the Constitution of Saarland (Article 2).
11. *BVerfGE* (=Collection of the decisions of the FCC), Vol. 65, pp.1ff.
12. *BAGE* (=Collection of decisions of the Federal Labour Court), Vol. 33, pp.140, 148ff; Vol. 48, pp.195, 200ff.
13. See with further references v. Mangoldt, Klein and Starck, *Das Bonner Grundgesetz, Kommentar*, 3rd edn., Vol. 1 (1985), Article 3, marg. no.29.
14. For references see ibid., Article 5, marg. nos. 231ff., 243ff.
15. *BVerfGE*, Vol. 35, pp.79, 125.
16. This problem is discussed in Christian Starck, *Praxis der Verfassungsauslegung*, (1994), pp.55ff.
17. Mangoldt, Klein and Starck, *Das Bonner Grundgesetz*, Article 5, marg. no. 265.
18. *BVerfGE*, Vol. 57, pp.295, 320; Vol. 83, pp.238, 296; Vol. 87, pp.181, 198.
19. Christian Starck, 'Europe's Fundamental Rights in their Newest Garb', *Human Rights Law Journal*, Vol. 3 (1992), pp.103, 114ff. referring to Article 18 (1) of the Portuguese Constitution and Article 53 (1) of the Spanish Constitution.
20. According to Articles 93 (1) no. 2 and 100 of the Basic Law.
21. *Deutscher Bundestag*, Drucksache 12/6000, pp.15, 65ff.

The Federal Constitutional Court: Facing up to the Strains of Law and Politics in the New Germany

NEVIL JOHNSON

The Federal Constitutional Court has since 1990 had to adjust to the consequences of reunification. It has done this without serious problems chiefly as a result of the fact that reunification involved in essentials the extension of West German law and political methods to the new Länder and their citizens. Examples of the Court's jurisprudence from the years shortly before reunification are discussed, followed by consideration of selected cases occurring since 1990 which reflect new problems and challenges. The conclusion is that the Court performs its complex legal political role with great success and a high regard for continuity.

I. Introduction

Amongst the institutions of the contemporary German state, the Federal Constitutional Court in Karlsruhe enjoys a remarkably high reputation with the public at large. As is well known, the Constitution embodied in the Basic Law in 1949 for the western part of the former German Reich provided for the setting up of a supreme court to exercise a specialised jurisdiction in constitutional matters only.[1] This was put into effect by the Federal Constitutional Court Act of 1951 which laid down in considerable detail the conditions governing the organisation and procedures of the new court.[2] There have subsequently been some amendments to the original legislation, for example in 1970 to provide for a single 12-year term of appointment to the Court, and to permit dissenting opinions. And as early as 1956, committees of three judges were empowered to sift constitutional complaints submitted by individuals and to reach decisions on those which are *prima facie* untenable, a method of internal delegation reinforced by recognition of these committees as chambers of the Court in 1986. But the basic characteristics of the Court's organisation – the presence of two Senates, one handling mainly basic rights cases brought by individuals, another dealing generally with disputes raised by and affecting institutions established under the Constitution – have remained unchanged, and the same goes for the procedures governing access to the Court and the terms under which it works and reaches its decisions.

The Federal Constitutional Court can now look back on a record of over 40 years of jurisdiction in the settlement of disputes involving interpretation of the Basic Law. A formidable body of case law has been built up over the years, and the decisions of the Court are now enshrined in nearly 90 volumes. It is to this source that one must look for the jurisprudence of the Court and the doctrines it has elaborated in order to interpret and adapt the founding constitutional document.

My main concern here is with the impact so far on the Court of German reunification and the problems presented by that change. So it will not be possible to engage at length in the perennial (but fascinating) argument about whether the Court is essentially a court of law, the decisions of which can be regarded simply as positive law and nothing more, or whether it is instead a hybrid judicial institution which, by its very terms of reference and the purposes it serves, is compelled to deal extensively in political and moral arguments and to ground its conclusions accordingly. But it is relevant to what will follow to mention that, in my view, it certainly does have such hybrid characteristics. Its form, methods and utterances seek with all rigour to maintain the claim to be exclusively a court of law, a body strictly concerned with applying legal principles to cases in hand and with such deductions as can be drawn from them. Often enough, this involves reference to previous cases and precedents established in the arbitration and resolution of specific disputes about what the original constitutional principles mean and how they should apply in the particular circumstances of each new case. As a result of this approach, there is little that is vague about the Court's findings: it does in a rather obvious way 'lay down the law'. Yet, at the same time, it would be unrealistic and even misleading to overlook the extent to which on many occasions the Court is inescapably engaged in an exercise in political arbitration. It is called on to interpret claims and values expressed in the broad and contestable language of basic human rights, and often enough it has to resolve conflicts between institutions and office-holders within the structures of government. In such circumstances, the Court has often to have resort to a mode of reasoning which makes use of political rather than legal categories, it has to draw on political evidence, and its conclusions are presented with careful regard to their possible political consequences.

Nevertheless, the relatively open involvement of the Court with many aspects of politics and political controversy seems to have had no ascertainable impact on the reputation it has established with the German public as the source of impartial and authoritative constitutional interpretation. It was intended to be the 'guardian of the constitution' – *der Hüter der Verfassung*, to echo a famous phrase[3] – and that is indeed what it has become. The evidence of opinion polls has repeatedly suggested that, at least in what used to be West Germany, most people have great confidence in the Court's effectiveness in performing precisely this role. It may be a matter of considerable political significance that the two institutions which have stronger claims than any others to enjoy the confidence of the majority of Germans are the Federal Bank and the Federal Constitutional Court, the guardians of the currency and of the Constitution respectively.[4] In contrast, the executive and legislative institutions of the German state currently command relatively little popular sympathy, whilst the political parties and politicians are objects of widespread criticism.[5] On these grounds alone, the capacity of the Court to cope with the demands presented by the new and larger German state emerging after reunification in 1990 is of great practical importance.

II. The Court's General Approach to Interpretation of the Basic Law

Unification has ostensibly presented many new challenges to the Court: the country has become larger, there are still marked disparities in living conditions and in outlook between the two parts of Germany, east and west, there have been many social consequences of unification which are hard to absorb, and there are plenty of signs that the full integration of two radically different societies will continue to be a slow process. But before considering some aspects of the Court's response to the new situation in which it finds itself, it is desirable to make some remarks about the broad thrust of its approach to the Basic Law and its interpretation in recent years, and to illustrate this by referring to a number of cases.

With some simplification, three main categories of cases coming before the Court can be distinguished: individual appeals or constitutional complaints alleging infringement of basic rights as set out in Articles 1–19 of the Constitution; disputes between institutions on which rights and duties are conferred by the Basic Law (*Organstreite*); and both concrete and abstract judicial review, that is, in the case of the former, referral of an issue of constitutionality from a lower court and, of the latter, a request from the Federal government or a state government or one-third of the members of the Bundestag to test the constitutionality of a law. The first category contains the greatest number of cases and represents the largest routine flow of work for the Court. The second category may involve disputes between major political institutions about jurisdiction or a challenge to the constitutionality of legislative decisions or executive acts. Typically, some of the Court's decisions on cases in this category have been lengthy and of great political significance. As to the third category, cases falling into it tend often enough to raise issues not dissimilar from those raised by individual constitutional complaints.

In relation to the questions raised in basic rights cases in the first category, the Court has, for the most part, developed in recent years what can be described as a moderately liberal jurisprudence. It has tended to adopt a position favourable to, and supportive of, individual claims, whilst it has also been very willing to apply the equality of treatment principle of Article 3 of the Basic Law rather rigorously. But it has to be remembered that in its interpretation of basic rights, the Court is also generally at great pains to weigh conflicting claims very carefully and to underline the need to set one *Rechtsgut* against another. It has done much the same thing in its treatment of the abortion issue, one of the most contentious matters to face the Court and one on which it has had to give major rulings several times, first in 1975 and again in 1992 and 1993.[6] (I note in parenthesis that the abortion issue did not come to the Court as a basic rights constitutional complaint, but in the shape of a request for abstract judicial review presented, for example in 1992, by a Land government and parties in the Bundestag. However, the issues that then had to be resolved resembled in many ways those that would have arisen had the matter been raised as a question of basic rights in a constitutional complaint.)

The same care to strike a cautious balance between conflicting values, especially in the absence of a clear constitutional commitment to the overriding importance of any one particular value in dispute, is usually to be observed in the Court's resolution of institutional conflicts. There are certain doctrines long established in the Court's jurisprudence which it seeks to maintain, for example the notion of 'federal comity' in relation to transactions within the federal structure of the state, and respect for a core sovereignty held to reside with the Länder.[7] Similarly, where powers have been unambiguously conferred on the Federal Government or Parliament, the Court will seek to respect that by defending the right of these institutions to exercise such powers to the full. Yet, at the same time, the Court has been very willing to intervene in procedural matters affecting the way in which Parliament (especially the Bundestag) and the political parties manage their affairs. It has done this to a large extent by applying its own elaborate and stiff standards of constitutionality to specific arrangements, for example the right of the Bundestag to exclude members not belonging to a party or collectively not constituting a *Fraktion* (parliamentary group) from its subordinate committees, or the terms on which financial contributions are made from public funds to political parties.[8] But even where it lays down detailed and often school-masterly guidelines for the amendment of a statute or the correction of the internal procedures of a major Federal institution like the Bundestag, the Court is concerned to do so in balanced and judicious ways.

It prefers painstaking persuasion and instruction to the sharp put-down.

The points just made can be briefly illustrated by mentioning one or two fairly recent decisions taken from the period shortly before unification. In a constitutional complaint decision of March 1990[9], the Court upheld the plea of a journalist that he had been injured in the enjoyment of his rights under Article 5 (1 and 3) of the Basic Law by a Bavarian court decision punishing him for publication of a scurrilous version of the *Deutschlandlied*. The Court annulled the lower court's decision, but also added riders to the effect that the third verse of the national anthem, the only one normally sung on official occasions, could legitimately be protected from abuse and derision. In a 1986 case on the tax concessions allowed in respect of contributions to political parties[10], the Green party sought to challenge existing upper limits of DM 100,000 for tax relief by both individuals and corporate bodies on contributions to political parties. In a lengthy judgement the Court decided, with two dissenting opinions, that this provision did not damage the principle of equality of chances *(Chancengleichheit)*. The decision was in line with the Court's earlier view of this matter, but it was to abandon this position within the framework of a more extensive judgement on party finance issued in 1992. In 1989, in a decision regarding the rights in the Bundestag of a member without party ties[11], the Court concluded that a member who had left his party (in this case the Greens) could not legitimately be excluded from all committees, but instead had the right to be allowed to attend and speak in at least one committee, though not necessarily with a right to vote. This decision neatly illustrates the Court's readiness to intervene in shaping the procedures of the Bundestag, something that members of that body seem to accept without demur.

In a different field, in its decision on voting rights in local elections in Schleswig-Holstein[12], the Court annulled in October 1990 a measure passed by the Schleswig-Holstein Landtag to allow certain foreign immigrants to vote in local elections. The Court here reaffirmed the institutional guarantee of German nationality as a condition of citizenship and the bar on any unilateral change in this by the Länder legislative authorities. In reaching this conclusion, the Court was staying well within the bounds set by precedent in such matters. (The position in this matter has, however, now been changed as a result of the Maastricht Treaty). There have also been a number of cases during the past decade or so in which the Court did not hesitate to become involved in very elaborate technical assessments, for example in relation to projects for the nuclear generation of electricity, or to dig deeply into the more arcane aspects of the qualifying conditions for university entry both in particular subjects and generally, an example being the decision in 1991 on the centralised allocation of places for the study of medicine.[13]

These fairly run-of-the-mill examples illustrate well the Court's capacity to ensure that constitutional norms are taken seriously and are respected. They suggest a judicial body which operates with some confidence in the precedents it has set, though, of course, it is not as a matter of judicial doctrine and practice bound by its own precedents. They also bring out the political character of the jurisdiction and the tendency of the Court to come to carefully qualified conclusions. Even if the answer it gives in a particular case is quite definite, it often finds it hard to resist the temptation to provide some further guidance for future contingencies as well.

III. Reunification: A Big Change or Not?

Ostensibly, the unification of Germany which took place on 3 October 1990 creates a new situation for the Court just as it does for so many other institutions in German public life. At the very least, there are in the new Länder moral and political perceptions and attitudes different from those in the west, there is an extended and, to some degree, less predictable federal structure which may give rise to tensions and controversies, there are some rather uncertain new political groups and certainly new people involved in the parties, and there is the fact that the new Germany is expected by the world around it to behave differently in some respects from its smaller West German predecessor. From these sources and others, there is at least the prospect that new challenges will face the Court in the interpretation of the Constitution. However, consideration of a number of decisions which have been taken since reunification and which illustrate some of the new demands imposed on the Court, suggests the conclusion that the direct effects and implications of reunification for the Court and the body of constitutional law which it safeguards have so far been very limited.

Basically what happened in 1990 was that the former German Democratic Republic ceased to exist and through its newly restored Länder it became part of the legal entity, the Federal Republic of Germany. This meant that the whole body of existing West German law, including constitutional law, was extended *en bloc* to the five new Länder, subject to a variety of qualifying conditions and transitional provisions set down in both the Treaty on Monetary, Economic and Social Union (*Staatsvertrag*) and in the exhaustive Unification Treaty (*Einigungsvertrag*) agreed and signed before reunification formally took place. This agreement, which also envisaged subsequent new national legislation on a number of difficult outstanding issues, including compensation for and in some circumstances return of property compulsorily taken over in the former GDR, effectively foreclosed a great deal of constitutional argument. It did this by regulating in advance what was to happen in many fields or what conditions and principles were to apply to particular problems with their origins in the past. In this way, reunification should be made a legally water-tight process. For example, the Unification Treaty embodied transitional arrangements for the application to the new Länder of the normal conditions governing the allocation of tax proceeds within the federal system, whilst later legislation was aimed at preventing the opening-up of interminable disputes regarding the property forcibly expropriated between 1945 and 1949 on the territory of what was then to become the GDR.[14] It is, therefore, reasonable to conclude that reunification is not likely to bring a great flood of new and contentious cases to the Court, though obviously some increase in its caseload will flow simply from the fact that the country is now significantly bigger. Nevertheless, despite all this, there are some new and difficult problems to be tackled, some of which have already been presented to the Court, notably the issue of abortion and, most recently, the constitutionality of any attempt to commit, without specific constitutional amendment, Bundeswehr forces to operations of any kind outside the NATO area and the task of self-defence.

Before turning to some of the questions raised by these very recent cases, it is worth making a remark on the Court's position *vis-à-vis* the citizens in the new Länder. It has remained firmly fixed in Karlsruhe – about as far west as one can get in Germany – and there is no prospect in the foreseeable future of it moving. Its membership has not so far been affected by reunification and thus it remains entirely 'western' in experience and orientation. Clearly, judges from the east will eventually be appointed, but this is bound to be a slow process owing to the lack of people in the new Länder adequately and acceptably qualified for appointment. And this limitation is likely to apply also to those vacancies which do not need to be filled by persons selected from the higher German courts, since even those usually nominated for such places still have to possess a traditional legal qualification. Given the nature of the former GDR regime, the terms of the Unification Treaty, and subsequent legislation in pursuance of it, the Court has no need to familiarise itself with a different body of law. It is entirely free to go on deciding cases within the traditions and doctrines it has long established, and there is no threat at all to continuity in interpretation. Naturally, there is what might be called a receptivity problem. The judgments of the Court are bound to be difficult to assimilate or even to grasp for many people in the new Länder. For two generations they have had no experience of effective judicial review, and there is, at the present time, no popular *Rechtskultur* ready to receive it. It is impossible to predict what will be the longer term effects of this situation or how long it will take before people begin to register the activity of the Court as impinging directly on their lives. Yet, it is worth noting that already the political class in the new Länder, and especially some of those active under the old regime, have shown that they are alive to the pos-

sibilities of appealing to the Court on matters in which they have an immediate interest.[15] Doubtless it is precisely the fact that the Court is exercising
a political jurisdiction which has helped such people to learn quickly how to
take advantage of its existence.

IV. Old Issues in New Forms: Some Court Cases After Reunification

We will now summarise a small number of cases which both illustrate the
changed circumstances in which the Court has to reach decisions and the
extent to which it has already been successful in preserving continuities. The
first one – and much the most significant so far – is the judgment on the
1992 amendments to the provisions in the Criminal Code on abortion. It was
necessary to amend the amendments of 1976 (which in turn resulted from
the Court's 1975 judgment)[16] because the two parts of Germany had had
very different conditions governing legal abortions. The GDR had a time-
based regulation, a *Fristenregelung*, of a fairly flexible kind. In the West,
abortion was possible legally only for specific reasons laid down in law and
subject to a variety of other limiting conditions, what was called the
Indikationslösung. It was necessary to arrive at conditions more or less
acceptable to both parts of the country, whilst paying due regard to the right
to life enshrined in Article 1 of the Basic Law. Abortion law is, however,
highly controversial in Germany as elsewhere in the Western world.
Because of the variable impact of religious affiliations, it does not establish
a clear dividing line between the major political parties, though the CDU
and CSU take, for the most part, a 'pro-life' stance in line with the position
of the Catholic Church, whilst the SPD and FDP tend to favour a liberal
view of the mother's claim to an abortion.

The legislative compromise eventually reached by the Bundestag was
something like a judgment of Solomon. What was, in principle at least, a
system of indicative regulation was to be replaced by what was in essence a
time-based regulation allowing abortions to be performed legally during the
first 12 weeks of pregnancy in certain circumstances. This was also to be
subject to new provisions for obligatory professional counselling for the
pregnant woman in advance of any permission to have a legally valid abortion. This solution in its final form was immediately challenged by the parliamentary group of the CDU/CSU and the state of Bavaria who gained a
temporary injunction from the Court in August 1992 preventing application
of the new provisions. Then, in May 1993, the Court issued its final judgment in the case.[17]

If the legislation itself represented a judgment of Solomon, it is tempting

to suggest that the Court went one better in the delicate balancing of conflicting values and demands, and in the refined formulation of that balance.
It upheld the newly proposed time-based solution, but in so doing reaffirmed the 'protective duty' of the state in respect of the unborn life and
the legal duty in principle of the mother to allow the pregnancy to proceed
to term in the absence of legally valid grounds for its termination. It
demanded that the new provisions should be amended to make it clear that
abortion within the agreed time limits (12 weeks) was only exempted from
the liability to punishment and that it was not referred to as 'not against the
law' (*nicht rechtswidrig*).

   Since abortion law could not be left in uncertainty and suspended anima-
tion pending further amendment to meet the Court's objections, it took the
relatively rare step of making use of its powers under the 1951 founding
statute to set out in detail provisional conditions which are to apply until the
Bundestag has taken action.[18] These tighten up in several ways the provisions for counselling, require serious efforts from the health and social care
authorities to make facilities available to encourage the mother to agree that
the pregnancy should continue, and contain a variety of supporting statements of principle. The Court's decision was greeted with a chorus of criticism from some quarters, though subsequently much of this seems to have
subsided. All in all, it would appear that this time the Court has sewn the
matter up so tightly that it will be hard to unpick the elaborate guidelines it
has laid down, though it has already been reported that there have been
efforts by the social service authorities of at least one Land to water down
the new conditions through the use of their powers to provide 'social help',
Sozialhilfe, to mothers applying for counselling.

   How the new abortion law – when it eventually takes effect in a final
form – will work out in practice is, of course, hard to predict: in all probability the three judges who offered dissenting opinions[19] will turn out to have
been justified in their scepticism about the effectiveness of seeking to
impose concepts which mean little in the context of contemporary social
attitudes towards abortion. The Court has offered a judgment which seeks to
calm passions on this issue and is very densely argued, especially in relation
to the state's 'protective duty'. But it also leaves the situation highly complex and perhaps for that reason it may turn out to be possible to neutralise
the intentions of the provisions for counselling or to render them a formal-
ity. Nor does the decision appear to pay much attention at all to the different
attitudes towards abortion of doctors in east and west: one would expect that
this is bound to influence the practical application of the new provisions.

   The abortion law decision demonstrates the skills of the Court in the
bridging of gaps and, even when it is striking out in a new direction, in the
maintenance of as many continuities as possible in its own collective view

of particular constitutional values. The decision of April 1992 on the financing of political parties also brings out the capacity of the Court to modify
previous positions[20] and to take account of changes in public attitudes and
the circumstances of party political activity. It is an exercise in political real-
ism, though it may be open to question whether the judges devoted as much
thought as might have been desirable to the possible longer-term implications of their findings. In essentials, the Court accepted the complaints put
to it by the Green Party which brought the case and took them as a basis for
reviewing party finance much more widely. Tax relief on donations from
firms to parties was held to be illegal (contrary to earlier judgments of the
Court), the rules for calculating the *Sockelbetrag* (the basic payment) were
held to be faulty and the same went for the treatment of the *Chancenausgle-
ich* (equalisation of chances) payments, the level for publishing individual
contributions in party accounts (DM 40,000) was said to be too high, and it
was held that the upper limit for tax relief to individual contributors should
not exceed DM 1,200.

The Court did not in this case declare null and void any of the statutory
provisions to which it raised objections. Instead, it demanded appropriate
legislative amendment by the end of 1993 and laid out again in considerable
detail in a judgment of 74 pages how this might be done and what principles
should be observed. In particular, the Court amended its previous doctrine
holding that only the election campaign activities of parties qualified for
public funding to the extent of concluding that state funding of the general
political activity of parties was also acceptable. It sought to qualify the possible effects of this (that is, a raising of the allowance per vote gained, then
set for Federal elections at DM 6.50) by stating that no party should receive
public financial support in excess of its own independent income, and that
the level of funding attained overall in the period 1989–92 should constitute
the *absolute Obergrenze* (absolute upper limit) for state support to the parties. It should be noted that this judgment relates only to funds flowing into
the parties as national or Land organisations, and excludes the large amounts
paid to them as *Fraktionen* (parliamentary groups) in the Bundestag and
other legislative bodies and to the various party-linked foundations for so-
called political education. Whether the judgment will have the long-term
effect of restraining the growth of state subsidies for parties must remain
doubtful. A ceiling set by reference to past levels seems to be a fragile bar-
rier to enlarged future demands, especially since the Court has now
expressly recognised that under Article 21 of the Basic Law it is legitimate
to fund from tax revenues the general political work of parties. Surely that
must leave the door open to Oliver Twist asking for more?

A very different case coming to the Court as a constitutional appeal concerned the rights of husband and wife in respect of the determination of a

family name after marriage and the birth of children. This was settled in March 1991 in the decision on family names.[21] This is not a case on which reunification has a direct bearing. But it does express well the Court's approach to the application of certain principles which is likely to have implications for attitudes in the eastern part of the country. The facts relating to the case are very complex and not without their humorous side. All that can be indicated here is that though a civil code amendment of 1976 did allow considerable freedom of choice in the selection of a family name after marriage, in the event of a failure to agree on such a name it did in some circumstances give precedence to the husband's name by reverting to the *deutsche Namenstradition*. The plaintiff objected to this on the grounds of unequal treatment.

In determining the complaint, the Court decided that this appeal to convention offended against Article 3 (2) of the Basic Law which had to be applied strictly. It then annulled the provisions complained of and laid down its own conditions to be applied until amendment of the law could be carried out. These provided that if no agreement could be reached on a family name each partner should for the time being retain his/her birth name. If this were still to be the position when a child was born, the parents were entitled to decide on one name or the other, or both names in whichever order they preferred. If they could not agree even at this stage, then the child was to receive both parental names, the order to be decided by lot. It is worth noting that in its judgment the Court denied that there are any relevant objective reasons for treating women differently from men in this matter, and explicitly rejected the relevance of what it called 'pre-existing social reality'. It also described a person's birth name as 'an expression of individuality and identity', not to be changed without important reasons. If this might be thought a bold assertion, the Court went on to claim that the procedure of drawing lots to settle the order of a double-barrelled name would not disadvantage either parent as would be the case if the alphabetical order of the two names were to prevail. This is perhaps as good an example as any of the Court's tendency sometimes to offer confident assertion rather than carefully constructed and well-founded argument. After all, the letter of the alphabet with which one's birth name begins seems to be eminently a matter of chance – no better than a lottery in fact. More seriously, the case does illustrate the Court's very strict views on the standards to be applied in respect of equality of the sexes, and its readiness to make maximum use of the principles of equal treatment enshrined in Article 3 of the Basic Law.[22]

Some of the issues which arise in relation to the foreign and defence commitments of the new Germany will now be discussed briefly. The country is larger than it used to be, yet relative to some of its neighbours accepts far fewer external security commitments, and especially any which might involve military support for UN peacekeeping operations or for its NATO allies outside the area of the alliance strictly defined for defence purposes. Several times since 1990 situations have arisen in which Germany has been subject to criticism from its allies and partners for its unwillingness to do anything more in a crisis than offer words of sympathy, cash contributions or promises of economic aid: the Gulf War with Iraq, the wars of succession in former Yugoslavia, and, most recently, UN operations in Somalia[23] come to mind as examples of the varying effects of the political and constitutional inhibitions affecting the German Government's capacity to accept external commitments which might entail the possibility of having to supply military support. Moreover, with the dissolution of the Soviet Union and the far-reaching changes in the world geo-political map stemming from that event, Germany faces, along with its partners, the challenge of re-thinking defence and foreign policies which have for 40 years or so been beyond question.

The problem of the role Germany should seek to play in international affairs is a hard nut to crack. Public opinion is divided and uncertain, and it raises issues which divide the parties and to some extent the present CDU/CSU/FDP ruling coalition. A majority in the SPD is against all military involvements on behalf of NATO outside the traditional continental European defence sphere intended to counter the one-time Soviet threat. But if an option of this sort is to be accepted as a possibility, the SPD wants it then to be covered by a constitutional amendment, and this demand is extended even to support for UN humanitarian activity, not to speak of UN peacekeeping. The FDP, which likes to see itself as a guardian of constitutional propriety, is divided: some of its leading figures are prepared to proceed pragmatically without insisting on constitutional amendment immediately, other members are mistrustful and want to see everything properly covered by explicit constitutional provisions in advance of any possible commitment. The CDU/CSU prefers on the whole to argue that constitutional amendment is not needed to authorise both reasonable support for UN operations and participation in NATO peace-keeping operations outside traditional limits. But it is also reluctant to get involved in the awkward business of constitutional amendment because agreement on that requires a two-thirds majority which could only be achieved in co-operation with the SPD. And it is worth noting *en passant* that as an exercise in drafting it might turn out to be virtually impossible to complete, not least because there is nowadays a widespread belief amongst German politicians that future contingencies of whatever kind can and should be provided for in the Constitution in exhaustive detail. Such a belief not only prolongs argument, but also tends to render amendments rigid and in some circumstances unworkable.[24]

To return now to the Court, it had to decide twice during 1993 whether to grant an injunction against the Federal Government. In April 1993, it rejected an SPD/FDP supported demand that it declare illegal the Government's decision to engage German air force personnel in AWACS surveillance flights over former Yugoslavia. Then, in late June 1993, it concluded that there was no constitutional bar on German participation in the UN relief operation in Somalia, though it did add that this ought to be covered by a formal vote of the Bundestag endorsing the decision. (This was then secured.) These are holding decisions and the Court is not expected to reach a final conclusion in the case until July 1994.

So far, the Court seems to have been guided in these matters by a principle of judicial restraint in relation to political questions: it has stuck to issues affecting competences and tried to avoid getting involved in a discussion of the merits of particular courses of action in external affairs and in relation to the use of German military forces overseas. It seems likely that the Court will try for one obvious reason to stick to this line in its final decision. If it were to enter into an elaborate consideration of the kind of constitutional amendment which might in a perfect world be needed to cover all Germany's conceivable commitments under the UN charter and other treaties, it would almost certainly be drawn into expressing views on the status and merits of particular policies. This is something it would wish to avoid. Moreover, it is obvious that, in principle, the German Parliament (acting through both chambers) could amend the Basic Law so as to confer on the executive or on some combination of executive and legislative organs the kind of discretion to deploy military forces in the national interest enjoyed by governments elsewhere. But this is a Pandora's Box which few want to open, and certainly not the Court. So it is likely that the Court will continue to maintain a careful political restraint in this matter, following essentially the lead given by the executive (which in turn has been very cautious).[25] If this is what happens, it does, however, follow that how the new Germany interprets and discharges its obligations in the world at large will depend very much on who is in power. Were Chancellor Kohl to lose his majority and leave office, the world might for some time be in for even more uncertainty about what defence role German governments are willing and able to undertake.

One more case falling in the foreign affairs field is worth mentioning briefly. This is the recent decision on the compatibility of the Maastricht Treaty with the Basic Law.[26] Here, again, the Court has maintained the restraint which it nearly always observes in relation to such highly political questions, and has upheld the Government's case that the Treaty is in accord with the Constitution. Indeed, it is hard to envisage the Court being ready seriously to call into question what so many regard as Germany's principal political commitment, that is to say the pursuit of political union in Europe. Nevertheless, the Court did garnish its judgment with several important *obiter dicta* which suggest that it is worried about the extent to which at some stage the process of European unification to which Chancellor Kohl appears to be so obstinately and passionately committed will come into conflict with principles enshrined in the Basic Law. The Court has in a slightly oblique way now advanced a case for the nation state, or at any rate for the independent, self-governing state as the only entity currently capable of providing effectively for the protection of civil rights and democratic values. It seems to recognise that, in principle, a European Union could at some stage provide these guarantees as well, but it also discerns that this is at best a very long way off. Meanwhile, the agreements of Maastricht are held to be essentially intergovernmental in nature and presumably, therefore, in principle revocable. For the foreseeable future, the possibility of a genuine conflict of values between the national and Community levels remains; the implication of the Court's comments is that this would have to be resolved in favour of the Basic Law as a national constitution.

V. The Court after Reunification: A Provisional Evaluation

Barely four years have passed since reunification and this is doubtless too short a time in which to be able to draw any definite conclusions about its impact on an institution so well established as the Federal Constitutional Court. Moreover, it is obvious that the flow of cases to a court of this kind is unpredictable in content, and on this account alone a substantial time must elapse before a pattern of responses to a new political and social situation will emerge and suggest definite conclusions about the character of the Court's responses. So provisionally it can be concluded that the Court has come through reunification remarkably unscathed: it is working as usual, though with an increased caseload, and delivering judgments in the familiar way. The Basic Law and the constitutional principles it enshrines seem little affected by the change, and the recent deliberations of the Joint Constitutional Commission do not offer the prospect of really significant constitutional amendment as a result of reunification.[27] Nor does the record of recent decisions suggest important shifts in the Court's thinking and its approach to constitutional interpretation. New problems have appeared, notably in the spheres of foreign affairs and defence, but whilst a consequence of reunification in a narrow sense these also reflect long familiar party controversies and rivalries. On that account, they invite that rather careful balancing of opposed viewpoints to which the Court is no stranger.

    If there are strains affecting the Court these almost certainly proceed from sources other than the direct effects of reunification. I would like to mention several which seem to me to be of some importance. First, there is the impact on the Court of the increasing risk of something like stalemate in

German political life. The established parties are dominant, even though the two largest ones are not as exclusively dominant as before. But all the parties have become so firmly built into the structure of public life that virtually all decisions have to be hammered out in intricate bargaining amongst them. Inevitably, this means that firm and decisive leadership becomes difficult and that politicians feel a temptation to avoid issues which they know are just too contentious to permit a bargain to be struck. This sometimes means that they are content to push a difficult matter in the direction of the Court: there is a readiness to invoke a judicial ruling partly in the hope of dishing one's rival, partly to escape from the blockages inseparable from intricate coalition politics.

Second, it seems that the Court has to some extent created difficulties for itself precisely because it is rather too willing to take on the responsibility for decisions which ought to be left to politicians. There are objections of legal principle in Germany to a refusal to offer a judgment on a valid plea, but there could be no objections of principle to a more robust and summary treatment of some of the issues put to the Court. Instead, the Court nowadays repeatedly errs in the other direction and is often all too ready to offer elaborate advice on matters of public policy and related administrative arrangements, even though this may not be strictly required by the case in hand. It is on this account that it sometimes sounds rather like a *praeceptor Germaniae*. But it has to be said that there is so far little evidence of popular hostility to that role. In the west, the Court is widely seen both as a high-minded moderator in contentious political issues and as a resolute defender of individual rights; in the east, attitudes towards its role have still not crystallised, but at least those of its decisions specifically affecting the former GDR have not presented too sharp a challenge to the somewhat suspicious and conservative outlook prevailing there.[28]

Third, there is some threat to the reputation and standing of the Court from the unbridled politicisation of appointments to it. As a result of the manner in which the appointment of members of the Court is shared between committees of the Bundestag and Bundesrat deciding by reinforced majorities, party political considerations have come into the selection of judges from the start. But in recent years the determination of the parties to ensure that they all get their share and that this goes automatically to those they recommend has made the exercise of patronage far more obvious than it used to be. The most remarkable example of a wrangle about an appointment occurred during 1993 when the succession to Vice-President Mahrenholz (SPD) was in contention. The CDU/CSU refused to support an SPD candidate, Frau Däubler-Gmelin, a deputy chairman of the parliamentary party, on the grounds that she was too actively engaged in political life to be a suitable appointee to the country's highest court. In retaliation the

SPD then vetoed other public appointments which the Government parties wished to make, and at one stage even refused to respond to proposals put forward by the plenum of the Court itself. Eventually the SPD gave way after its preferred candidate decided to withdraw her name and two seats on the Court (both 'reserved' for the SPD) were filled amicably. Such arguments, which are the common currency of German political life, appear out of place when conducted in relation to the Federal Constitutional Court and seem likely to undermine its authority.

Finally, there is the aspect of the Court's increasing caseload. This is a problem which has been there for many years and has often been raised.[29] The relegation of constitutional complaints initially to committees of three, who in effect sieve them and identify those which can be rejected, was adopted over 20 years ago as a way of mitigating the impact of the heavy caseload. It is doubtful whether there is now much further scope for the internal delegation of work. But equally there is little desire to increase the number of judges or to contemplate a break with the time-honoured division of labour between two Senates of eight judges. So it looks as if the Court will simply continue to do its best to prevent the waiting time before cases are decided becoming inordinately long. And presumably it must hope that the gradual assimilation of the new Länder to the *Rechtskultur* of the West does not encourage a long-term growth in litigiousness in the population there.

The Federal Constitutional Court has so far coped with the backwash of reunification remarkably well. There are stresses affecting it, and there is some tendency in political life to expect too much of it. It remains, however, perhaps the most successful and respected institutional innovation in the reconstruction of the institutions of German public life and the reinvigoration of constitutional values which have taken place since the Second World War. But it owes its strength and reputation in part to the fact that it has revived and developed further traditions already present in earlier periods in the German approach to the rule of law and constitutional government.[30] These traditions accept and even welcome efforts to translate political questions into the categories of *Recht* and, more particularly, constitutional law. Here, they contrast sharply with British political and legal traditions which set great store by trying to keep the spheres of law and politics separate. The Federal Constitutional Court's methods of legal interpretation, with its readiness to call in aid wide-ranging and necessarily imprecise concepts resonant of political and moral value judgements, and to rely on open-textured assertion rather than strict legal deduction and the appeal to evidence, vividly expresses this difference. The Court is engaged in a delicate and often contentious exercise in which it still acquits itself with some distinction.

NOTES

This paper is an extended version of an address given to the Europa Institute at the Faculty of Law, University of Edinburgh, on 5 November 1993.

1. Basic Law, Articles 93 and 94 specify in detail the competences of the Court and how it is to be constituted.

2. A convenient summary of the terms in which the Court was set up is to be found in Donald P. Kommers, *The Constitutional Jurisprudence of the Federal Republic of Germany*, (Durham, NC: Duke University Press, 1989), Chapter 1.

3. *Der Hüter der Verfassung* was the title of an influential essay by Carl Schmitt, (Tübingen, 1931), in which he advanced his theory of the presidential prerogative in relation to the protection of the Constitution.

4. It is certainly indicative of German attitudes towards the Court and the judiciary in general that there was no serious or widespread objection to the candidature of Professor Herzog, President of the Federal Constitutional Court, for the office of President (to which he was duly elected in May 1994). It was widely believed that in a popular vote his SPD rival, Herr Rau, Minister President of North-Rhine Westphalia, would have been elected. But few questioned the appropriateness of selecting under a party label the country's highest judge for the office of head of state.

5. *Parteienverdrossenheit* – disillusionment with parties – is a familiar German complaint. However, often enough it expresses little more than the changing attitudes of the voters towards particular politicians and events rather than any deep-seated feelings of hostility or rejection in relation to parties.

6. The two earlier decisions were BVerfGE 39, pp.1ff. (1975), and BVerfGE 86, pp.390ff. of 4 Aug. 1992.

7. These matters are discussed in Philip M. Blair, *Federalism and Judicial Review in West Germany* (Oxford: OUP, 1981), Ch. VII and VIII.

8. There have been numerous decisions on matters affecting the rights of parties and their claims to public financial support, e.g. BVerfGE 8, pp. 51ff. (tax deduction in favour of parties), BVerfGE 20, pp.56ff. (the major party finance case of 1966), BVerfGE 24, pp.300ff. (equalisation of chances decision of 1968), BVerfGE 41, pp.399ff. (on the claim of an independent candidate to a share of public financial support), and BVerfGE 84, pp.304ff. (on the recognition of groups as *Fraktionen*).

9. *Bestrafung wegen Verunglimpfung der Hymne der Bundesrepublik Deutschland*, BVerfGE 81, pp.298ff.

10. *Steuerliche Abzugsfähigkeit von Mitgliedsbeiträgen und Spenden an politische Parteien*, BVerfGE 73, pp.40ff.

11. *Rechtsstellung eines fraktionslosen Abgeordneten des Deutschen Bundestages*, BVerfGE 80, pp.188ff.

12. *Wahlrecht für Ausländer bei den Gemeinde- und Kreiswahlen in Schleswig-Holstein*, BVerfGE 83, pp.37ff.

13. *Zentrale Prüfung für Studierende der Medizin in Form des Antwort-Wahlverfahrens*, BVerfGE 84, pp.59ff.

14. The decision not to expose property expropriations undertaken in the Russian zone of occupation between 1945 and 1949 to a general challenge by former owners prompted substantial criticism from some sources, not least those who lost property at this time or their descendants. There were, however, reasons of legal principle for the decision as well as political considerations stemming from a desire to avoid giving too much offence to the former Soviet Union.

15. A clear example of this was the challenge by the Greens and various other political groups in the former GDR to the electoral law intended to apply in the first all-German elections in December 1990. The Court endorsed the challenge to the extent of requiring special provisions to be enacted which exempted parties in the new Länder from the application of the five per cent threshold calculated on a national basis: BVerfGE 82, pp.322ff.

16. B VerfGE 39, pp.1ff.
17. B VerfGE, 88, pp.203ff.
18. A statutory revision of the law on abortion had by June 1994 still not got through both chambers of the legislature.
19. Dissenting opinions were recorded by Judges Mahrenholz and Sommer jointly, and by Böckenförde singly.
20. *Parteienfinanzierung*, B VerfGE 85, pp.264ff.
21. *Ehenamen und Gleichberechtigungsgebot*, B VerfGE 84, pp.9ff.
22. Amending legislation was passed in October 1993 which in fact departed from the Court's proposals in several respects, notably by substituting reference to Wardship courts for the drawing of lots.
23. A contingent of troops strictly limited to the distribution of relief aid was sent to Somalia for a short period in 1993.
24. The 1992 amendment to the asylum provisions of the Basic Law (Article 16) provide an illustration of the new style of prolix drafting, running as it does to more than 300 words. However, it has to be said that this amendment seems to be having a real impact on the number of asylum seekers, though its effectiveness depends heavily on the co-operation of Germany's immediate eastern neighbours.
25. The preceding passage was completed before the decision of the Court of 12 July 1994 on the use of the Federal Armed Forces outside the NATO area. The Court's decision appears generally to sustain the position taken by the Federal Government, subject to the need on such occasion to secure endorsement by the Bundestag of specific decisions to deploy German armed forces outside the NATO area. The comments made here about the Court's likely approach appear on the whole to be in line with its reported conclusions.
26. B VerfGE of 12 Oct. 1993 (2 BvR 2134/92; 2 BvR 2159/92).
27. Since the legislative organs had, at the time of writing (June 1994), not yet reached a final decision on constitutional amendments consequential on consideration of the Joint Commission's recommendations, no account has been taken of this matter here. But all the signs point to very modest changes: *parturient montes, nascetur ridiculus mus.*
28. For perceptive comment on public attitudes towards the Court's political impact see Friedrich Karl Fromme, 'Immer nahe bei der Politik', *Frankfurter Allgemeine Zeitung*, 17 May 1994.
29. In his annual review of the work of the Court in 1993, President Herzog noted that of 5,440 new cases which came in, 5,246 were constitutional complaints. (Average success rate 2.7 per cent for earlier years.) As against 1992, there was an increase of 1,300 in the flow of new cases, much of this due to asylum appeals. The Court's backlog of undecided cases did not, however, increase significantly. See *Frankfurter Allgemeine Zeitung*, 7 March 1994.
30. See Nevil Johnson, 'Law as Articulation of the State in Western Germany', *West European Politics*, Vol.1, No.2 (1978), pp.177–192.

The Frontiers of Constitutional Law: Identity Politics in Reunified Germany

NEIL WALKER

This article examines the changing significance of constitutional law in post- unification Germany. It asks whether the importance of constitutional discourse and processes within the Federal Republic will be sustained or exceeded in post-1990 Germany. On the one hand, the emergence in Germany and elsewhere of a politics of cultural identity alongside the traditional left–right politics suggests an increasingly pivotal role for constitutional law, which has always been closely concerned with identity questions. On the other hand, in so far as it makes constitutional actors the focus of political controversy and encourages a distorted view of law's regulatory potential, this same development might in the longer term undermine the legitimacy and effectiveness of constitutional law.

I.

British observers of contemporary Germany often remark upon the extent to which its social and political culture appears to be shaped by its system of constitutional law.[1] In part, this may reflect the atypical nature of the British experience. While the unwritten constitution undoubtedly influences the conduct of political life in Britain, it is a somewhat negative influence. Many of the salient features of the British political system, including the importance of political parties, the tradition of strong government, the formal legislative supremacy of parliament, the centrality of a network of extremely pliable constitutional conventions and the lack of a robust role for the judiciary in constitutional adjudication, arise precisely because of the permissiveness and flexibility of the basic constitutional settlement.[2] By contrast, the idea of a constitution as a source of fundamental values and of a comprehensive institutional design, performing a more positive, directive function in respect of the conduct of political life, is an alien one.

Thus, when one attempts to assess the limits of constitutional law in Germany, the British experience provides a largely unhelpful benchmark. By comparison, the German case is suggestive of a more central role for constitutional law, as indeed are all political systems which evince a strong tradition of the state-under-law (*Rechtsstaat*), where the devices of political competition and the pursuit of the ends of government are restricted in accordance with the dictates of an entrenched constitution. The inquiry becomes more interesting, however, not to mention controversial, when we ask just *how* robust? Is there anything singular about the German experience which suggests a stronger – or, indeed, a weaker – role for constitutional law in shaping the wider society than is true of other Western democracies with comparable constitutional settlements? What of the underlying secular trend? Does this suggest a rise or a decline in the prominence of the Constitution in German political life? And can we point to any particular events or episodes which might accelerate, or reverse, this process? In particular, has reunification made a significant difference? This article represents a preliminary attempt to address these various questions.

II.

Informed commentators in both Germany and Britain appear to be in agreement that the centrality of constitutional processes and debates which characterised the development of the West German polity has been reinforced by the experience of reunification and its aftermath.[3] In 1949, with the institution of the Basic Law, West Germany bore all the hallmarks of an 'invented state'.[4] Required and eager to renounce the ethnic nationalist past, the new political forces in post-war West Germany sought to establish 'a post-nationalist or even anti-nationalist state'.[5] This tended to place the new constitutional order at the centre of political and cultural life, for both negative and positive reasons. Negatively, the absence of nationalism as a candidate to provide an affirmative ideology for the new state created the cultural space within which there could develop a 'constitutional patriotism'[6] – that is, the treatment of the Constitution itself is an object of allegiance and a means of lending cohesion to and providing a set of values for the reconstructed social and political system. Positively, the sentiments underlying the post-nationalist ethos also produced a commitment to what Thomas Mann termed a 'militant democracy'.[7] The recent German experience of an absolutist ideology and a totalitarian political system, and the massive development to the east of a new political bloc – embracing the GDR – that exhibited similar traits, distilled a sense of the importance of designing institutions which would offer firm protection to the liberal democratic order: the Basic Law, which sought to place the rudiments of representative democracy and social pluralism beyond political debate, was ideally suited to this agenda.

   As the new state developed, these abstract supports were supplemented by more concrete allegiances to the maturing institutions of the new constitutional order, including the system of courts with the Federal Constitutional Court as its apex,[8] and the dense network of structures and processes within which evolved the distinctive German concoction known as 'co-operative federalism'.⁹ The legitimacy of the new order gradually became less linked to grand historical concerns, more grounded in the everyday empirical workings of the political system. Accordingly, in the atmosphere of intensive political debate surrounding reunification, in the words of Goetz and Cullen,

> However much proponents and opponents of far-reaching reform differed in their views on the necessary extent and content of constitutional change, few doubted the centrality of national constitutional law for the political, economic, social and cultural life of the country and its capacity to influence and guide ... the course of the polity.¹⁰

The Basic Law has been a key text and the Federation Constitutional Court and the Joint Constitutional Commission leading actors in a political event which not only has thrown up difficult questions of adapting the framework of government to meet the novel circumstances of the extended state, but also has prompted substantive reconsideration of themes as disparate as abortion, asylum, environmental protection, property restitution and the legitimacy of Germany's military role.

However, as Goetz and Cullen also remind us,¹¹ we should not confuse discursive centrality with objective significance. The Constitution may be at or near the centre of political discussion and may be generally perceived as an important political resource, but it does not follow that the Constitution in fact exerts a profound influence over the social and political life of the community. Indeed, there may even be an inverse relationship between the two; the increasingly noisy debate may reflect 'a diffuse sense of unease' that the Constitution is in fact becoming an empty vessel, with a 'declining ability to perform its traditional functions'.¹²

We will return in due course to some of the points which these authors put forward in accounting for the supposed gap between rhetoric and reality. The more basic significance of their argument, however, is to remind us of the necessity of having some theoretically informed method of interpreting constitutional evidence. As their discussion makes clear, it is not enough simply to point to a flurry of constitutional activity and deduce from this that constitutional politics is in a healthy state. We must look beneath the surface to try to discover some more fundamental significance in constitutional events.

III.

One promising method of investigating the 'deep structure' of constitutional transformation is suggested by Bruce Ackerman in his landmark study of American constitutional history.¹³ Briefly, Ackerman argues that the

American political system has a dual framework. It accommodates two levels of politics, normal politics and constitutional politics. As the terminolo-
gy suggests, constitutional politics are atypical. Constitutional debate only
moves centre-state at moments of profound political rupture, where near-
revolutionary change to the political system is effected. According to
Ackerman, there have only been three such 'constitutional moments' in
American political history: first, the Federalist moment, involving the enact-
ment of the 1789 Constitution in the post-independence period; secondly,
Reconstruction following the Civil War between North and South; thirdly,
the New Deal welfare state following economic depression in the 1920s and
1930s. In each case, once the constitutional moment passes, the new system
which has been put in place defines the shape of normal politics until the
next constitutional moment arises. Through restructuring the relationship
between the different organs of government and resetting the broad limits of
acceptable political conduct, although rarely its substantive outcomes, the
successful constitutional moment establishes 'a kind of grammar of political
action'[14] for the new political generation.

    Applied in the German context, such a dualistic model might suggest that
reunification following the collapse of Soviet Communism has provided the
first redefining 'moment' of constitutional politics since Germany's own
earlier reconstruction, signalled by the establishment of the Basic Law in the
aftermath of the Second World War.[15] The advantage of such an approach is
that it guards against inferring from a short period of intense constitutional
activity the relative preponderance of constitutional politics in the longer
term. It implies, instead, that once we have passed through the rarified
atmosphere of reunification we can expect to return to the flatlands of normal politics, albeit now somewhat altered in form by the new constitutional
settlement.

    But in cautioning against reading too much into contemporary events, per-
haps such an approach risks the opposite error of reading too little. Even if
we accept the plausibility of Ackerman's basic approach, why should we
assume that the transformation wrought in any particular constitutional
moment allows the distinction between normal politics and constitutional
politics, which is the cornerstone of his analytical model, to be preserved in
the same basic dichotomous form? It may well be that the new grammar of
politics issued in by a particular constitutional moment is one which trans-
forms the very relationship between normal politics and constitutional politics. In the new order of normal politics, constitutional law may no longer
have the same background structuring role as is assumed in Ackerman's dualist metastructure. It may be more marginal, or more prominent; it may relate
to normal politics in an entirely novel way. That is to say, Ackerman's model
may well be useful, but only if we concede its self-transforming potential.

If we remain open to this possibility, we may discern some interesting trends in the constitutional moment represented by reunification. However, in order to understand these we must introduce a further qualification to Ackerman's thesis. Ackerman's approach assumes that the dynamic underpinning the relationship between normal and constitutional politics is state-specific. The American story is deemed to be unique, as indeed would be German or British constitutional narratives. However, it may be that the appropriateness of this assumption is itself historically contingent, and that there are new international forces a work which influence constitutional change in similar ways across different states.

This, at least, is the message which may be drawn from Vincent Cable's recent innovative analysis of the political structure of the new world order.[16] Cable's thesis holds that the division between left and right, which traditionally has formed the basis of normal politics within states, is gradually being displaced, or at least supplemented, by a new *politics of identity*. If we map this new politics onto a continuum, at one extreme we may place those who define their own and other people's identities in exclusive, closed terms. For racists, tribalists, religious fundamentalists, extreme ethnic nationalists and so on, 'cultural identity is of all-embracing importance'.[17] At the other extreme are those whose overriding commitment is to individual choice in personal morality and lifestyles. For them, 'cultural identity is flexible, multiple or essentially superficial',[18] and always informed by the liberal principle of toleration. As with the economic politics of left and right, with its choices between social ownership and market, redistribution and property rights, labour protection and deregulation and so on, many and complex intermediate positions are possible along the new 'political fault line'[19] of identity politics.

For Cable, a number of factors lie behind the exponential development of identity politics. There is the negative factor of disillusionment with the traditional left–right divide, reinforced by the collapse of the 'Cold-War' ideological oppositions orchestrated under the old world order. But there are other more direct causes, in particular the interrelated trends of globalisation, liberalisation and class fragmentation. Globalisation of technology, economic organisation, transport, communications, and so on, undermines notions of national sovereignty and other forms of local identity; the liberalisation revolution in economic thought causes dislocation and exacerbates inequalities; the ensuing fragmentation of class, and of communities and industrial and political associations organised around class, undermines a previously potent form of collective consciousness. The linking theme is the threat to existing forms of social belonging and the institutional mechanisms through which they are nurtured and consolidated, and the cultivation of new forms of social identity in response to this threat. Further, a crucial strength of those involved in such cultivation is, as Cable remarks, 'that they inherit well-fertilized ground'.[20] Ideologies of ethnic or national identity are typically based upon notions of 'imagined community'[21] – timeless myths of social solidarity unendingly available to successive generations.

In practice, Cable argues, the new politics of identity co-exist and interact with the old left–right politics. Indeed, contemporary political movements are best understood in terms of the combination of these two axes, and from this we can identify four archetypes:[22] 'Communitarians' combine left-wing economics with liberal ideals in identity politics; 'national socialists' (or perhaps, less provocatively, socialist nationalists) link left-wing economics to an exclusive politics of identity; 'libertarians' combine the right-wing politics of economic freedom with an equivalent belief in freedom in the cultural domain; 'cultural conservatives' are market liberals whose cultural politics tend to be more authoritarian and exclusive. Again, beyond these crude models, we can imagine more complex variations and combinations.

Although not a line that Cable himself pursues, it is arguable that his thesis has profound implications for our understanding of constitutions and constitutional politics. Constitutional texts and discourse have traditionally been characterised by their emphasis upon nationality, citizenship and other aspects of membership of the political community; upon the geographical boundaries of the state and sub-state units; upon the internal distribution and dispersal of political power on territorial lines, and in accordance with other criteria of group identity such as race and religion; and upon the classical rights and freedoms of individuals, and to a lesser extent groups, to express and defend their own sense of cultural identity. *In short, constitutions have always been centrally concerned with identity politics.* In an age when normal politics was dominated by economic questions, these questions of identity provided an indispensable and periodically profoundly contested part of the background context within which day-to-day economic politics took place, defining the rules of the game and the identities and capacities of individual and institutional players. In this sense, Ackerman's dualist model is, indeed, well suited to the conventional structure of political debate. However, in the newly emergent context where identity politics are now part of the *foreground* of political debate, situated alongside and overlapping the key questions of economic politics, constitutional questions inevitably move towards the centre of the political stage.

If we apply Cable's thesis (and our extension of it to constitutional questions) to the German context, an interesting picture emerges. Many of the main themes of the debate surrounding unification have, indeed, been located within the domain of identity politics, and, as such, have tended to be articulated and treated in predominantly constitutional terms. The protracted controversy over the restructuring of German federalism resulting from the economic weakness of the eastern Länder and differing conceptions of regional autonomy in the various parts of the Federation is a case in point.[23] So, too, the debate surrounding the new Article 23 of the Basic Law, which regulates the relationship between Germany and the European Union, addresses a more complex issue of multi-layered allegiances which is on the contemporary political agenda of every European state; this is the question of overlapping regional, national and supranational identities, and of the most appropriate relationship between these three tiers.[24] On the one hand, Article 23 responds to the aspirations of the more powerful Länder to play a semi-autonomous regional role in the European Union; on the other hand, as the decision of 12 October 1993 of the Federal Constitutional Court on the constitutionality of the Treaty on European Union makes clear, Article 23, read together with Articles 20, 38 and 79, also reasserts the ultimate authority of national law and institutions to determine whether European institutions have acted within their competence, using the broad standard of democratic legitimacy as a key criterion.[25]

Questions of national identity are also to the fore in discussions over Germany's military role and its asylum law, discussions which again have been predominantly articulated in constitutional terms. The debate concerning the legitimacy of the deployment of German armed forces outside Germany in an active military support capacity came to a head in the AWACS case.[26] A central theme in this controversy concerns the nature of the reunifi German state; is it now fully restored as a 'normal' state,[27] and, if so, does this normalcy imply something more than a purely defensive military capability? Similarly complex questions about the evolving meaning of German national identity attend the asylum debate, which has been conducted around the introduction of the new Article 16a of the Basic Law restricting the categories of persons competent to seek asylum in Germany. As Ignatieff has argued, the asylum debate and the subsequent constitutional amendment has been, for many German liberals, 'the first moment in the post-war period where they feel forced to renounce the utopia of a post-nationalist state and think more soberly of Germany's national interest'.[28]

Many of the questions of individual rights highlighted in the unification debate also relate to the politics of identity. For example, the question of restitution of property confiscated in the area of the former GDR, although ostensibly primarily concerned with economic matters, also registers within the politics of identity. The decision of 23 April 1991 of the Federal Constitutional Court regarding the irreversibility of Soviet-authorised expropriations is partly predicated upon the Court's view as to the limited responsibility of the Federal Republic for what happened in the East prior to reunification, which in turn depends upon a particular conception of the degree of continuity or otherwise of German national identity during the years of divided statehood.[29] The abortion question, controversially resolved by the Federal Constitutional Court against the enacted will of the all-German legislature in its judgment of 28 May 1993, also relates to questions of identity, in this case the entitlement or otherwise of the individual to make decisions about her own body as against the authority of the majority to impose its collective morality. In this case the cultural conservatism of the West prevailed over the more liberal traditions of the East.[30]

IV.

While certain of the questions referred to above may become less urgent as the drama of reunification fades, most are likely to remain firmly on the agenda. The German example, does, therefore, tend to support Cable's thesis as to the growing significance of identity politics, and, consequently, the importance of the constitutional framework as a primary means through which such politics are articulated. Accordingly, we can no longer with any confidence employ the Ackerman approach to predict that, following a brief period in the harsh spotlight, constitutional politics will again retreat into the background. However, while this suggests that the increased discursive centrality of constitutional politics is no mere transient phenomenon, it still does not answer affirmatively the question of the efficacy of the Constitution as a directive influence over social and political life.

One important argument against such a connection has been advanced by Goetz and Cullen. They suggest that the fact that most of the issues considered above are not within the exclusive jurisdiction of national constitutional actors, but are shared with the European Union (asylum, Eurofederalism) or with other international authorities, such as the signatories to the Two - plus - Four Treaty anticipating reunification (military capacity, property restitution), is itself evidence of the marginal and declining efficacy of constitutional law in this field.[31]

On one level, this is a semantic issue to which there are different answers, each with respectable backing in conventional usage. If one chooses to view constitutional law as an exclusively domestic preserve, then Goetz and Cullen are undoubtedly correct. However, this is only helpful if one considers that the limits of constitutional law are determined by the extent to which national entities retain sovereignty over their own affairs. This is a perfectly reasonable investigative standpoint, but one which, I fear, is increasingly likely to yield a negative answer, and to that extent become less interesting and unduly exclusionary. Another, perhaps more fruitful starting point, is to suggest that the frontiers of constitutional law, rather than being restricted to the jurisdictional boundaries of any particular territorial authority, should instead reflect the extent to which the sorts of issues which have traditionally fallen within the domain of constitutional law remain capable of effective regulation by *any* authority or combination of authorities. In other words, it is the object of legal analysis rather than the source of the law that matters. After all, as Ascherson has argued, and as the decision of the Federal Constitutional Court on the legality of the Maastricht Treaty rather reinforces, in the new Europe we are entering a period of 'fuzzy democracy' where the sources of legal and political authority are unlikely even to be arranged in an ordered hierarchy, still less identifiable in terms of exclusive sovereign jurisdictions.[32] In a period when the relationship between the various domains of political power becomes ever more complex and opaque, it may be that our conceptions of the disciplinary boundaries of constitutional law, supranational law and international law also have to become suitably fuzzy, otherwise we will be in danger of trying to understand the world with out-of-date instruments.

If, the, we concede the desirability of a multi-tiered conception of its sources and an open-ended understanding of its limits, to what extent is constitutional law capable of exploiting its privileged position *vis-à-vis* an increasingly axiomatic politics of identity in order to forge a more effective regulatory role? In large part, this depends upon the ability of constitutional actors to define and act upon the agenda of the new politics of identity. As Cable argues,[33] in order to respond effectively to the underlying fears and aspirations of the various constituencies of the new politics of identity, it is vital to develop certain guiding principles. In particular, he stresses that if identity politics are to be channelled to productive and harmonious ends, it is important to facilitate the development and maintenance of multiple identities on the part of individuals, as well as to encourage democratic decentralisation, anti-discrimination initiatives, less unequal distribution of material goods across groups, and collective measures of international order maintenance. In each of these areas, law has an obvious role to play.

On the negative side, however, constitutional law's centrality to the new politics of identity creates difficulties and dangers as well as opportunities. More specifically, there are three sets of problems and pitfalls that constitutional lawyers in Germany and elsewhere must confront in grappling with the new political configuration suggested above. I will conclude by briefly considering each of these in turn.

First, there is the danger of an increasing instrumentalisation of constitutional law, mirroring the 'enhanced visibility of policy in law' generally within the Western democracies.[34] The legitimacy of Western law has traditionally depended to some extent upon its formal independence – the fact that it is no mere 'instrument' of political will. Indeed, it is legal formalism, the distinctiveness of legal language, methods and actors from the everyday political process, which helps to underpin the authority of law over that process.[35] To the extent, however, that there develop areas of substantive overlap between constitutional questions and mainstream public policy questions around issues of identity, some of that distinctiveness, and, ensuingly, some of that legitimacy, may be lost. Asylum and abortion are cases in point where matters of partisan dispute between major political parties have recently become thoroughly constitutionalised. More specifically, the criticism directed towards the Constitutional Court in the wake of its decision in the abortion case against the tide of political consensus points to the danger of a progressive disillusionment with the overall political system, including the legal system (*Systemverdrossenheit*), to match the disillusionment with political parties (*Parteiverdrossenheit*) which has become a widely acknowledged feature of the German political landscape in recent years.[36]

It is important, however, to retain a sense of perspective when advancing this argument. In public opinion polls, the Court regularly emerges as the most trusted of German public institutions. Indeed, despite a steady diet of cases implicating the Court in controversial party political issues, its prestige appeared to grow during the 1980s.[37] If, therefore, the more recent accentuation of this politicising trend has triggered a decline in the Court's public standing, it is a decline from a very high baseline. It may be, moreover, that this relatively healthy general picture reflects the comparative insignificance of legal formalism in the German context. Analysts of mainstream German politics in the post-war period have often emphasised the importance attached to consensus-building.[38] Historical experience has convinced the political class of the importance of harmony and reconciliation in the public sphere, both as a principle guiding (and rhetoric accompanying) action and as an imperative built into the design of the constitutional system itself. From this perspective, the Court can be seen to have occupied a pivotal role from the outset as umpire and mediator between competing levels of government and rival social and political interests. Its involvement in politics, rather than compromising its independence, is simply proof of its 'constitutional patriotism' – its commitment not to any particular regime or substantive political ideology but rather to the maintenance of a stable and widely legitimised political order. Acceptance of this line of argument does not make the Court impervious to the allegation of partisanship and usurpation of democratic authority typically levelled against judicial institutions viewed as instrumentalist. It does, however, suggest that the threshold of tolerable political involvement is relatively high,[39] and in consequence that the dangers associated with aggressive judicial engagement with the new politics of identity are likely to be relatively low and slow to surface.

A second, less equivocal, difficulty associated with the increasingly prominent politics of cultural identity concerns law's intrinsic incapacity to address effectively many of their core themes. As we have seen, reunification has precipitated a wide-ranging debate about the nature of German identity.[40] Many of the questions raised and solutions sought, concerning, for example, the scope and meaning of citizenship and the nature of Germany's military role, turn as much upon self-understanding as upon material self-interest.[41] Arguably, law is less effective in aiding the search for self-understanding than it is in expediting the pursuit of self-interest. For instance, law, through institutions such as contract and property and through devices such as criminal sanctions and administrative regulation, is often effective in resolving social co-ordination problems in a manner which optimises the attainment of the often differing interests of multiple parties.[42] By contrast, in the domain of self-understanding, law can often reflect, and so reinforce, certain meanings which are derived from other cultural sources, but is less able to generate new meanings.[43] In short, law, constitutional law included, has only limited influence over the affective and symbolic aspects of social life, yet it is these aspects which are often implicated in the politics of identity.

Finally, just as it is important, as the property restitution question demonstrates, that the implications for questions of cultural identity of issues which appear to be predominantly economic in character are not neglected, so it is equally important that the economic dimension of issues which appear to be more closely bound up with identity concerns is not obscured or ignored. As has been indicated, identity politics may be rooted in experiences of dispossession or dislocation which have economic ramifications. There is a danger, therefore, that identity politics, and the legal and constitutional mechanisms which address them, will focus upon the construction of symbolic responses to problems which can only be fully resolved through the transformation of material life-chances. For example, the message of ethnic equality conveyed in the new Germany by the retention of relatively liberal asylum laws and the introduction of less strict naturalisation laws for those seeking German citizenship,[44] may be eclipsed in the perceptions of racist groups by their experience of material deprivation, restricted opportunity, and acute competition for scarce jobs from guestworkers. Similarly, granting former citizens of the GDR the full panoply of rights available under the Basic Law may make them the formal equal of their West German fellow-citizens, but it is unlikely to overcome a sense of envy and resentment born of material inequality.

In conclusion, therefore, it is important to reiterate the need to look at deeper currents as well as surface movements in coming to terms with the ebb and flow of constitutional politics. The new emphasis upon questions of cultural identity may indeed have guaranteed constitutional issues a more central position within Germany's political agenda. By the same token, however, the altered understandings, strategies and expectations that accompany the new politics threaten to expose more acutely than ever the limits of legal regulation. It may be that an increasingly transparent instrumentalism will threaten the broad legitimacy of constitutional law and practice. Even if not, the capacity of public law to transform understandings and attitudes in many of the areas of identity politics in which it is implicated is likely to be restricted both by the general limitations of the method of formal regulation in pursuing objectives in the sphere of affective and symbolic relations, and also by the incomplete analysis of the underlying social problems upon which the identification of such objectives tends to be based.[45]

NOTES

1. See e.g. P. J. Cullen, 'Constitutional Change in Germany', in W. Paterson and C. Jeffery (eds.), *German Unification* (Oxford, Blackwell, forthcoming): W. Paterson and D. Southern, *Governing Germany* (Oxford: Blackwell, 1991), pp. 73–4; D. P. Kommers, 'The Federal Constitutional Court in the German Political System', *Comparative Political Studies*, Vol. 26, No. 4 (1994), pp.470, 485–9.
2. See e.g. M. Foley, *The Silence of Constitutions; Gaps, 'Abeyances' and Political Temperament in the Maintenance of Governments* (London: Routledge, 1989).
3. See e.g. K. H. Goetz and P. J. Cullen in this volume.
4. Paterson and Southern, op.cit., p.75.
5. M. Ignatieff, *Blood and Belonging: Journeys into the New Nationalism* (London: Chatto and Windus, 1993), p.75.
6. Kommers, op. cit., p.488; P. Pulzer, 'Unified Germany: A Normal State?', *German Politics*, Vol. 3, No. 1 (1994), pp.1, 5–11.
7. Quoted in Paterson and Southern, op. cit., p.60.
8. C. Landfried, 'Judicial Policy-Making in Germany: The Federal Constitutional Court', *West European Politics*, Vol. 15 (1992), p.50.
9. C. Jeffery, 'Plus Ca Change: The Non-Reform of the German Federal System after Unification', Discussion paper in Federal Studies (Leicester: Centre for Federal Studies, 1993).
10. See Goetz and Cullen in this volume.
11. Ibid.
12. Ibid.
13. See B. Ackerman, 'Constitutional Politics/Constitutional Law', *Yale Law Journal*, Vol. 99, No. 3 (1989), p.453; *We the People; Foundations* (Cambridge, Mass.: Harvard, 1991).
14. J. Simon, 'Columbus in the Twilight Zone: Bruce Ackerman's "Discovery" of the Constitution', *Law and Social Inquiry*, Vol. 14 (1992), pp.501, 515.
15. For a more comprehensive periodisation of German political and constitutional history using a similar analytical framework, see Pulzer, op. cit.
16. V. Cable, 'The World's New Fissures: Identities in Crisis', Demos Paper No. 6 (London: Demos, 1994).
17. Ibid., p.8.
18. Ibid., p.9.
19. Ibid., p.4.
20. Ibid., p.29.
21. B. Anderson, *Imagined Communities* (London: Verso, 1991, 2nd edn.).
22. Ibid., p.76.
23. See C. Jeffery, op. cit.
24. See C. Jeffery and J. Yates, 'Unification and Maastricht: The Response of the Länder

Governments', *German Politics*, Vol. 1 (1992), p.71. For the more general Europe-wide debate, see e.g. C. Harvie, *The Rise of Regional Europe* (London, Routledge, 1994); A. Scott, J. Peterson and D. Millar, 'Subsidiarity; a "Europe of the Regions" *v.* the British Constitution', *Journal of Common Market Studies*, Vol. 32, No. 1 (1994), p.47.

25. *Brunner v. European Union Treaty* [1994] 1 C.M.L.R. 57; see also G. Ress, 'The Constitution and the Maastricht Treaty' in this volume.

26. Die Öffentliche Verwaltung (DÖV), Vol. 47, No. 19, October 1994, pp.824–29; and see Goetz and Cullen in this volume.

27. See Pulzer, op. cit.

28. Ibid., p.75.

29. See D. Southern, 'Restitution or Compensation: The Open Property Question', *German Politics*, Vol. 2 (1993), p.436. The meaning of German national identity has been a key constitutional issue since the inception of the Basic Law, with Art. 116 – the Citizenship clause – as the textual focus; see R. Brubaker, *Citizenship and Nationhood in France and Germany* (Cambridge, Mass.: Harvard, 1992), Ch.8.

30. See M. Prützel-Thomas, 'The Abortion Issue and the Federal Constitutional Court', *German Politics*, Vol. 2 (19930, p.467.

31. Goetz and Cullen suggest a second basis for the declining efficacy of German constitutional law, namely changing state–society relations within national boundaries (pp.26–32). In the context of the present article I am unable to do justice to their arguments on this theme, suffice to say that their overall approach would seem to echo the 'regulatory crisis' thesis advanced by writers such as Luhmann and Teubner, with which I have broad sympathy (see note 45 below).

32. N. Ascherson, 'Fuzzy Democracy', *New Statesman and Society*, 11 March 1994, p.24.

33. Ibid, pp.59–76.

34. R. Cotterrell, 'Law's Community: Legal Theory and the Image of Legality', *Journal of Law and Society*, Vol. 19 (1992), pp. 405, 410.

35. See e.g. J.H.H. Weiler, 'Journey to an Unknown Destination: A Retrospective and Prospective of the European Court of Justice in the Arena of Political Integration', *Journal of Common Market Studies*, Vol. 31 (1993), p.417.

36. See e.g. Prützel-Thomas, op. cit., p.481.

37. See Kommers, op. cit., pp.485–9.

38. See e.g. P. Pulzer, 'Too Big for Europe? The Unexpected Achievement of German Unity', *Times Literary Supplement*, 7 Jan. 1994, p.3; T. Garton Ash, *In Europe's Name: Germany and the Divided Continent* (London: Jonathan Cape, 1993). It is a prominent aspect of Garton Ash's thesis that the post-war German political class also stressed the need for harmonization in international relations; ibid., pp.40–41, 175.

39. See also, C. Landfried op. cit.

40. See e.g. Garton Ash, op. cit.; D. Gow, 'Germany: The Unruly Giant', *Scottish Affairs*, No. 6 (1994), p.5.

41. R. Brubaker, op. cit., p.182.

42. Within the philosophy of law, the idea of law as a solution to problems of social co-ordination, rather than as an independent source of values, is one which tends to be emphasised and explored by legal positivists.

43. The theme of reinforcement is well captured in Bohannan's concept of 'double institutionalization', whereby legislation serves to reinforce existing social customs or understandings. See P. Bohannan, 'Law and Legal Institutions', in W.M. Evan (ed.), *The Sociology of Law* (London: Routledge, 1980).

44. R. Brubaker, op. cit., Ch.4.

45. Probably the most sophisticated contemporary analysis of the methodological and cognitive limitations of law as a mechanism of social regulation are provided by the German social theorists Niklas Luhmann and Gunther Teubner. See e.g. N. Luhmann, *A Sociological Theory of Law* (London, Routledge, 1985); G. Teubner (ed.), *Autopoietic Law: A New Approach to Law and Society* (New York, Walter de Gruyter, 1988).

Concluding Theses on Constitutional Policy in Unified Germany

PETER J. CULLEN and KLAUS H. GOETZ

The Basic Law has neither been fundamentally amended nor radically reinterpreted as a result of unification. Constitutional continuity has been the major response to the challenge of national integration. There has been an ambiguous response to the problems posed by the emerging European constitution. The reform debate has also failed to address systematically a number of issues of constitutional theory, with negative consequences for the quality of constitutional regulation. In particular, insufficient consideration was given to questions concerning the proper scope, limits and form of constitutional regulation.

1. The Constitution and the National Question

The question, then, is not whether the Germans are a nation, but how they respond to it and what they make out of it.[1]

A number of the issues addressed in the constitutional reform debate can be explained as facets of the process of responding to the changed nature of the German state following unification. Unification has put paid to the idea of the Federal Republic as a 'post-national state'.[2] The Basic Law of course reflected the division of the German nation into two states. In what proved to be a successful way of helping to overcome such division, the Federal Republic willingly undertook to transfer sovereign powers to (Western-oriented) international institutions.[3] The Basic Law has, in particular, always expressed an openness to European unity; this is a constitutional commitment of historic, and therefore symbolic, importance but it also has important substantive legal implications, as the recent judgment of the Federal Constitutional Court on the Maastricht Treaty illustrated.[4] The new state and its Constitution were also inevitably burdened with the tragic inheritance of the Third Reich. The asylum clause was part of the response to this inheritance; along with the other basic rights, this clause embodied a renewed commitment to a code of moral values. As Nevil Johnson has observed, the Basic Law had 'an eminently political role to play'[5] in the new state. The dispersal of power from the centre to the new federal states which finds

expression in the institutional provisions of the Basic Law was also a defining feature of the new political and constitutional order. The establishment
of a Federal Constitutional Court to guard against abuse of human rights and
over-centralisation of state powers provided an important balance to legislature and executive in the system of separation of powers; the new democracy was set firmly in a *Rechtsstaat.*

The 'constitutional patriotism'[6] which this system of government engendered grew out of its success in delivering political stability and, especially,
economic recovery in the post-war Federal Republic. West Germans became
comfortable with the Western democratic model, and even proud of their
constitutional organs (especially the Constitutional Court[7]). The internal
consolidation of democratic practices occurred at the same time as Adenauer
steered a consistent course of integration with the European Community and
wider Western political and security frameworks. The end of division will
result in a clearer definition of German foreign policy interests and, gradually, the emergence of a new all-German identity, necessary if the two halves
of Germany are to unite in more than a purely legal sense. There are also
greater expectations of the unified Germany among the international community, in particular in relation to the contribution it might make in helping
guarantee stability and security in Europe and in other parts of the world
troubled by political or economic crises. President Clinton's remarks on his
recent visit to Germany were unequivocal in this regard.[8]

What are the consequences of these changes for the Basic Law? To begin
with, the Constitution may not be a very promising vehicle to further the
integration of east Germans in the new Germany. While the Basic Law
meets many of the political concerns at the root of the East German 'revolution' of 1989, it is a western product and part of the west German legal and
institutional tradition which is still foreign to the people of the new Länder.
The Basic Law has not been amended in any respect, however minor, to
reflect the East German experience of political renewal. The inclusion of a
clause like Article 35 of the 'New Constitution of the GDR', drafted by the
Round Table,[9] specifically encouraging and conferring legal recognition
upon citizens' action groups such as 'New Forum', which played a significant role in the events of 1989–90, would have facilitated easier identification by East Germans with their new Constitution. A clause like this would
also have the advantage of stressing the importance for the former GDR of
developing its own structures of civil society, though one should not exag-
gerate the role the Basic Law can play in helping to overcome the many historical and societal difficulties which stand in the way of that process.[10] The
population of the new Länder have of course opted to submit themselves to
the Basic Law, and their acceptance of the western constitutional framework
of government will be an essential part of the growing together of eastern-

ers and westerners.[11] But initially their concerns will focus on the progress of economic transformation; confidence in the Basic Law in West Germany grew steadily as the economy improved,[12] and the same can be expected in the former East Germany. A shared nationality and the common rights of political participation as citizens which stem from it will contribute to national unity. Nationality remains rooted in the cultural concept of 'Volk'; the Constitutional Court has declined to redefine this notion in the light of the multi-national character of modern German society, with the result that non-Germans can achieve political participation through the ballot box only by virtue of naturalisation.[13] The legislative changes of 1990 broke with the principle of *ius sanguinis*, to allow foreigners settled in Germany for 15 years or more, or foreigners between the ages of 16 and 23 with eight years' residence (and at least six years' schooling) in Germany to apply for naturalisation.[14] But the requirement to give up one's existing nationality remains a significant disincentive and it is doubtful that the discouragingly low numbers of naturalisation applications will be enhanced by the further minor changes made in conjunction with the asylum reform.[15]

In the decision on the Maastricht Treaty, the Constitutional Court had occasion to consider the concept of 'Citizenship of the Union' which, by conferring voting rights in local elections on nationals of member states while resident in any EU country, necessitated a constitutional amendment in Germany.[16] This change calls into question the Court's previous emphasis of the link between the 'Volk' and the democratic legitimation of government in the localities,[17] but Karlsruhe quietly accepted that the closer relations between the peoples of the European Union developed in the process of European integration justified the departure from principle. This development has the negative effect that it exacerbates the de facto discrimination suffered by the eight or so per cent of the total population of Germany from outside the European Union. It seems particularly important that the task of national integration should not forget the need, identified for example in the recent 'Report on Foreigners in Germany' submitted to the Bundestag, to improve integration of foreigners.[18] The treatment of foreigners in Germany has come under particularly close international scrutiny as a consequence of the large number of racially-motivated attacks made against asylum-seekers and other foreigners in Germany since 1990. The amendment of Article 16 has changed the tone struck by the Basic Law with regard to foreigners in general; President von Weizsäcker and others reacted to this by invoking the protection of human dignity clause (Article 1) in their defence.[19] Resettlers (*Aussiedler*), that is ethnic German immigrants whose German ancestors settled in Russia and other parts of eastern and central Europe from the eighteenth century onwards, continue to benefit from the acquisition of citizenship rights by virtue of Article 116, whereas their links with the Federal Republic are usually weaker than those of non-German immigrants who have been contributing to the state and economy over a long period.[20]

The Joint Constitutional Commission paid scant attention to the nationality question.[21] It did look at the position of minorities in Germany[22] but missed an opportunity to link its examination of this matter with the broader issues of immigration and national identity. The proposal of the Commission to require the state, in a new Article 20b, to 'respect the identity of ethnic, cultural and linguistic minorities' was adopted by the Joint Commission with non-German as well as German ethnic minorities in mind.[23] But its aim of excluding any 'pressure to assimilate' conflicts with an approach to integration of foreigners which positively encourages naturalisation: the Commission's stance on the nationality question suggests it favours such an approach.[24] While it has been argued in this volume that many issues of 'identity politics' may be best addressed by ordinary legislation,[25] the elimination of the instances of discrimination against foreigners evidently present in such legislation in Germany may be assisted by a more overtly 'foreigner-friendly' Constitution.[26]

German military history is such that the Bundeswehr is unlikely for the foreseeable future to provide a focus for national pride or patriotism. This is evident from the rather muted reaction of politicians and public to the decision of the Federal Constitutional Court of 12 July 1994[27] that Germany's armed forces may be deployed for purposes other than the defence of the federal territory as required by commitments undertaken under frameworks of collective security. The Court indulged in this case in creative interpretation worthy of comparison with some of the most teleological endeavours of the European Court of Justice, whose judicial activism it recently chose to criticise;[28] it gave preference to Germany's treaty commitments to participate in systems of collective security over the apparently clear wording of Article 87a that any use of the Bundeswehr for purposes other than defence must be 'expressly' authorised by the Basic Law. Opinions in the Joint Commission on this question, including among the experts called upon to give evidence, had been seriously divided; even those arguing the line eventually taken by the Constitutional Court favoured a textual amendment of the relevant articles to clarify the law.[29] It is difficult not to agree with the observation that the Constitution should be 'the product, not the departure point',[30] of the political reorientation of Germany's policy on military matters, but once again in Germany the judges (of course at the behest of the politicians) have set the legal framework within which policy must be implemented.

As a result of the decision of the Court, Germany now enjoys a degree of freedom of action on military matters more typical of other European nation states, though the balance of institutional powers stipulated by the Court requires that Parliament must authorise out-of-area military deployments, which will also be collective in character, that is usually under United Nations mandate. It is unlikely that hasty steps will be taken to expand German military involvement in multilateral operations: a 'culture of restraint'[31] is set to be adopted, which might in fact lead to disappointed expectations for some of Germany's allies. Moreover, the coercive power of the state in respect of military matters which is regarded as an important attribute of national sovereignty is mitigated in the German case by the limitations on military capacity stipulated by the Two-plus-Four Treaty.[32]

Germany is unaccustomed to being a nation state and will take some time to settle into its new role.[33] The constitutional implications of this change have not yet been fully digested. Conceptions of national identity and military sovereignty are likely to be affected by further European developments in the areas of common citizenship and common foreign and security policy, once again raising the issues of substitution and marginalisation of national norms addressed elsewhere in this volume.[34] The Basic Law will, however, begin to play an increasingly important role in cementing a consensus around a core set of values as part of the process of integration of the former GDR; as it stands, it appears less suited to be able to do that for Germany's foreign population.

2. Constitutional Continuity and New Departures

It is in the interest of both opponents and proponents of comprehensive constitutional reform to emphasise the limits of constitutional change in response to and following unification. For those seeking to minimise changes to the Constitution, the fact that unification could be achieved without requiring large-scale adaptations provides further evidence of the enduring quality of the Basic Law. A legal framework which could accommodate a political event of such momentous import without serious difficulties is evidently not in need of 'repair'. Conversely, those who criticise the lack of substantial change in the Basic Law tend to equate continuity with stagnation. The less constitutional change there has been, the greater the need for comprehensive reform.

Certainly, the amendments to the Basic Law contained in the Unification Treaty left all its defining features intact. However, even in the absence of a grand reform design, the Basic Law has since been substantially amended on a number of occasions. Topics have included the privatisation of air traffic control (14 July 1992); the adaptation of the Basic Law to the Treaty on European Union (21 December 1992); asylum law[35] (28 June 1993); the privatisation of the public railways[36] (20 December 1993); and the privatisation of the Bundespost[37] (August 1994). In September 1994, the Bundestag and Bundesrat adopted most of the recommendations of the Joint Constitutional Commission and these were formally incorporated into the Constitution by law on 27 October 1994 (see Appendix).

Moreover, textual amendments, though undoubtedly of key significance, provide only part of the answer to the question of how much the German Constitution has changed. Of equal importance are the decisions of the Federal Constitutional Court. Placed 'at the epicenter of the Federal Republic's political system',[38] the Court, through its interpretation of the Basic Law, creates constitutional law. There has been no dramatic shift in the Court's jurisdiction in the wake of unification;[39] but its judgments have continued to define central constitutional principles of the German state. The decision of the Court of 12 July 1994 on the deployment of German armed forces outside the NATO area is a particularly illustrative example in this respect. On this occasion, the Court pushed aside what had for decades been the dominant interpretation of the Basic Law amongst constitutional scholars. Textual change to the Basic Law is, therefore, but one indicator of change in constitutional law.

It is also worth re-emphasising in this context that German constitutional law is not coterminous with the Basic Law. Länder constitutions and their interpretation by Länder constitutional courts represent an essential part of the German constitution. It is, therefore, not surprising that the constitutionalisation process in the new Länder has attracted political and scholarly attention; importantly, it has resulted in a number of substantive innovations[40] which affect the constitutional landscape. But constitutional change at the Länder level has not just been restricted to the new East German states. Shortly before unification, in May 1990, for example, Schleswig-Holstein adopted a new Constitution, as did Lower-Saxony, in May 1993. Other states, such as Berlin and Bremen, are in the process of preparing major reforms. Since Land Constitutional law cannot contravene or override Federal constitutional law, the practical implications of constitutional diversity at the Land level should not be overestimated; even sceptical commentators, such as Josef Isensee, however, acknowledge the importance of Land constitutions on account of their integrative capacity and their value as symbols of the Länder's statehood.[41]

Finally, as is argued below (4), domestic constitutional law is increasingly complemented by a European and international legal framework, which, in terms of its domestic consequences and its implications for German sovereignty, could be said to possess quasi-constitutional status. In this respect, the coming into force of the Maastricht Treaty, in particular, has constitutional implications which outstrip those of many minor amendments to the Basic Law.

In sum, therefore, any analysis of constitutional continuity and change needs to take account of both the different layers of constitutional regulation and the role of judicial interpretation in shaping constitutional law. Viewed from such a perspective, constitutional change since unification would appear to have been rather more far-reaching than textual amendments to the Basic Law might suggest.

3. State Objectives: No Limits to the State?

The intensive attention devoted to state objectives (*Staatsziele*) has certainly been one of the most striking features of the German constitutional reform debate, and one which is perhaps also amongst the most perplexing to foreign observers. In its deliberations, the Joint Constitutional Commission adopted the definition of state objectives put forward by the Expert Commission on State Objectives and Legislative Responsibilities of 1983, which defined state objectives as follows[42]:

> State objectives (*Staatszielbestimmungen*) are constitutional norms of a legally binding character, which prescribe for state activity the permanent consideration or fulfilment of certain tasks, i.e. substantively defined objectives. They describe a certain programme of state activity and thus constitute a guideline or directive for state activity, and also for the interpretation of laws and other legal norms. Typically (*im Regelfall*), a state objective is addressed to the legislature, though this does not exclude the possibility that the norm is also an interpretative guideline for the executive and the judiciary ... A state objective leaves it to the political discretion of the legislature, how and when the stipulated state task is fulfilled through a law and whether it wishes to create individual claims to public services or against third parties.

According to this definition, a state objective differs from a mere suggestion for legislative action, but it is also unlike a basic right, which creates individual rights protected by the courts.

By the early 1990s, the academic debate on the merits and the demerits of constitutionalising state objectives had already been so extensive that the topic could be regarded as 'written out' or exhausted;[43] but the political controversy reached a peak with the discussions in the Joint Constitutional Commission. State objectives deemed worthy of consideration included, *inter alia*, the protection of the environment; animal welfare protection; the protection of ethnic minorities; an array of social state objectives, such as the right to work, the right to adequate housing, the maintenance of a system of social security and access to education and culture; and, finally, human fellowship (*Mitmenschlichkeit*) and public spiritedness (*Gemeinsinn*).

Moreover, the Commission considered some state objectives within the context of its discussions on basic rights, notably the equal treatment of women and men.

In the event, the Joint Commission could only agree on compromise formulations for three state objectives: the protection of the environment, the equal treatment of women and men[44], and the protection of ethnic minorities; but the latter failed to win approval in the Bundestag vote on 30 June 1994, since the Christian Democrats insisted on a textual change to the Commission's proposal. This would have made it clear that the clause 'The state respects the identity of ethnic, cultural and linguistic minorities' refers to the minorities of German nationality, that is the Sorbs, the Friesians and the Danish minority. By contrast, the call for the constitutionalisation of a common public obligation to human fellowship and public spiritedness resurfaced in Parliament's discussion of the Commission's report[45], gathering cross-party support[46], though it ultimately failed to win a necessary two-thirds majority.

Considered from the perspective of state theory, the emphasis on state objectives in the German constitutional debate is illuminating in two respects. First, it underlines that there is a fairly broadly based political consensus, extending well into the liberal-conservative political spectrum, about the desirability of state action to shape economic, social and cultural reality far beyond the protection of basic rights and the obligations deriving from the Federal Republic's definition as a 'democratic and social federal state' (Article 20 (1) of the Basic Law). In this sense, constitutional law is not so much about protecting spheres of societal autonomy and self-organisation, as about creating obligations on the state to use the legislative, administrative and financial capacities at its disposal to realise specific political goals.

Whilst this positive recognition of state obligations might be unsurprising against a background of a strongly statist political history, the great trust of proponents of state objectives in the state's capacity to fulfil such a directive role is more difficult to explain. The contrast between expectations placed on state authorities and capacity to act might appear most pronounced in the case of the new Länder, the constitutions of which contain extensive state objective catalogues[47] even though their legislative powers (along with those of the old Länder) and their financial and administrative potential are very limited. In this connection, it is interesting to note that critics of state objectives have tended to base their arguments primarily on the twin dangers of an undue restriction of the scope for ordinary legislation and of the increased judicialisation of politics; by contrast, the question of whether the state possesses the necessary means of effectively promoting the realisation of state objectives has often been given less prominence.

4. Shared Sovereignty: International and European Relationships

As has been illustrated by a number of the contributions to this volume, the Basic Law finds itself in a changing international legal environment which is having a profound impact on the relationship between national and supranational legal orders. It is partly the uncertainty surrounding the 'constitutional direction' of the European Union that has brought about the rather ambiguous responses by the constitutional legislator and the Federal Constitutional Court to the managing of that relationship. Put more simply, how can the Basic Law respond coherently to the challenges posed by the legal order of the European Union when the Union does not know where it is heading? Maastricht is not the unequivocally centralist treaty that some hold it to be, though it does 'deepen' the process of integration in a number of important respects.[48] This treaty framework will be reviewed in 1996 when a different balance may be struck between centralisation and the preservation of member state competences.

New interpretations and applications of international treaty commitments have been necessitated by changed demands on bodies such as the United Nations since the transformation of the world political order in 1989–90. These developments have created new legal challenges for the signatory states. In the judgment of 12 July 1994 on the scope for Bundeswehr military action abroad, the Federal Constitutional Court was split down the middle on the question whether the roles of the UN and the Western European Union since the political upheavals in central and eastern Europe had so changed as *de facto* to modify the treaty bases on which Germany might be called upon to act. Half the judges took the view that this had occurred and argued as a result that Article 59 of the Basic Law had been infringed when the Bundestag had not been called upon to ratify these changes.

One of the important objectives of the drafters of the new Article 23 (and of the Federal Constitutional Court in the decision on out-of-area activities of the Bundeswehr) was to shift the balance of institutional powers within the processes of German foreign and European policy-making somewhat in favour of the legislature (Bundestag and Bundesrat) and away from the executive. This development raises the questions of coherence and effectiveness of policy response, factors which have traditionally been invoked by governments to justify substantial discretionary powers for the central executive in foreign policy (especially in the United Kingdom[49]). German commentators have not been slow to draw attention to the complexity of the new Article 23;[50] how Bundestag, Bundesrat, Federation and Länder coordinate their respective roles under the new provisions will be interesting to watch. Ordinary legislation, which is more easily altered than the Basic Law, would have been a more flexible means of regulating the respective rights of the parties concerned. In their quite understandable and legitimate anxiety to provide watertight constitutional protection for the principles of democratic accountability and Länder autonomy, the constitutional legislators may in fact have made the German policy-making processes on European Union matters more cumbersome and less transparent.

The Federal Constitutional Court has issued rather conflicting signals in its reactions to Germany's expanding international and European legal obligations. On the one hand it has been ready to interpret the Basic Law purposively to conform with important aspects of the Government's foreign policy as embodied in international treaty commitments: the property expropriations and Bundeswehr cases may be cited in favour of this proposition.[51] It probably sees less of a threat to national constitutional automony in the requirements of public international law than in those of European Community law, in relation to which, by contrast, its Maastricht judgment sounds a note of considerable caution. As Ress has noted in this volume, it may well be premature to interpret this opinion as presaging a serious conflict between the two legal orders (and more particularly the German Constitutional Court and the European Court of Justice). It also remains to be seen whether the vigour with which the Federal Republic has pursued political integration within the Community under Chancellor Kohl will be diminished by the constitutional restraints imposed by the Constitutional Court.[52] One of the most important issues in this regard is how the terms of the first sentence of Article 23 will be interpreted and applied by the organs of government; it is wholly unrealistic to expect the other Member States of the European Union to adopt without further ado the German interpretations of democracy, federalism, 'Rechtsstaat' or (perhaps especially) the social state principle.[53] Having said this, the richness of West Germany's post-war constitutional tradition offers considerable scope for constructive and influential German input into the continuing process of European constitution-building.[54] This German tradition has already made itself felt, for example, in the jurisprudence of the European Court of Justice on the protection of fundamental rights[55] and, more specifically, in the pervasive influence in such jurisprudence of the principle of proportionality.[56] The tone and thrust of the Maastricht judgment and the new Article 23 are, however, more suggestive of a defensive approach to the further constitutional development of the European Union.

5. Substance and Form of Constitutional Regulation

Constitutional policy since unification has suffered from some deficits in constitutional theory which, if they remain unaddressed, threaten the authority of constitutional regulation. The first deficit relates to what one might

172 CONSTITUTIONAL POLICY IN UNIFIED GERMANY

call 'constitutional teleology', that is the purpose of constitutional regulation. The reform debate has underscored the fact that there is no political or
academic agreement on this question. Some wish to see the Constitution
essentially restricted to providing fundamental rules for the functioning of
the state and the political system and to ensure the protection of basic rights;
as a law, the Constitution is not considered the place for the expression of
political and philosophical beliefs, but should be restricted to stable justi-
ciable norms. Others, however, stress the constitutional function of both
expressing and helping to create a sense of political, social and cultural identity, which goes much beyond the task of organising state authority.
Moreover, the limitation of constitutional regulation to basic principles with
a high degree of permanence can be seen as unduly restrictive; rather, the
Constitution should be a 'work in progress'[57], reflecting the changes in state
and society.

Strong arguments can be advanced in favour of and against both positions. Constitutional theory which stresses the state as the prime addressee
of constitutional regulation seems based on a duality and, indeed, hierarchy
between state and society which, in reality, does not exist;[58] its assumptions
about the internal and external sovereignty of the state are at odds with a
highly decentralised, deconcentrated, internationalised and increasingly
amorphous statehood. Moreover, the restriction to fundamental constitutional principles, which leave broad scope of discretion to the ordinary legislator, might well undermine the directive capacity of the Constitution. On
the other hand, turning the Constitution into a 'catechism'[59] raises the danger of undermining its legal authority. As Grimm has argued in his intervention in the debate on the constitutionalisation of human fellowship and
public spiritedness as general obligations on all citizens[60], burdening the
constitution with extraneous elements is likely to damage both its normativ-
ity and its capacity to fulfil its core functions:

> If the Constitution is characterised by its legal validity, its orientation
> to the state and its fundamental nature (*Grundsätzlichkeit*), then other
> elements cannot be imposed without harm. Since the Constitution
> claims to be legally valid and realisable (*Durchsetzbarkeit*) and derives
> its meaning and acceptance from this fact, each sentence which does
> not satisfy this damages it.

Constitutional policy will inevitably respond to these conditions and, to a
certain extent, reflect these conflicting views and demands. The constitutional legislator cannot be expected, and should not be required, to argue
with the precision of the constitutional theorist. Yet, it is legitimate to expect
that careful thought be given to the question of what subjects require constitutional regulation and how detailed such regulation should be. In this

respect, the new Article 16a of the Constitution has come in for particular criticism. Not only is it so detailed as to render the distinction between constitutional and ordinary law virtually meaningless[61], it can also be argued that in this instance 'the Basic Law has been used for the stipulating of a temporary party political compromise, which programmes the need for further amendment'.[62] Similarly, some of the recommendations of the Joint Constitutional Commission, for example, those relating to territorial reform or legislative procedures, show little appreciation of what marks out constitutional legislation in either substance or form.

6. Where Should Constitutionalisation Take Place?

A second fundamental point of constitutional theory which constitutional policy will need to address in coming years is the question of where constitutional regulations are best located. Can and should all matters of essential importance be addressed in the Basic Law? Or do not Länder constitutions, on the one hand, and European and international legal frameworks, on the other, constitute often more appropriate frameworks of regulation? As far as the relations between the Federal and Länder constitutions are concerned, one important, though rarely discussed, way of strengthening the Länder would be to increase the scope for Land constitutional policy-making, by restricting regulations in the Basic Law to matters which clearly affect, and require uniformity throughout, the territory of the Federal Republic as whole. In the deliberations of the Joint Constitutional Commission it was, for example, argued that there was no need to include a clause on the protection of ethnic minorities in the Basic Law, since the states in which such minorities are concentrated already have or could easily adopt equivalent regulations in their own constitutions. Perhaps surprisingly, however, the Länder have shown very little interest in demanding constitutional subsidiarity from the Federation.

Just as the potential for constitutional decentralisation seems so far largely unexplored, so are the implications of the existence of a quasi-constitutional framework partly superseding, partly rivalling and partly complementing the Basic Law. Where domestic political controversy makes it desirable, such as in the case of the asylum law, the German constitutional legislator may be tempted to seek a 'European' solution; but it is difficult to find evidence in the constitutional debate since unification of a serious consideration of the implications of Europeanisation and internationalisation not just for the scope, but also for the necessity of national constitutional regulation.

There is little danger that by taking full account of the scope for constitutional decentralisation, on the one hand, and Europeanisation and internationalisation, on the other, the Basic Law's authority would be undermined. On the contrary, it might be argued that by concentrating on what it does best, its legitimacy would be strengthened.

7. Processes of Constitutional Change

Some might argue that the outcome of the constitutional reform debate was pre-ordained by the decision taken in Article 5 of the Unification Treaty to entrust the deliberation of constitutional questions raised by unification to the legislative bodies of the unified Germany. Political bargaining characterised the Joint Commission's search for consensus; the 'exchange processes' identified by Benz in this volume frequently resulted in constitutional stalemate; the breadth of the discussions contrasted with the paucity of the concrete recommendations. Given the more or less entrenched positions of the main political parties and the need for two-thirds majorities for formal proposals, a forum like the Joint Commission was always unlikely to endorse an agenda for far-reaching constitutional reform. The Commission was also prone, because of its composition, to emphasise party political standpoints and interests in a way which alienated a public displaying signs of considerable dissatisfaction with the established parties. President von Weizsäcker drew attention to the failure of the constitutional debate to address the public's loss of faith in party government and called for more stringent legal controls of party activities, especially political patronage.[63] He also probably gave voice to a more widespread public perception that much of the constitutional debate was self-serving, in particular the great stress placed by Länder politicians on strengthening the federal system of government.[64]

A number of our concluding theses have criticised the fact that too little attention has been given by constitutional policy-makers in Germany to the directive capacity of the Constitution and the proper scope and limits of constitutional regulation. The Joint Commission was almost bound to lose sight of such theoretical issues when it moved beyond the remit suggested by Article 5 of the Unification Treaty, that is the consideration of constitutional adaptation in the light 'in particular' of unification. Ultimately, of course, Article 79 of the Basic Law dictates that political preferences will determine the outcome of deliberations on constitutional reform (subject to the direct intervention of the *pouvoir constituant* in the unlikely event of the application of Article 146). But in the case of such a defining 'constitutional moment'[65] as unification, a strong argument could be made in favour of the prior evaluation of the constitutional consequences of Germany's political transformation by a body or bodies which were genuinely free from the instructions of political masters. Far less compelling pretexts have been found in the past to justify the setting up of non-partisan Commissions of Enquiry (*Enquete-Kommissionen*)[66] in order to conduct studies for the Government on certain aspects of policy. Any institution given the task of elaborating proposals for constitutional reform has an obligation to go beyond narrow sectionalist or party interests and appeal to the wider public for participation in and acceptance of its work. One could not accuse the Commission of neglecting this obligation entirely. But when it invited outside assistance, from scholars of constitutional law, for example, this was often in order to seek opinions on positions already formulated by the parties rather than to encourage original contributions to points of debate.[67] The many public petitions submitted to the Commission were taken by it as evidence that it succeeded in establishing an intensive 'constitutional dialogue'[68] with the public. In fact, one of the consequences of the overall lack of transparency of Commission proceedings was that it is not clear how carefully these petitions were considered and taken on board by the Commission. Practical pressures of limited time and resources combined with political pressures to limit the scope for a real 'conversation' between Commission and public.

The wide jurisdiction of the Federal Constitutional Court of course ensures, through constant interpretation and reinterpretation of constitutional norms, that the gap between constitutional law and 'constitutional reality' is kept under review. But objections on the ground of democratic legitimacy may be raised against excessive judicial stipulation of the legal framework for political action. The frequency with which the Constitutional Court has been called upon to adjudicate on questions arising from unification has exposed the danger of its becoming embroiled too closely in political controversies, though Karslruhe does not lack skill in charting these troubled waters. In any event, in responding to the facts of the cases brought before it, the Court can only offer piecemeal solutions to constitutional problems. The continuing evolution of state and society in the new Germany and the further development of supranational government in Europe will pose a series of difficult challenges for constitutional policy. The Constitutional Court and the politicians would be better placed to address them effectively with the assistance of reformed structures of constitutional review enjoying a broad remit to interpret and analyse the constitutional implications of such challenges dispassionately.

NOTES

1. Heinrich August Winkler, 'Rebuilding of a Nation: The Germans Before and After Unification', *Germany in Transition, Daedalus*, Journal of the American Academy of Arts and Sciences (Winter 1994), pp.107–27 (122).
2. Ibid., p.107.
3. See paragraphs 1 and 2 of Article 24.
4. Decision of 12 Oct. 1993, *Neue Juristische Wochenschrift*, 1993, pp. 3047–58 (3051).
5. Nevil Johnson, 'Law as the Articulation of the State in Western Germany: A German Tradition Seen from a British Perspective', *West European Politics*, Vol. 1, No. 2 (1978), pp. 177–92 (184).
6. *Verfassungspatriotismus*: cf. Winkler, 'Rebuilding of a Nation, pp.121.
7. See the evidence for this in Klaus von Beyme, *Das politische System der Bundesrepublik Deutschland nach der Vereinigung* (Munich: Piper, 7th ed., 1993), p. 67.
8. *Frankfurter Allgemeine Zeitung*, 13 July 1994, pp.1–2.
9. The text of this document is reproduced in Ingo von Münch (ed.), *Dokumente der Wiedervereinigung Deutschlands* (Stuttgart: Kröner, 1991), pp.122–62.
10. Cf. Claus Offe, 'German Unification as a "Natural Experiment"', *German Politics*, Vol. 1, No. 1 (1992), pp.1–12 (2–5).
11. Winkler 'Rebuilding of a Nation', p.122.
12. Werner Weidenfeld and Karl-Rudolf Korte, *Die Deutschen – Profil einer Nation* (Stuttgart: Klett-Cotta, 1991), pp.131–3.
13. See decision of the Federal Constitutional Court of 31 Oct. 1990, BVerfGE 83, 37 (52).
14. Law of 9 July 1990, BGBl. I, 1354, paras. 85 and 86 (as amended by the Law of 30 June 1993, BGBl. I, 1062).
15. See on figures for naturalisations both Manfred Kuechler, 'Germans and "Others": Racism, Xenophobia, or "Legitimate Conservatism"?', *German Politics*, Vol. 3, No. 1 (1994), pp. 47–74 (52–53) and Helmut Rittstieg, 'Staatsangehörigkeit und Minderheiten in der transnationalen Industriegesellschaft', *Neue Juristische Wochenschrift*, (1991), pp.1383–90 (1385).
16. Decision of 12 Oct. 1993, (see note 4), p. 3051 and see Article 28, Basic Law, as amended.
17. BVerfGE 83, 60 (72–3).
18. See *Das Parlament*, Nos. 26–7, 1/8 July 1994, p.7.
19. Richard von Weizsäcker, 'Mitverantwortung aller Deutschen für die Wahrung der Menschenwürde', *Bulletin des Presse-und Informationsamts der Bundesregierung*, No. 122, 12 Nov. 1992, pp.1121–3 (1121).
20. Cf. Kuechler, 'German and "Others"' on recent changes concerning the resettlers (p. 50) and Rittstieg, 'Staatsangehörigkeit', pp.1387ff. on the policy aspects of naturalisation laws.
21. Cf. the final report's brief discussion of the subject: Bericht der Gemeinsamen Verfassungskommission (Hereafter *GVK Report*) (Bundestag-Drucksache 12/6000, 5 Nov. 1993), pp.112–13.
22. Ibid., pp.71–5.
23. Ibid., p.72.
24. Ibid., pp.112–3.
25. See Neil Walker in this volume.
26. The legislative discrimination is highlighted in remarks made by the Federal Commissioner for Foreigners in the debate on her report (see note 18).
27. Not yet officially reported at the time of writing; cf. the extracts and summaries reproduced in the *Frankfurter Allgemeine Zeitung*, 13 July 1994, pp.1–2.
28. See note 4, p.3057.
29. See GVK Report, pp. 101–6 and *Gemeinsame Verfassungskommission, Stenographisches Protokoll*, 7. Anhörung, 11 Feb. 1993, esp. pp.149 ff.
30. Karl Kaiser, *Deutschlands Vereinigung – Die Internationalen Aspekte* (Bergisch Gladbach: Bastei-Lübbe, 1991), p.114.
31. The phrase of the Foreign Minister, Klaus Kinkel, *Frankfurter Allgemeine Zeitung*, 14 July 1994, p.3.

32. See Goetz and Cullen in this volume.
33. Cf. Gregor Schöllgen, *Angst vor der Macht* (Berlin, Frankfurt: Ullstein, 1993), p.152.
34. By Goetz and Cullen.
35. Friedrich Schoch, 'Das neue Asylrecht gemäß Art. 16a GG', *Deutsches Verwaltungsblatt*, Vol. 108, No. 21 (1993), pp.1161–70.
36. G. Fromm, 'Die Reorganisation der Deutschen Bahnen', *Deutsches Verwaltungsblatt*, Vol. 109, No. 4 (1994), pp.187–95.
37. Susanne K. Schmidt, 'Reforming the Federal Postal and Telecommunications Services: The Second Wave', in *Transforming Governance in Germany*, Klaus H. Goetz and Arthur Benz (eds.) (Aldershot: Dartmouth, forthcoming).
38. Donald P. Kommers, 'The Federal Constitutional Court in the German Political System', *Comparative Political Studies*, Vol. 26, No. 4 (1994), pp.470–91 (471).
39. Nevil Johnson in this volume.
40. See Christian Starck in this volume.
41. See the contribution of Josef Isensee to the discussion of Länder constitutions at the 1987 meeting of the Association of German Public Lawyers: *Veröffentlichungen der Vereinigung der Deutschen Staatsrechtlehrer*, Vol. 46 (Berlin: de Gruyter, 1988), pp.120–3. He argued that 'The Länder constitutions have, in practice, been reduced to organisational statutes; and even in this residual area there has only remained a standardised (*konfektionierte*), equalised uniform constitution for all Länder, apart from certain Länder-specific modificiations in the area of the parliamentary system of government... The Länder constitutions are languishing in the shadow of the Federal Constitution' (pp.120–1).
42. Bundesminister des Innern/Bundesminister der Justiz (Hrsg.), *Staatszielbestimmungen/ Gesetzgebungsaufträge* (Bonn, 1983) RZ7.
43. Fritz Ossenbühl, 'Probleme der Verfassungsreform in der Bundesrepublik Deutschland', *Deutsches Verwaltungsblatt*, Vol. 107 (1992), pp.8–7 (475).
44. Initially, Article 3 (2) of the Basic Law stipulate that 'Men and women shall have equal rights'. To this the amendment of 27 October 1994 adds that 'The state promotes the actual (*tatsächliche*) realisation of the equal rights (*Gleichberechtigung*) of women and men and works towards the removal of existing disadvantages'. Whilst part of the basic rights catalogue of the Basic Law, this new sentence does not create an individual right and it is, therefore, classified as a state objective. See Winfried Brohm, 'Soziale Grundrechte und Staatszielbestimmungen in der Verfassung', *Juristen–Zeitung*, Vol. 49, No. 5 (1994), pp. 213–20 (219).
45. Whilst commonly referred to as a state objective, this new clause would actually have been addressed to all citizens rather than the state.
46. 'Mitmenschlichkeit und Gemeinsinn', *Frankfurter Allgemeine Zeitung*, 8 June 1994.
47. See Starck in this volume; and Peter Häberle, 'Die Verfassungsbewegung in den fünf neuen Bundesländern', *Jahrbuch des Öffentlichen Rechts der Gegenwart*, Vol. 41 (1993), pp.69–92.
48. Cf. Ulrich Everling, 'Überlegungen zur Struktur der Europäischen Union und zum neuen Europa-Artikel des Grundgesetzes', *Deutsches Verwaltungsblatt*, Vol. 108 (1993), pp. 936–47 (940-941).
49. See e.g. E.C.S. Wade and G. Phillips, *Constitutional and Administrative Law* (New York: Longman, 9th edn. by A. W. Bradley, 1977), pp.296ff. (304: '..the Executive has a largely unfettered power to enter into treaty obligations....').
50. Everling, 'Überlegungen', p.945; Thomas Oppermann and Claus-Dieter Classen, 'Die EG vor der Europäischen Union', *Neue Juristische Wochenschrift* (1993), pp.5–12 (11–12).
51. Cf. von Beyme, 'Das politische System', p.384, who refers to academic criticism of the Court's lack of restraint in foreign policy questions in the past.
52. Cf. Matthias Herdegen, 'Maastricht and the German Constitutional Court: Constitutional Restraints for an 'Ever Closer Union'', *Common Market Law Review*, Vol. 31 (1994), pp. 235–49 (248–9).
53. Everling, 'Überlegungen', p.945.
54. Werner von Simson and Jürgen Schwarze, *Europäische Integration und Grundgesetz –*

Maastricht und die Folgen für das deutsche Verfassungsrecht (Berlin, New York: de Grutyer, 1993), p.77.

55. See Daniel Wincott, 'Human Rights, Democracy and the Role of the Court of Justice in European Integration', *Democratization*, Vol. 1, No. 2 (1994), pp.251–71 (255–9).
56. Jürgen Schwarze, *European Administrative Law* (London: Sweet & Maxwell, 1992), p.855.
57. Bernd Guggenberger, 'Wie "zeitgemäß" ist die Verfassung?', in Bernd Guggenberger et al. (eds.), *Eine Verfassung für Deutschland* (Munich: Hanser, 1991) pp.8–13 (9).
58. Wolf-Dieter Narr, 'Verfassungsdenken über den Staat hinaus', in Bernd Guggenberger and Andreas Meier (eds.), *Der Souverän auf der Nebenbühne: Essays und Zwischenrufe zur deutschen Verfassungsdiskussion* (Opladen: Westdeutscher Verlag, 1994), pp.66–70.
59. Ossenbühl, 'Probleme der Verfassungreform', p.476.
60. Dieter Grimm, 'Was zuviel ist, ist von Übel: Wie man beim besten Willen eine Verfassung verderben kann', *Frankfurter Allgemeine Zeitung*, 15 June 1994, p.37.
61. Ibid.
62. Schloch, 'Das neue Asylrecht', p.1162.
63. *Richard von Weizsäcker in Gespräch mit Günter Hofmann und Werner A. Perger* (Frankfurt: Eichborn, 1992), pp.137–47.
64. Ibid., p.143.
65. See Neil Walker in this volume.
66. Rule 56 of the Rules of Procedure of the Bundestag governs the setting up of such commissions. The commission which reported on constitutional reform in 1976 was such a body: see Schlußbericht der Enquete-Kommission Verfassungsreform, *Bundestag Drucksache* 7/5924, Dec. 1976.
67. This was true of the submissions invited from experts heard in relation to the Bundeswehr's out-of-area jurisdiction: see *Gemeinsame Verfassungskommission* (note 29), pp.149ff.
68. *GVK Report*, p.13.

APPENDIX

A. LIST OF AMENDMENTS TO BASIC LAW MADE SINCE UNIFICATION

AMENDING LAW	REASONS FOR CHANGE	ARTICLES DELETED/AMENDED/ INTRODUCED
1. Unification Treaty of 31 August 1990 and Federal Statute of 23 September 1990.	Alterations consequential on the unification of Germany.	Article 23 (deleted); Preamble, Articles 51(2), 146 (amended); Articles 135a (2), 143 (introduced).
2. Federal Statute of 14 July 1992.	To facilitate privatisation of air traffic control.	Article 87d(1) (amended).
3. Federal Statute of 21 December 1992.	Alterations consequential on ratification of Maastricht Treaty.	Articles 28 (1), 50, 88, 115e(2) (amended); Article 23, 24 (1a), 45, 52 (3a) (introduced).
4. Federal Statute of 28 June 1993.	Tightening of asylum law.	Article 16 (2), sub-section 2 (deleted); Article 18 (amended); Article 16a (introduced).
5. Federal Statute of 20 December 1993.	To facilitate privatisation of public railways.	Articles 73 (No. 6), 74 (No. 23), 80(2), 87(1), (amended); Articles 73 (No. 6a), 87e, 106a, 143a (introduced).
6. Federal Statute of 30 August 1994.	To facilitate privatisation of posts and telecommunications services.	Articles 73 (No. 7), 80 (2), 87 (1) (amended); Articles 87f, 143b (introduced).
7. Federal Statute of 27 October 1994	Adoption of recommendations of Joint Constitutional Commission (in part) and new clause concerning disabled persons.	Articles 3 (2) and (3), 28 (2), 29, 72, 74, 75,76 (2) and (3), 77, 80, 87 (2), 93 (1) (amended); Articles 20a, 118a and 125 (a) (introduced).

Note: In the compilation of the above table reference was made to the table of amendments to the Basic Law which appears on p.17 of *Das Parlament*, No. 2, 14 Jan. 1994.

B. <u>TEXT OF NEW ARTICLES ON ASYLUM AND EUROPEAN UNION</u>

Article 16a (Asylum)

(1)   Anybody persecuted on political grounds has the right of asylum.

(2)   Paragraph 1 may not be invoked by anybody who enters the country from a member state of the European Communities or another third country where the application of the Convention relating to the Status of Refugees and the Convention for the Protection of Human Rights and Fundamental Freedoms is assured. Countries outside the European Communities which fulfil the conditions of the first sentence of this paragraph shall be specified by legislation requiring the consent of the Bundesrat. In cases covered by the first sentence measures terminating a person's sojourn may be carried out irrespective of any remedy sought by that person.

(3)   Legislation requiring the consent of the Bundesrat may be introduced to specify countries where the legal situation, the application of the law and the general political circumstances justify the assumption that neither political persecution nor inhuman or degrading punishment or treatment take place there. It shall be presumed that a foreigner from such a country is not subject to persecution on political grounds so long as the person concerned does not present facts supporting the supposition that, contrary to that presumption, he or she is subject to political persecution.

(4)   The implementation of measures terminating a person's sojourn shall, in the cases referred to in paragraph 3 and in other cases that are manifestly ill-founded or considered to be manifestly ill-founded, be suspended by the court only where serious doubt exists as to the legality of the measure; the scope of the investigation may be restricted and objections submitted after the prescribed time-limit may be disregarded. Details shall be the subject of a law.

(5)   Paragraphs 1 to 4 do not conflict with international agreements of member states of the European Communities among themselves and with third countries which, with due regard for the obligations arising from the Convention relating to the Status of Refugees and the Convention for the Protection of Human Rights and Fundamental Freedoms, whose application must be assured in the contracting states, establish jurisdiction for the consideration of applications for asylum including the mutual recognition of decisions on asylum.

Article 23 (European Union)

(1)   With a view to establishing a united Europe, the Federal Republic of Germany shall participate in the development of the European Union, which is committed to democratic, rule-of-law, social and federal principles as well as the principle of subsidiarity, and ensures protection of basic rights comparable in substance to that afforded by this Basic Law. To this end the Federation may transfer sovereign powers by law with the consent of the Bundesrat. The establishment of

the European Union as well as amendments to its statutory foundations and comparable regulations which amend or supplement the content of this Basic Law or make such amendments or supplements possible shall be subject to the provisions of paragraphs (2) and (3) of Article 79.

(2)   The Bundestag and, through the Bundesrat, the Länder shall be involved in matters concerning the European Union. The Federal Government shall inform the Bundestag and the Bundesrat comprehensively and as quickly as possible.

(3)   The Federal Government shall give the Bundestag the opportunity to state its opinion before participating in the legislative process of the European Union. The Federal Government shall take account of the opinion of the Bundestag in the negotiations. Details shall be the subject of a law.

(4)   The Bundesrat shall be involved in the decision-making process of the Federation in so far as it would have to be involved in a corresponding internal measure or in so far as the Länder would be internally responsible.

(5)   Where, in an area in which the Federation has exclusive legislative jurisdiction, the interests of the Länder are affected, or where in other respects the Federation has the right to legislate, the Federal Government shall take into account the opinion of the Bundesrat. Where essentially the legislative powers of the Länder, the establishment of their authorities or their administrative procedures are affected, the opinion of the Bundesrat shall be given due consideration in the decision-making process of the Federation; in this connection the responsibility of the Federation for the country as a whole shall be maintained. In matters which may lead to expenditure increases or revenue cuts for the Federation, the approval of the Federal Government shall be necessary.

(6)   Where essentially the exclusive legislative jurisdiction of the Länder is affected, the exercise of the rights of the Federal Republic of Germany as a member state of the European Union shall be transferred by the Federation to a representative of the Länder designated by the Bundesrat. Those rights shall be exercised with the participation of and in agreement with the Federal Government; in this connection the responsibility of the Federation for the country as a whole shall be maintained.

(7)   Details regarding paragraphs (4) to (6) shall be the subject of a law which shall require the consent of the Bundesrat.

Note: The above extracts from the Basic Law are taken from the official English translation (revised and updated edition, August 1993) as it appears in: *Documents on Democracy in the Federal Republic of Germany*, published by the Press and Information Office of the Federal Government, Bonn, August 1993. The editors would like to thank the Press and Information Office for their kind permission to reproduce these extracts.

C. RECOMMENDATIONS OF THE JOINT CONSTITUTIONAL COMMISSION

The Joint Constitutional Commission proposed changes to twenty-three articles of the Basic Law. We list the articles concerned below. The purpose of each proposal is briefly stated, together with an indication whether or not the proposal has been incorporated into the Basic Law, following adoption by the Bundestag and Bundesrat, (this is indicated by the word "adopted").

(1)   *Article 3:* Proposal to strengthen the obligation of the state to eliminate gender discrimination. (Adopted).

(2)   *Article 20a:* Proposal to strengthen the obligation of the state to protect the environment. (Adopted).

(3)   *Article 20b:* Proposal to require the state to respect the identity of ethnic, cultural and linguistic minorities. (Not Adopted).

(4)   *Article 23:* Proposal to stipulate conditions for German participation in the European Union and to enhance participation of the Länder in European policy and decision-making processes. (Adopted).

(5)   *Article 24:* Proposal to permit the Länder to transfer sovereign powers to transfrontier institutions in neighbouring regions. (Adopted).

(6)   *Article 28:* Proposal to amend paragraph 1 to enable nationals of Member States of the European Community to vote and to stand as candidates in local elections (Adopted); also proposal to amend paragraph 2 to declare that the right of communal self-government extends to the basic structures of financial autonomy. (Adopted).

(7)   *Article 29:* Proposals to simplify procedures for changing Land boundaries. (Adopted).

(8)   *Article 45:* Proposal to provide that the Bundestag shall establish a new Committee on European Union with the power to act for the Bundestag as a whole. (Adopted).

(9)   *Article 50:* Proposal to amend existing article to emphasise that the Länder shall participate through the Bundesrat in matters concerning the European Union. (Adopted).

(10) *Article 52:* Proposal to provide that the Bundesrat may form a chamber for European Affairs with the power to act for the Bundesrat as a whole. (Adopted in part).

(11) *Article 72:* Various proposals intended to strengthen Länder legislative powers by making more stringent the criteria which the Federation must satisfy before it may adopt concurrent or framework legislation. (Adopted in part).

(12) *Article 74:* Various proposals to amend catalogue of concurrent legislative

matters: deletion of obsolete matters, transfer of some matters into framework category in order to strengthen Länder legislative powers, and introduction of some new concurrent matters. (Adopted in part).

(13) *Article 75:* Various proposals designed to increase scope for Länder legislation by tightening definition of framework laws and restricting scope for federal action, inter alia by excluding university constitutional law as subject of framework legislation. (Adopted).

(14) *Article 76:* Various proposals mainly designed to give the Bundesrat more time to consider and decide on federal legislation; this would also, in theory, work to the benefit of Land parliaments. (Adopted).

(15) *Article 77:* Proposal to make clear that Bundesrat should consider and decide on legislative proposals within reasonable time (Bundestag placed under similar obligation by proposed amendment to Article 76, above). (Adopted).

(16) *Article 80:* Proposals to increase powers of Bundesrat and Länder in respect of delegated legislation. (Adopted).

(17) *Article 87:* Proposal to allow for Land administration and supervision of social insurance institutions where their jurisdiction extends beyond the territory of one Land but not beyond the territory of three Länder. (Adopted).

(18) *Article 87d:* Proposal to facilitate privatisation of air traffic control. (Adopted).

(19) *Article 88:* Proposal to allow the powers of the Bundesbank to be transferred to a European Central Bank (as envisaged in the Maastricht Treaty on European Union). (Adopted).

(20) *Article 93:* Proposal to extend jurisdiction of Federal Constitutional Court to disputes between the Länder and the Federation concerning the fulfilment of the criteria for adoption of concurrent or framework legislation as set out in the (revised) Article 72. (Adopted).

(21) *Article 115e:* Proposal for amendment consequential on adoption of new Article 23, to make clear that Joint Committee of Bundestag and Bundesrat enjoying emergency powers during state of defence may not enact legislation transferring sovereign powers to the European Union. (Adopted).

(22) *Article 118a:* Proposal to enable the Länder of Berlin and Brandenburg to merge by agreement between themselves, without satisfying complicated procedural requirements set out in (revised) Article 29. (Adopted).

(23) *Article 125a:* Proposal for amendment consequential on adoption of proposals for redistribution of legislative competencies between Federation and Länder which would make possible the replacement of existing Federal law by Land law. (Adopted in part).

Notes on Contributors

Arthur Benz is Professor of Public Administration at the University of Constance. His publications include *Kooperation als Alternative zur Neugliederung* (1991, with F. W. Scharpf) and *Kooperative Verwaltung: Funktionen, Voraussetzungen, Folgen* (1994).

Peter J. Cullen is Jean-Monnet Lecturer in European Community Law at the Europa Institute, University of Edinburgh. He has published on various aspects of European Community law and German constitutional law and has been a participant in a major study on 'European Police Co-operation', funded by the ESRC.

Klaus H. Goetz is Lecturer in Government at the London School of Economics. He is the author of *Intergovernmental Relations and State Government Discretion* (1992) and co-editor (with A. Benz) of *Transforming Governance in Germany* (forthcoming).

Nevil Johnson is Reader in the Comparative Study of Institutions at the University of Oxford and a Professorial Fellow of Nuffield College. His publications include *State and Government in the Federal Republic of Germany* (1983) and *The Limits of Political Science* (1989).

Uwe Leonardy is Head of Division (*Ministerialrat*) in the Mission of Lower Saxony to the Federation in Bonn, with special responsibilities for legal and constitutional affairs, Federal-Länder relations and European integration. He is the author of several articles in German and English on the German federal system.

Georg Ress is Professor of Public Law at the University of Saarland and Director of the Europa-Institut, Saarbrücken. The author of numerous studies on German constitutional law and European Community law, Professor Ress has recently been appointed to serve on the European Commission of Human Rights.

Christian Starck is Professor of Public Law at the University of Göttingen. His publications in English include *Basic Principles of the German Basic Law* (ed., 1983) and *New Challenges to the Basic Law* (ed., 1991).

Neil Walker is Senior Lecturer in the Department of Public Law, University of Edinburgh. He has written widely on questions of constitutional theory and the relationship between law and public policy and has recently been involved in a major study on the law and practice of transnational policing within the European Union.